Table of Contents

PROLOGUE

March 12, 1953

It had been seven years since the start of the First Indochina War between the Viet Minh rebels and their French overlords. Both sides were exhausted, and yet both refused to yield. France was stretched to its limit after the devastation of Nazi occupation during World War II. To survive and rebuild its country, France needed the wealth generated from the rice and opium crops grown in its colonies in Indochina. Their colonists had other ideas. They wanted their freedom.

To stop the growing reach of communism, the Americans supported the French. The Russians and Chinese supported Ho Chi Minh and his rebel army, called "Viet Minh." Both sides fought bravely and with conviction, but to end the conflict, one side needed to bring the other into submission. This is the story of the final battle in the war before the war. This is the story of Dien Bien Phu.

KICKING THE HORNET'S NEST

It was late morning, and the sky was overcast and grey. The northern highlands of Vietnam were a rolling sea of green. The mountains were covered with dense forests, and the hills were terraced with rice fields. The valleys were spotted with tiny villages divided by muddy rivers with wooden monkey bridges. All was covered with a primordial fog that protected the young rice plants and the people from the heat of the day.

A Russian-made sedan wound its way down a steep mountain road. The road was a single lane of packed dirt that turned to mud when it rained, making the drive even more treacherous. In the back sat a man in his early sixties and slight of build. His clothes were neatly pressed and simple. He was born Nguyen Sinh Cung. It was later in life that he became Ho Chi Minh, the leader of the Democratic Republic of Vietnam, and affectionately nicknamed Uncle Ho by his followers. The driver, Phung The Tai, was Ho's bodyguard, and he also dressed simply. Phung always carried a British revolver under his shirt and a Chinese submachine gun under the front seat. Ho had little doubt Phung would die for him without a second thought. The car was a gift from the Russians and was painted green, which made it hard to spot from the air. The French ruled the air and were known for strafing any vehicle in areas they did not control. Ho felt the car was too fancy with its chrome hubcaps and gave the wrong impression. It was, however, more reliable than the Chinese cars, so he tolerated it. Besides, he needed the Russians and didn't want to insult them by refusing such a gift, even if its oversized engine used too much fuel.

The road led to a valley, and the car rolled to a stop in front of a wooden footbridge on the far side of a village. Ho and Phung got out and stretched for a moment. The air smelled like smoke and freshly cooked rice. There was no official party to greet him. Nobody knew he was coming. Phung crossed the bridge first, checking to ensure its wooden planks were stable and there were no booby-traps. Ho followed. In the center of the village was a community house. Ho could hear the political officer inside drone on about the communist philosophy and the latest party policies. Phung climbed the stairs and entered first. Ho followed.

Inside the community house, ninety men and women dressed in worn but clean and carefully patched civilian uniforms sat on a wooden floor in rows. They listened to the Chinese political officer at the front of the re-education class speaking in Vietnamese. The matching uniforms took away the students' individuality and gave the class a sense of unity and belonging to a higher purpose.

Upon seeing Ho, the political officer stopped his lecture mid-sentence and blinked as if he could not believe what he was seeing. The students and other officials turned to see what had captured the instructor's attention and immediately prostrated themselves upon seeing Ho. Ho hated this. They were all brothers and sisters; no one better than the other. He thought about correcting them, but there were more important matters to attend to. The building fell silent. The entire class laid on the floor with their heads down and their hands clasped, all but one man who remained seated and looked straight ahead. He did not need to turn. He knew who was behind him. The man still seated was in his early forties and short, even for a Vietnamese. Ho took several steps forward until he was even with the row where the man sat. Ho stared straight ahead and did not look at the man. Ho was angry but controlled. The man seated was General Vo Nguyen Giap, commander of the Northern Army of Vietnam, and considered by many to be the greatest military strategist of the 20th century. "Enough," said Ho.

"You do not approve of the committee's order for my re-education?" said Giap quietly.

"You give me a headache."

"It was not my intention."

"I care not for your intentions."

"I lost over fifteen hundred of our best at Na San."

"Yes. You failed. And now your self-pity leaves our army leaderless."

"You are their leader, not I."

"The people need you elsewhere. I need you elsewhere."

And there it was. Giap could refuse the people he loved and even the political committee he loathed, but he could not refuse Ho.

Ho and Giap sat in the back of the Russian sedan as it made its way back up the mountain road. They rode in silence, each contemplating what would come next. Twenty years apart in age, Ho and Giap had attended Quoc Hoc, the National Academy of Hue, and both had been incarcerated in Lao Bao prison for their political protests as young lyceens. They had met in China while in exile from the Japanese and Vichy French during WWII. Together, they studied Mao's philosophy and learned of his strategy and tactics to further the communist revolution. They often had political discussions that lasted long into the early morning hours.

There were some in the military that believed Giap's rise in rank was due to his longtime friendship with Ho Chi Minh, but Ho knew otherwise. It was Giap's early successes in battles against small French outposts that gave Ho and his followers' legitimacy and allowed the underground communist movement to rapidly progress. Nothing promoted a cause like a victory against an oppressor. Ho needed Giap, and Giap needed Ho. Giap was not perfect and had lost many of the Viet Minh under his command, but Ho knew that Giap was not one to forget the lessons of his defeats. Giap was an investment, and the currency was life and death.

"I hope your time has not been completely wasted," said Ho, breaking the silence.

"My mind is clear," said Giap, measured and steady.

"The French have asked for a peace conference in Geneva."

"I was informed."

"Their generals will want a big military victory to better their position in the negotiations."

"Yes. It is to be expected."

"Your task is to deny them that victory by winning one of our own."

"I will do my best."

"The new heavy artillery division is ready. Use it judiciously. I doubt the Chinese will be so generous a second time."

"We must kick the hornet's nest if we hope to choose our ground."

"You have a plan?"

"I have the beginning of a plan," said Giap. "We will see if the French cooperate."

It was noon, and the sun was already out in full strength. The sky was blue and without form. A French Panhard armored car rolled along a winding road at the head of a 100-vehicle supply column snaking its way through the mountains of North Vietnam. With a turret-mounted 75mm cannon and a

7.5mm machine gun, the Panhard was ideal for fighting in the hills and mountains. It was quick, reliable, and with 4-wheel drive, could climb even the roughest terrain when needed. The 2 ½-ton trucks in the column were U.S. hand-me-downs from the Second World War and the workhorses of the French army. The French sent overland supply convoys to their military outposts throughout Vietnam, but the convoys that traveled through the Northern Highlands were especially important because of the lack of airfields. Strategy and tactics win battles, but logistics wins wars.

At the end of the column was a second Panhard with its guns facing backward to guard the rear. Convoys always traveled in daylight, when French aircraft could hover above like guardian angels and spot the enemy. The French owned the day, but the Viet Minh owned the night. It was crucial that the convoy make it to a French outpost before sunset. The French knew that the Viet Minh scouts were tracking the convoy, looking for any opportunity to attack, looking for the French to make a mistake. Traveling at night--for whatever reason--was a mistake that the French would not easily survive.

The column emerged from a thick forest of bamboo that had given them an all-too-brief reprieve from the merciless heat of the sun. The trucks and their armored car escorts traveled along the edge of a steep ravine. Below, the dark brown waters of the Ky Cong River were lined by an impenetrable forest. Above, five limestone karsts capped the top of the ravine-like watchtowers along a castle wall. The karsts were covered with shrubs and small trees, with vines that grew in the pockets of the porous limestone formed from ancient fossils and seashells.

The convoy was protected by Foreign Legionnaires. The Legion, as it was known, was made up of soldiers from dozens of different nations, many of which were veterans and some even former enemies of France. Unlike most armies, the Legionnaires swore their allegiance to the Foreign Legion, not to France itself. They were glorified mercenaries, contracted by the French government to fight in France's interest. Many in its ranks were fleeing from their own home country to avoid criminal prosecution or debt, while others were colonists living under the French flag. Upon three years of loyal service, or the shedding of blood during battle, a Legionnaire was offered citizenship in France and the potential for a new life. More than anything, the Foreign Legionnaires were known for their esprit de corps. Their fellow Legionnaires were their family and all that mattered. It's why they fought.

Inside the lead Panhard were four Legionnaires. The convoy commander, Lieutenant Julian Travers, was from Côte d'Azur in the South of France. He sat in the front next to the driver while the main gunner and the machine gunner sat in the turret. It was cramped, and the smell of sweat and unwashed uniforms was palpable. The Panhard was noisy, and the heavy steel doors clanked in unison when the armored car rolled over a bump or hit a pothole. The engine whined under the strain as the vehicle climbed up the mountainside.

"Jane Russell, of course. Those breasts..." said the main gunner, giving each imaginary breast an air kiss.

"Christiane Martel, I think," said the driver. "Yes, Martel over Russell."

"Why?" asked the machine gunner.

"She is French and knows what to do with her breasts. Besides, I am a patriot," said the driver.

"Lieutenant, what do you think? Jane Russell or Christiane Martel?" asked the machine gunner.

"I think you should stop this foolishness and keep watch as ordered," said Travers. Travers had joined the Legion when he got a young girl pregnant and didn't want to marry her. He liked the girl well enough but loathed her father, who was a stone cutter from Corsica and always smelled of cheese.

The machine gunner reached up and opened the turret hatch. He stood on his seat and poked his head up through the hatchway to look outside. The slope above and the valley below were motionless, except for the river and a light breeze that rustled the patches of grass on the barren hillside.

Satisfied his men were now performing their jobs correctly, the Lieutenant reconsidered the question. "I won't kick either out of bed for eating crackers," said Travers. His men grunted their approval.

A gunshot cracked the air. The machine gunner fell back down through the hatchway and sat limply in his chair. A single bullet hole through his throat prevented him from talking. Blood flowed down his uniform. He would be dead within a minute. "Contact!" said the main gunner.

"Where?" said Travers.

"I don't know. I didn't see where the shot came from," said the main gunner. He put his hand on his friend's wound to help stop the bleeding, but it was hopeless. The dying man gurgled a bloody bubble that popped and spattered the main gunner's face with red specks.

"Where was he facing?"

"Downhill, I think."

"And the bullet's entry point?"

The main gunner wiped away the blood as best he could and examined his friend's neck. There was a small entry hole in the back of the neck and a much larger hole in the front of the throat where the bullet had exited. "Back of neck," said the main gunner.

The driver slowed the Panhard.

"Don't stop, for God's sake. Keep moving," said Travers.

The driver stomped on the accelerator. The armored car lurched forward and picked up speed. Travers grabbed his radio handset. "Break, break. All Oscar Three Francois elements. This is Francois Twenty-Five. We have contact on the uphill slope. I say again, uphill slope. Mark your targets, and keep moving. Out."

The main gunner swung the turret to face the uphill slope. He peered through the gun sight, searching for a target. Nothing was visible. The driver watched the road through the front viewing port. Travers climbed out of his seat, pulled the dead machine gunner from the turret, and climbed up into his place to watch through the machine gunner's porthole. The Panhard approached two staggered trenches dug into the road. The driver slammed on the brakes, and the vehicle lunged to a stop.

"I told you to keep going, you fool. You're going to get us killed," said Travers.

"Piano keys in the road, Lieutenant."

"Go around."

"There's no way."

"Find a way, or we are dead."

The driver cranked the wheel and crept up the slope, avoiding the trenches. An RPG whistled through the air and slammed into the Panhard's front viewing port. The explosion rocked the vehicle and created a football-sized hole in the armor plating. The molten shrapnel hit the driver in the face, killing him instantly. The Panhard's front left wheel collapsed and folded under the vehicle's body, exposing the thinly-armored underbelly. The cabin filled with smoke mixed with the odor of burning flesh.

"You all right?" asked Travers.

"I'm still alive," said the main gunner.

"And the gun?"

"Still functional."

"Gunner, find me a target."

"Yes, sir."

The turret swung around and the cannon lowered to match the angle of the hillside's slope. The main gunner caught a glimpse of the Viet Minh sapper in his gunsight just as he rose up from behind a boulder and launched the second rocket toward the crippled armored car.

"Merde," said the main gunner.

The RPG hit the vehicle's underbelly and found the gas tank. The Panhard exploded, killing Travers and the main gunner. The front of the column was blocked by the burning hulk.

At the opposite end of the column, two more Viet Minh sappers sprung up from behind a fallen tree and fired their RPGs into the rear Panhard. The first glanced off the turret's slanted armor and exploded in mid-air. The second rocket found the front wheel well and crippled the vehicle. A third sapper rose up from behind a boulder and fired. The vehicle exploded, killing everyone inside and trapping the column between two burning vehicles.

One by one, the trucks were forced to stop. The driver and guard in each truck grabbed their rifles, dismounted, and took up firing positions behind whatever cover they could find along the hillside. Except for the occasional bullet or shell baking off in the two burning Panhards, the mountainside was silent.

"They've got us trapped. Why don't the little bastards attack?" said a driver.

"How the hell should I know?" said the guard.

A French scout plane swooped down from above and flew along the length of the column. It was a single-engine Morane with an overhead mono-wing, nicknamed "Criquet" for its long, spindly landing gear. It was unarmed. The best the pilot could do was radio in the ambush.

The truck driver and guard watched the plane pass overhead.

"Maybe they're afraid of the plane?" said the truck driver.

"It's a scout plane. It has no guns," said the guard.

"They don't know that."

"How long before help arrives?

"Help? We're thirty kilometers from the closest outpost. There's not going to be any help."

"So, what do we do?"

"Do? We fight and win."

The two readied themselves for the brawl they knew was coming.

On the hillside above, a Viet Minh sapper hidden behind a boulder finished attaching two wires to a handheld detonator. He inserted the T-handle into the top of the detonator and twisted it several times to wind the spring inside. He glanced over the boulder to ensure the column had not moved. Satisfied, he ducked down behind the boulder and pushed the T-handle on the detonator. The spring was unleashed and drove the magneto, producing an electrical charge.

In just three milliseconds, the electrical charge traveled down the bridgewire to blasting caps inserted in TNT bundles attached to the base of the limestone karst towers capping the top of the mountainside. The ground shook from the power of five simultaneous explosions. Only three of the karsts toppled like decapitated stone knights, but three was enough to achieve the desired effect of a massive landslide. A tidal wave of rock and soil rolled down the mountainside, gaining speed and mass. It smashed into the column of trucks and soldiers like a freight train knocking them from the road to merge with the rolling chaos. Nothing survived the landslide's fury.

The sapper that set off the chain reaction stared down the mountainside and could hardly believe his eyes. He was a rice farmer by trade, but now he was a warrior that had defeated over two hundred French soldiers. His smile was missing several teeth. It was a good day for the Viet Minh.

It was night and hot in Saigon. The rains had come too early that afternoon and had done little to cool off the evening. The air smelled of flowers from the garden and freshly cut grass. Dinner was served on the patio of the French-style villa that served as the headquarters for the French Far East Expeditionary Corps and residence of Lieutenant General Henri Navarre. The general's table was always the finest, with the tablecloth starched and ironed, the plates and bowls of fine china, and the silverware polished to a mirror finish.

A Vietnamese butler served white wine from a bottle wrapped in a white cloth napkin. Navarre and his dinner guest, Major General Rene Cogny, finished their evening meal of game hen with gravy over wild rice with sautéed vegetables. A Siamese cat was curled up and asleep on the cool tile floor next to Navarre's left foot. Navarre was neatly dressed in his everyday uniform and led the conversation about his latest trip back to Paris and the politics of the capital.

Cogny listened to his superior with the occasional comment when appropriate. Navarre liked Cogny because he was well-educated, with dual degrees in engineering and political science and a doctorate in law, and because Cogny knew how to handle the press, a task Navarre scorned whenever possible. Known for being somewhat aloof, Navarre was a deep-thinker and prized strategy, while Cogny was organized and proficient at execution. They made a good team.

A French captain stepped onto the patio and snapped to attention with a crisp salute. Cogny motioned him over but continued to listen to Navarre's story. The captain handed Cogny a communiqué and stepped back to stand at attention and wait for any instructions. Cogny read the note, and his face tightened.

"What is it, Rene?" asked Navarre.

"You should finish your meal, General," said Cogny.

"That bad?"

Cogny signaled to the captain that he was dismissed.

"We've lost another supply column," said Cogny. Navarre was taken aback by the news.

"The highlands?"

"Yes, sir. Near Cao Bang."

"I see," said Navarre. "Is the garrison in danger of falling?"

"No, sir. We will resupply by air. It won't be enough, but they will make do."

"Yes. Our men can always 'make do,' but what of offensive operations?"

"They will need to be postponed until a complete resupply can be achieved."

"Honestly, Rene, what good is having a garrison if our men are prevented from protecting the area because of supply shortages?"

"Yes, sir. I am acutely aware of the issue, and I will correct it."

The men continued their meal in silence, each deep in thought. When Navarre had replaced General Raoul Salan as commander and chief of Indochina, he was told that winning the war was no longer France's main objective. Stabilizing the war effort to negotiate a peace with the Viet Minh is what the French politicians wanted. Navarre had other plans. This was his third war, and he had no intention of losing it.

"Perhaps it is time for 'Castor'?" said Navarre.

"The airhead in Dien Bien Phu?" said Cogny.

"Why not? It's time to shake things up a bit, don't you think?"

"Sir, when I originally designed the operation, it was for one or two battalions."

"Yes, yes, Rene," Navarre said. "I am aware of the original design, but that doesn't mean it can't be used for something larger. We need something more tempting than a couple of battalions if we are going to draw Giap into a major battle."

"But General, we still have no serviceable roads that far east. Five battalions supported by air?"

"I was thinking more like eleven, or even twelve."

"Twelve battalions? That's almost ten percent of our forces in all of Indochina."

"Which is what we will need to defeat Giap if he takes the bait."

"What of the spring offensive in the South?"

"Yes, well… It will be stretching things, but we can do both. We will need to shorten the men's downtime between missions and use some of our reserves if necessary."

"General, any garrison in the highlands would be a sideshow to the defense of the Red River Delta or any attacks in the South."

"Of course. But if Giap takes the bait…"

"You are resolved, then?"

"I always value your counsel, Rene."

Cogny knew what that meant. His commanding officer had made up his mind, and they were going to move forward with the plan no matter what Cogny had to say. He knew when arguing was useless and preferred to save his military capital for when it could tip the scales.

"Have you considered commanders?" said Cogny.

"Gilles has recommended Langlais for the initial assault."

"Of course. And the garrison?"

"De Castries."

"The cavalry officer?"

"Yes."

"An excellent officer, but he will be fighting from a fixed position and has no engineering experience."

"Yes, but he is aggressive. I do not plan to let our men sit on their behinds in the highlands. They must engage the Viet Minh to draw them away from Laos. We cannot lose Laos."

"No. Of course not. And the required aircraft?"

"I've already talked with the Americans and they will send more."

"Yes, but the pilots. We are desperately short on pilots."

"I will discuss it with Dechaux. He will find the pilots we require."

"Yes, sir."

"Now. I have an excellent dessert wine that I purchased in Bommes. You must try it, Rene."

"Of course, General."

It was a cloudy day with patches of blue sky and an occasional glimpse of the sun. A lone C-47 cargo plane flew high over the Red River Basin in North Vietnam. The reddish-brown silt that colored the water gave the Red River its name. The land around the river was a patchwork of low earthen dikes that separated the vivid green fields and allowed the rain to form the knee-deep ponds so vital to rice production. The farmers and water buffalo that worked the rice fields were no longer frightened by the sound of the overhead planes. They had grown accustomed to the French and their flying machines. They had crops that needed tending and no time for such madness.

The Douglas C-47 Skytrain was another American hand-me-down from World War II and nicknamed the "gooney bird" after its massive wingspan. Poor quality roads in many parts of Vietnam made the C-47, with its dual Pratt & Whitney Wasp engines, the backbone of the French Army's logistical support, and troop transport. In addition to the four crew members, the C-47's cavernous hull could hold 27 paratroopers, 18 medical stretchers, or 3 tons of cargo. It was a reliable workhorse and would usually stay in the air even when heavily damaged.

Tom Coyle sat alone in the plane's windowless cargo hold, surrounded by cases of rifle ammunition, grenades, and mortar shells. His seat was made of aluminum tubes covered with canvas, and he felt every bump. The hold smelled musty, like old books, and the bare interior walls had dozens of bullet holes patched with small sheets of aluminum. It was a strange feeling for Coyle to ride in the back of a plane and not in the pilot's seat. He didn't like it much, although it was a bit more relaxing. The unpressurized hold was cold at twelve thousand feet, and he was thankful for his leather flight jacket.

Coyle felt the aircraft descend and buck as it passed through the clouds. He knew that the pilot didn't want to lose any airspeed as he descended and would keep the engines throttled up. That was the choice in Vietnam, fly high out of range of the snipers or fly low and fast to keep the snipers from getting a clear shot. Higher was safer, but not always an option. They must be getting close to the airfield, Coyle thought. The pilot wouldn't risk flying below three thousand feet within sniper range if he didn't need to. It would only take one unlucky bullet hitting a grenade or mortar fuse to blow the aircraft to smithereens.

The C-47 touched down at Haiphong Cat Bi airfield just outside of Hanoi. There were two anti-aircraft gun emplacements stationed on opposite ends of the airfield. Not that the French were afraid of an aerial attack. The French Air Force controlled the sky over all of Vietnam. That would all change if the Chinese ever fully committed to the war and brought in their fighter jets. For now, the Chinese, like the Americans, were content to let the French and the Viet Minh duke it out and kept them equipped with the weapons and supplies required to kill each other.

The American-made machine guns that defended the airfield were quad-mounted on an electric turret and used for direct fire against ground targets. Nicknamed "Meat Grinders," the four .50 caliber machine guns were rigged to fire in unison and had a massive rate of fire that would discourage any wave attack of Viet Minh, no matter how brave the soldiers.

The C-47 turned around at the end and headed back down the runway until it turned onto a taxiway. The pilot followed the signals of the ground crew and parked his aircraft next to the five other C-47's on the airfield's apron. The French did not stagger their military aircraft in Vietnam. They were not concerned with enemy strafing since the Viet Minh had no aircraft. Besides, it was visually more pleasing to have their planes lined up in rows, and the French appreciated good aesthetics.

When the cargo door opened, Coyle stepped down the ladder with his duffel bag and took a moment to stretch. It had been a long flight from the American airbase in the Philippines. The airfield smelled of fuel and exhaust mixed with rotting vegetation. Coyle saw a bear-sized man walking toward him. He smiled on seeing Jim "Earthquake McGoon" McGovern, usually the largest man in a room and always the loudest.

"Coyle, you beautiful bastard," said McGoon.

"Hey, McGoon," said Coyle.

McGoon reached out with his massive open arms.

"Oh God, wait—" said Coyle.

McGoon lifted Coyle off the ground with a bear hug, "Boy, it's good to see ya."

"Ribs, McGoon. Watch the ribs."

"Oh, right," said McGoon releasing Coyle. "I'm telling you, Coyle. You ain't gonna regret this. The money's great, the beer's cheap, and the women ain't shy."

"Sounds good."

"It ain't just good, Coyle; it's great. It ain't nothing like flying for Chiang Kai-shek and the Chinks, running around all the time getting shot at and landing out in the boondocks with nothing to do. Here, ya fly your mission and come back to civilization safe and sound. Our contract with the Frenchies says 'No Combat Missions.' Best whore houses are just a hop-skip-and-a-jump from the airfield, and all the good bars store their beer on ice to keep the customers coming back. It's like living in Jersey." McGoon picked up Coyle's duffel and started walking, "Come on. I got us a car waiting. You hungry?"

"I could eat," said Coyle, following McGoon.

"Good. I'll take ya back to my place so you can clean up, then I'm gonna take you someplace special. In the meantime, you want a Vietnamese hotdog?"

"A Vietnamese hotdog?"

"Yeah. They sell 'em all over Hanoi. Yellow folk can't get enough of 'em."

"Okay."

Just outside the main gate, Vietnamese hawkers lined up along both sides of the street. This was precious space and known for its territorial skirmishes between the established vendors and interlopers. It was serious business selling to the Westerners and often meant the difference between a hawker's family eating or going hungry that night. McGoon walked over to a woman wearing a conical hat to shade her from the sun and roasting satays on a small BBQ grill. He grabbed one of the bamboo sticks that skewered five chunks of roasted meat and handed her a coin. He handed the satay to Coyle, "Watch out. They're kinda hot."

Coyle carefully took a bite of the top chunk of meat and chewed. "Mmm... not bad. But it ain't no hotdog, Vietnamese or otherwise."

"Sure it is. It's hot--dog."

Coyle looked confused.

"You know... ruff, ruff," said McGoon.

Coyle coughed out the meat. "McGoon, you bastard."

McGoon howled, "Oh yeah. Just like old times."

A taxi dropped Coyle and McGoon off in front of a bungalow by the river in Hanoi's Old Town neighborhood. The one-story building was painted in a traditional French yellow with green shutters and doors. Dark mold invaded the paint wherever water had trickled down the side of the house, giving the structure a time-worn feeling. Trees shaded the home and kept the rains from pounding the roof tiles to dust. The house sat on the bank of a river and smelled of rotting fish and human waste. It wasn't overpowering, but not pleasant.

They walked inside, and McGoon called out, "Girls, we're back."

The interior was decorated with traditional Vietnamese furniture and WWII-style pinup posters of American women wearing bathing suits and lingerie. Incense burned next to a little jade statue of Princess Lieu Hanh and helped combat the smell from the river.

Two Vietnamese women in their early twenties, each wearing a long dress with a slit on both sides, revealing silk pants underneath, ran through a doorway. Upon seeing Coyle, they stopped and stood next to each other with their heads slightly lowered. Stealing quick glances at Coyle, they whispered to each other and giggled.

"These two beauties came with the bungalow. Leftovers from the last renter. This is Chau. She cleans and cooks. And this is Nguyet. She feeds the cat."

"You have a cat?"

"Well, I did 'til it went missing a few months back. The girls will draw you a bath. Tub's in the back."

McGoon made a couple of hand gestures like drawing a bath. Both girls nodded that they understood. Nguyet was from Can Tho in the Mekong Delta of southern Vietnam, while Chau was from a small village near Lao Cai in the Northern Highlands. Although she would never admit it, Chau was jealous of Nguyet's lighter skin color and stayed out of the sun whenever possible. Both were good girls and sent money to their families from the money they borrowed from McGoon's pants while he was sleeping. They exited.

"Their English ain't too good, but we're working on it. If you want something, just show 'em with your hands. They'll understand. You can bivouac here 'til we find you a place of your own. You'll be sleeping in the extra bedroom."

"I don't want to put anyone out."

"Oh, you won't. Sleeping arrangements are kinda loose when we have visitors. More of a sharing situation," said McGoon, moving behind a rustic bamboo bar that looked more Polynesian than Asian. "So, what's your poison? I got Mekong whiskey, Lychee vodka, and I think the girls have a stash of sticky wine someplace. I don't drink it. Nasty stuff. Tastes like fermented snake."

"How 'bout a beer?"

"Beer it is." McGoon punched holes in the top of two cans of Bia hoi, a local beer, and handed one to Coyle. "Tomorrow we gotta head over to flight ops and let the Frenchies check you out. Officially, we'll be under the command of Captain Soulat. He's in charge of the CAT detachment."

"What's CAT?"

"Civil Air Transport. But there ain't nothing civil about it. It's a covert CIA operation run by General Chennault. CAT signs contracts with civilian pilots, most of which are former American combat veterans, and then contracts with the French Air Force for aircraft crews. It's a real nice arrangement that keeps things hush-hush. The interview ain't no big deal. Frenchies lost a bomber and two C-47's last week alone. Americans keep shipping over replacement aircraft, but the Frenchies got a real shortage of pilots. They've been hiring anyone that knows the difference between an aileron and an altimeter. Veterans like us are a real commodity around these parts. So, I figure we get in, make some real money for a change, then get the hell out before we get our asses shot off."

"I like the part where we don't get our asses shot off."

"Amen."

With a towel wrapped around his waist, Coyle walked out the back of the bungalow and onto the patio's bamboo floor. Nguyet and Chau, wearing towels, were waiting next to a large soaking tub filled with cool water.

"Thank you," said Coyle. Nguyet and Chau bowed. Coyle bowed back and waited for them to leave. They didn't. Nguyet walked over and gently pulled Coyle to the tub and removed his towel.

"Okay. I guess you do things a little different here," said Coyle, and climbed into the tub.

Nguyet and Chau removed their robes and climbed into the tub with him. Nguyet immediately went to work, scrubbing Coyle down with soap. Chau scooped up a handful of water and added a few drops to a shaving soap bowl, and lathered up the shaving brush. She soaped up Coyle's beard stubble and opened a straight razor. Coyle reached out and stopped her for a moment, "Just so I'm clear… you're on our side, right?" Chau pushed his hand away and shaved his face.

It was late afternoon and raining lightly. General Cogny's Hanoi headquarters were located within the crumbling walls of the nine-hundred-year-old citadel, the imperial home of the ancient emperors of Vietnam. The wet tile that covered the ground within the high walls of the compound gave off an earthen smell.

Inside the main building, Cogny stood over a map of the Northern Highlands, taking it in, analyzing. Cogny was pragmatic. While he was hesitant at the size of 'Castor' and had made his opinion known, he was a professional and would do his best to execute Navarre's orders successfully. After all, it was his plan originally, and Navarre would probably give him some of the credit if it was successful.

The HQ's furnishings were humble compared to Navarre's villa in Saigon. Filled with maps, aerial recon photos, and a large operational staff, the two-story building was more about function than style. Not that Cogny didn't have style. He was six-foot-four with chiseled good looks and considered the most desirable bachelor in Indochina. But Cogny was first and foremost a warrior. As commander of ground forces in North Vietnam, Cogny oversaw all Army operations.

A military sedan passed through a guard gate protected by stacks of sandbags and a light machine gun squadron of Vietnamese Legionnaires. The vehicle pulled up in front of the headquarters' entrance, where a guard stood by the doorway. Colonel Christian De Castries, wearing a scarlet sidecap from the 3rd Moroccan Spahis--his mechanized command in North Africa during WWII--climbed out and entered the building's front doors. De Castries was an aristocrat born into a distinguished military family and graduated from the prestigious Saumur Calvary School. As a young sergeant, he had served under then-Lieutenant Navarre and had been wounded several times while leading assaults on the enemy's lines. He had a measured amount of panache and carried himself like a swashbuckler.

De Castries was escorted into a conference room where Lieutenant Colonel Pierre Charles Langlais, Airborne Commander of GAP 2, was already seated with three cigarette butts in the ashtray and the fourth burning in his lips. Born in Brittany in Northwest France, Langlais was stubborn and known for arguing with his superiors. He liked his whiskey straight and shaved his skull to look more menacing. Langlais rose and saluted De Castries. Both were unquestionably brave veterans, but there was a sharp contrast between De Castries recently pressed uniform and Langlais well-worn fatigues. The two colonels shook hands and exchanged pleasantries, as was the custom. Langlais didn't care about a soldier's decoration, his family's history, or even what he said. He cared about a soldier's actions, especially in battle. Langlais did not suffer fools. Although they had only met once before, Langlais liked and respected De Castries. He was aggressive and known to be a real fighter.

"I assume you are to lead our little cabal?" said Langlais.

"I have not received any orders as of yet," said De Castries.

Cogny entered, and the colonels saluted.

"You two have met?"

"Briefly, in North Africa. I was riding an armored car, and Colonel Langlais, a camel. I'm not sure which was more comfortable," said De Castries.

"The armored car, I assure you," said Langlais.

"Please be seated, gentlemen," said Cogny, and crossed to a map of North Vietnam on the wall. "Colonel De Castries, Colonel Langlais has already been fully briefed, but I thought it important that you two meet before operations begin. As you are aware, we have been facing particularly active engagement against our supply conveys in the highlands. We believe these attacks to be preparations for a new enemy front with the objective of overrunning Laos. The loss of Laos would threaten our northern garrisons and give the Chinese a protected supply route into central Vietnam and even Cambodia. We, of course, cannot let this happen. Are you familiar with Dien Bien Phu, Colonel?"

"The abandoned airstrip near the Laotian border?" said De Castries.

"Exactly," said Cogny. "We are going to retake it and rebuild the airstrip."

"An airhead?"

"With a heavily fortified garrison. It will become our new base of operations in the Northern Highlands. From it, we will be able to resupply any of our existing northern garrisons, and more importantly, reinforce Laos when and if any attack takes place. Colonel Langlais, with his GAP2 paratroopers, will oversee the retaking of the airfield and secure the area. You, Colonel De Castries, will be responsible for building and defending the garrison."

"And the size of my force?"

"Twelve battalions."

"That's over ten thousand men. How will you supply such a force?"

"Once the airstrip is rebuilt, we will fly in the supplies you require. Until then, we will supply by airdrop."

"Do we have the aircraft for such an operation?"

"I have been assured that we will."

"Enemy strength?"

"There are currently four Viet Minh battalions in the area, two regular and two local militia."

"Nothing we cannot handle," said Langlais.

"But with luck, more will come," said Cogny. "Your mission is to engage and destroy the enemy using your garrison as a base of operation."

De Castries rose to study the map more closely.

"Artillery?" said De Castries.

"You will be given all you need to accomplish your objectives," said Cogny.

"And the enemy artillery?" said De Castries.

"One of the Viet Minh battalions already in the valley has heavy mortars, plus some recoilless rifles, but no artillery."

"Yet," said Langlais. "Intelligence reports that the Chinese have supplied the Viet Minh with a division of heavy artillery."

"True, but Intelligence also reports that it is impossible to transport heavy artillery through the three hundred kilometers of mountains on existing roads. And even if they could, the Viet Minh are not yet trained in indirect fire and would therefore be ineffective."

De Castries turned to Langlais. "Can you hold them until our artillery arrives?"

"We'll hold them," said Langlais.

"We are calling it 'Operation Castor,'" said Cogny, "and it kicks off in one week. Your thoughts, Colonel?"

"It is a great honor, General," said De Castries.

"Excellent," said Cogny. "Gentlemen, I hope you brought your appetites. We dine at Le Beaulieu with some of the other commanders in the operation."

The streets of Hanoi were a cacophony of police whistles directing traffic, street vendors heralding their latest wares, and spattering oil from the iron woks of curbside cafes. And then there were the bicycles, hundreds of them weaving between the buses and military vehicles with little regard for the rules of the road and all the riders ringing their handlebar bells like someone was actually listening and would get out of their way.

In Hanoi's European quarter, Coyle and McGoon, both wearing freshly ironed shirts and slacks, rode on the front seat of a trishaw pedaled from behind by a Vietnamese man. The driver, his face heavily lined from a lifetime working in the sun, wore dark blue silk pajamas and rope sandals. His trishaw was old and maintained to the best he could afford, which wasn't much.

The cobblestone streets were lined with French colonial villas, manicured lawns and black cast-iron street lamps. It's as if the entire neighborhood was lifted from the streets of Paris and transplanted into the center of Hanoi. On the boulevard, Henri-Rivière immediately opposite the Tonkin Résidence Supérieure sat the Grand Hôtel Métropole. Designed in French colonial style with smooth white stucco and forest green shutters, the 3-story Métropole was considered by most westerners to be the most illustrious hotel in Southeast Asia and had an excellent wine cellar stocking the finest French vintages. The trishaw pulled to a stop at the front entrance of the hotel. Coyle climbed down first. As McGoon climbed off the back tire of the trishaw lifted off the ground. Once off, the trishaw slammed back down on the street, and McGoon paid the driver.

McGoon and Coyle walked into the hotel lobby and through an open glass doorway into Le Beaulieu, a French restaurant with parquet floors, crystal chandeliers, and large windows overlooking the street. Pastry carts stacked with petit fours, bright-colored macarons, rum baba, and religeuse topped in ganache were wheeled slowly through the aisles for patrons to view. Vietnamese chefs with tall white hats stood tableside and sautéed Steak Diane and Crepe Suzettes in butter and cognac as blue-orange flames leaped up from their copper pans. The smell was heavenly.

"Nice digs, huh?" said McGoon.

"I'll say," said Coyle.

"Best chow in Hanoi," said McGoon. "I like eating in the bar. Grub's the same as the restaurant, but ya don't need a reservation and the waitresses are prettier. You like snails?"

"To eat?"

"Yeah. Frenchies cook 'em nice with garlic and butter. You really need to widen your palate, Coyle."

"I like what I like."

Coyle and McGoon sat at the bar.

"They got a full bar and I'm buying the first round, so drink up."

"I'll have a beer."

"Didn't really hear me on the whole expand your palate thing, did ya?"

"I like beer."

McGoon signaled the bartender, a Vietnamese man dressed in a white tuxedo.

"I'll have a martini cocktail light on the vermouth with three olives, and he'll have a beer."

Coyle looked out into the restaurant at the French patrons dressed in dinner jackets and long gowns. On a bandstand, a Vietnamese woman in a long white gown sang in perfect French accompanied by a 7-piece band of Vietnamese men dressed in white tuxedos.

"These people realize they're fighting a war?"

"Oh, they realize. They just choose to ignore it during supper. Hell of a thing, ain't it?"

McGoon looked outside through the window and saw a woman stepping from a trishaw.

"Uh oh."

"What's wrong?"

"Trouble's coming."

McGoon turned his back to the restaurant's entrance and put his hand up to shield his face. Coyle turned to see what McGoon was looking at, but the woman had already disappeared from the window.

"I don't get it."

"Just look away, and maybe she won't notice us."

"Kinda hard not to notice you, McGoon."

"Well, I can't help my healthy physique."

Coyle watched as Brigitte Friang entered the restaurant, wearing a strapless cocktail dress that revealed a small scar above her left breast. She was proud of her scars, especially that one, because it was from a German bullet shot while she was trying to escape from the Gestapo in WWII. Her natural beauty only paled in comparison to her self-confidence. She walked toward the maître d' who, upon recognizing her, immediately blocked her from entering the restaurant and asked her to leave at once. She didn't. The maître d' signaled for the hotel's security guards to remove her, and still, she held her ground.

"Hey, McGoon, where's the head?"

"Out the door and to the left. Do you want some oysters?"

"Sure. Whatever you want."

Coyle walked toward the entrance and turned at the last moment to approach Brigitte, the security guards, and the maître d'.

"Darling, I'm sorry I didn't see you," said Coyle, offering her his arm. "I was waiting in the bar." She grabbed Coyle's arm, and the security guards released her. The maître d' scolded Coyle for interfering.

"Sorry. Don't speak French," Coyle said and led Brigitte into the bar.

McGoon turned to see Coyle coming into the bar with Brigitte. "Coyle, you attract trouble like bears to honey," he said to himself.

"Thank you, but I assure you I didn't need any help," said Brigitte.

"You speak English," said Coyle.

"So do you."

"Well yeah, that's cuz I'm--"

"--an American."

"You say that like it's a bad thing."

"Bad? No. Just different."

Brigitte looked back over her shoulder to see the maître d' escorting a couple into the restaurant.

"You American men enjoy saving damsels in distress, yes?"

"Can't really speak for all of us, but in general... yeah. Especially if the damsels are beautiful."

"Ah, yes. Now, if you will excuse me."

"I was hoping we could have a drink."

"Yes, you were."

Brigitte walked away and slipped into the restaurant. She avoided the maître d' as he returned to his stand at the entrance to the restaurant. She searched the sea of white tablecloths for her intended target.

Cogny, De Castries, and Langlais sat with the one-eyed Brigadier General Giles, Commander of Airborne Operations, and General Jean Dechaux, Northern Tactical Air Group Commander. The conversation was easy, veteran fighters swapping war stories.

"After the Maginot Line fell, eight-hundred-thousand of us were shipped off to prison camps. It took me a year to finally escape. I crawled naked through a drain pipe. I traveled through Bavaria and finally joined the French Resistance," said Cogny.

"And your stick?" said Langlais referring to Cogny's walking cane.

"Mmm… that old thing," said Cogny, remembering. "The Gestapo picked me up in Paris. Six months of interrogation in Fresnes before they finally sent me to Buchenwald to starve with the Jews and Poles. Wasn't much left of me when we were finally liberated."

"Sadist bastards," said Dechaux.

"Yes, but effective," said Cogny. "Colonel Langlais, you served with the camel corps in Northern Africa?"

"Yes. The Méhariste in the Ahaggar Mountains of southern Algeria. It was my first assignment after the academy at St. Cyr," said Langlais. "Everyone rode their camel barefoot, officers, and soldiers alike. Filthy animal, the camel, but tough like the Chaamba troopers that rode them. Good fighters, the Chaamba, and brave."

Cogny was the first to see Brigitte approach the table and stood. "Mademoiselle Friang." The others stood.

"Gentlemen, please. I do not mean to interrupt such a distinguished gathering of officers," said Brigitte.

"I doubt that," said Langlais.

"Colonel, you know Mademoiselle Friang?" said Cogny.

"Brigitte parachuted with my battalion into Tu-Le. That was your second combat jump, I believe?"

"Third, actually," said Brigitte.

"Well, the press is always welcome," said Cogny.

"Especially when you are winning, no?" said Brigitte.

"Of course. Then you are most welcome," said Cogny.

"And when do you jump next, Colonel Langlais?"

"When ordered, Brigitte."

"And on that day, will I be welcome?"

"Perhaps."

"The heads of the air force and paratroopers dining with their commanding officer. Gentlemen, if I did not know better, I would say you are planning a drop and an important one at that. Perhaps with two para battalions and sixty-five aircraft?"

The officers exchanged surprised glances.

"How did you come upon such detailed falsehood, Mademoiselle Friang?" said Dechaux.

"By not revealing my sources, General Dechaux."

"And you would print such fabrications?" said Cogny.

"I am a patriot first, General Cogny. I would never report anything that would endanger the lives of Frenchmen. I have proven that time and time again, as Colonel Langlais has witnessed."

"Brigitte can be trusted," said Langlais.

"Thank you, Colonel," said Brigitte.

"In that case, you might want to check your chute, Mademoiselle Friang," said Cogny.

"Thank you, General, I shall. Gentlemen, if you will excuse me, I shall let you get back to the business of war." She turned and walked away.

"How does she find such information?" said De Castries.

"She's a good reporter," said Langlais.

"And attractive," said General Gilles. "A useful attribute to get men to talking."

"The people like her and her magazine," said Cogny. "You will keep her safe, Colonel Langlais?"

"As best as I am able, General," said Langlais. "But she is strong-willed. She will not be easily deterred when danger comes."

"Let's hope it is so, Colonel," said Cogny. "History needs a credible witness."

Coyle sipped his beer as he listened to McGoon. "…and after a minute, the ol' girl starts a shuttering and a bucking. I look at the window and see my number two engine is smoking like a butcher's oven," said McGoon. "I'm still ninety or so miles away from the frontlines, and I've got a full load of ammunition in the hold. I can't bail out because the damn Chinese communists have a bounty on my head. 'Sides, I'd just gotten my chair good'n broken in and didn't want to lose it. So, I feather number two's prop, and I drop a thousand feet like a rock."

Coyle watched as Brigitte walked out of the restaurant and crossed the reception area. She glanced in his direction before disappearing out the front door. Coyle smiled to himself.

A P-38 Lightning, with its twin tail booms, disappeared and reappeared as it flew through the tops of clouds with blue sky above. The aircraft was armed with a 20mm cannon and four 50-cal machine guns in its nose, and four triple-rocket tubes under its wings. It packed a formidable punch and was often used for air-ground support. It had been nicknamed "Fork-Tailed Devil" by the Germans that feared it during WWII.

Coyle sat in the cockpit and could see the silver reflections of a river below. It was a beautiful day, and he was feeling the rush that comes with flying a powerful war machine. He felt a little cocky, like a gunslinger that wanted to slap leather and kill someone just to prove he was the fastest. A village appeared, the target he had been assigned. He pushed the yoke forward, and the aircraft's elevators lowered, kicking the twin tails up. He kept the engines at full-throttle and the aircraft picked up speed as it dove down through the clouds toward the village. He could see the thatched roofs on the bamboo-walled huts, surrounded by their animal pens and fenced gardens. The people looked like ants and scurried for cover inside the huts when they heard his plane's engines.

An anti-aircraft machine gun hidden in one of the huts opened fire through a hole torn in the roof. Tracer bullets streamed up into the sky. Three bullets hit Coyle's left wing, leaving half-dollar sized holes torn in the aluminum skin. Coyle remained in his dive, and the aircraft picked up speed as it headed downward. He glanced at the armament selector switch on the top of the yoke and flipped it from "Gun" to "Rocket." He lined up his sight on the hut with the anti-aircraft gun, pulled the trigger button and launched his under-wing rockets.

Three seconds later, the rockets hit the hut and the surrounding ground. The explosions shook the earth, and the fireballs set other nearby huts on fire.

His aircraft was right over the village when Coyle pulled up from his dive. He felt the heavy pull of gravity and sunk back into his seat. He was confident he had destroyed his target but looked back over his shoulder to confirm his kill. He could see the outline of the gun through the burning roof of the hut and heard the gun's shells baking off with little explosions like firecrackers.

Out of the corner of his eye, a swift motion caught his attention. It was just a blur, but it frightened him, and he turned away, not wanting to see. He was a pilot, and pilots flew too high and too fast to witness the destruction they caused. And that's what he wanted right now, to fly away and not look back.

Coyle was suddenly standing on the ground in a village. It all looked too familiar. He had been there before, on the ground, in that very spot. There was fire everywhere, burning everything. He was terrified and wanted to close his eyes, but he couldn't. For some reason, he had to watch. He had to know. And there it was again... the blur... and a scream.

Coyle shot straight up in bed. His body was drenched in a cold sweat. The bedsheets stuck to his wet chest and arms. He struggled to catch his breath. His mouth was dry. He mustered what spit he could and swallowed hard. It was dark, and he could only see glimpses of things outlined by the moonlight coming through the open window. It took a few moments to realize where he was and that he was safe.

He looked over and saw Nguyet asleep beside him, her naked body exposed from having kicked off the bed sheet from her side of the bed. She stirred, reached up, and tried to pull him back down into her arms. Coyle gently batted away her hands and rose from the bed. He walked over to the window in hopes of a breeze to cool him down and dry the sweat. There was none. He looked out at the river below. Wisps of a light fog were starting to form over the water. Only a few of the sampans that lined the river banks still had their lights on. He could hear voices conversing in Vietnamese mixed with the hum of a distant boat engine and frogs calling for their mates along the river's edge.

Most nights were like this one. Coyle knew it was useless to try and sleep again. He rarely slept the whole night through. Each night's dream was different but always ended the same... in the burning village with a blur and a scream. He did as he always did. He took out his penknife, picked up the piece of wood he had been working on, and whittled. Anything to occupy his mind and let him forget, if even for a few moments. Oblivion was what he wanted most.

In a sweltering office on Cat Bi airbase, Coyle sat across from Captain Soulet. With all the windows open and the ceiling fan spinning at its top speed, both men were still sweating like racehorses. "You flew in the Pacific during World War Two, and again in Korea," said Soulet, reviewing Coyle's paperwork. Soulet was French but spoke good English. It was the main reason why he was assigned the position of riding herd over the American pilots contracted to fly supply missions for the French Air Force.

"That's right," said Coyle.

"Your commendations are impressive."

"I did my duty."

"Why did you leave the military?"

"Lousy food."

"You trained on the C-119?"

"In Manila before I resigned my commission."

"Why did you stay in Southeast Asia?"

"I went home for a bit. Things just weren't the same. My people didn't understand. At least here, I know who I've become."

"One last question, Monsieur Coyle. Is it true you hold the Navy record for most aircraft crashes?"

"Yes, sir."

"Would you mind explaining?"

"I'd rather not if it's all the same."

"It is not all the same."

"Okay. I flew a lot of missions. At times, things got squirrely, and I crashed."

"You find that amusing?"

"Not at the time."

"Monsieur Coyle, this is not the US Navy. Our resources are limited. Do not crash our planes."

"I'll do my best," said Coyle.

Soulet had no choice. The French needed pilots like Coyle. He stamped his application 'APPROVED.' "Welcome to the French Air Force, Monsieur Coyle."

THE VALLEY

The sun was filtered by a thick morning haze and rose slowly over Haiphong–Cat Bi airfield. The sky was blanketed with a high layer of cirrocumulus that gave it a grey-gloomy feeling and held in the cool nighttime air. The airfield's apron was lined with Quonset huts that served as offices and hangers for small aircraft. A concrete control tower was positioned near the center of the two runways. The runways were configured in an X that allowed aircraft to avoid crosswinds while taking-off and landing. It was quiet at that time of the morning. Only birds hunting for crickets and seeds landed and took off from the grass between the runways. The tarmac was covered with parked cargo aircraft with all their doors open and their ladders down as if waiting.

A Vietnamese artist stood on a ladder and painted the final touches on Daisy Mae, a buxom cartoon character from the Li'l Abner comic strip, on the nose of a C-119 cargo plane. The C-119 was nicknamed the "Flying Boxcar" because the fuselage was in the shape of a long square box with rounded edges, like someone with a bad sense of style had attached a pair of wings to a freight train's boxcar. It wasn't the prettiest of aircraft, but it was a workhorse with a massive payload. With its twin tail booms and powerful dual engines, the C-119 could haul almost three times as much weight as the next largest aircraft in the French fleet. It was easy to see why they were so prized by the French, who needed to transport large amounts of cargo and troops around a country with few roads.

Standing on the tarmac below, McGoon observed the artist's work while Coyle finished the pre-flight check.

"Ailerons are a bit loose, but the rest seems pretty solid," said Coyle.

"Ya think her breasts are big enough?" said McGoon.

"I don't know. How big ya need 'em?"

McGoon raised his massive hands to form a pair of imaginary breasts in the air. "Mmm… I suppose ya got a point."

"Frenchies say a woman's breast should be no larger than a champagne glass; otherwise it's a waste."

"Humph. I don't know about that," said McGoon. "Sides, you've been here a week. How do you know what the Frenchies say?"

"I've been reading up," said Coyle.

Coyle and McGoon turned to the sound of a distant cadence in French. Hundreds of French and Vietnamese paratroopers wearing pristine uniforms, jump helmets and their parachute packs marched in perfect unison onto the airfield and to their assigned aircraft waiting on the tarmac. Each carried a MAS 36 rifle or a MAT 36 submachine gun with a folding stock. The officers, always keen to look their best, carried the latest model MAT 49 submachine gun and wore their red berets, while their jump helmets hung from their web belts.

"Frenchies sure are a pretty bunch," said McGoon.

Brigitte approached, wearing a khaki uniform with a jump pack on her back, a portable typewriter in one hand, and a jump helmet in the other. Her hair was up in a tight bun, and she wore no makeup.

"I'll be damned," said Coyle.

"Bonjour," said Brigitte.

"Yeah, Buenas dias to you, too. Look, lady, this is a military airfield," said McGoon. "You could get that pretty little head of yours lopped off by a – "

"I ride with the First Colonial Paras in the second wave," said Brigitte handing McGoon her orders.

"You're a war correspondent," said Coyle.

"You say that like it is a bad thing," said Brigitte.

"No, but it explains a lot."

"Such a shame. We've only just met, and you already have me figured out."

"Actually, we still haven't met. And as for figuring you out… I have serious doubts that's even possible."

Brigitte offers her hand. "Brigitte Friang, reporter for the magazine Indochine Sud-Est Asiatique."

"Tom Coyle, cargo pilot, and this is Jim McGovern. We call him "McGoon.""

McGoon handed back her orders. "I don't give a damn what those say. We ain't dropping no civilians outta our aircraft, especially during a war."

"I assure you, the Mademoiselle is quite capable," said Major Marcel Bigeard, the hawk-nosed commander of the 6th Battalion of French and Vietnamese paratroopers. He was beyond brave and openly flirted with death to the point where many of his cohorts couldn't stand him.

Brigitte walked over and gave him a hug, "My little Bruno." Bruno and Brigitte exchanged pleasantries in French.

Bruno offered his hand to Coyle and McGoon, "Major Marcel Bigeard. 'Bruno' to my friends."

"Bruno and I were together at Tu Le," said Brigitte.

"What a mess that was, yes?" said Bruno.

"Bruno's battalion was used as bait to lure the Viet Minh away from the French garrisons on the Thai highlands," said Brigitte. "They dropped us behind an entire division of Viet Minh regulars."

"Nothing like five thousand angry Viet Minh to get your blood pumping, eh?" said Bruno. "We were… how you say… running and gunning all the way down the mountain."

"With your permission, I will stow my gear," said Brigitte.

McGoon looked to Coyle for support. Coyle shrugged, "She's jumped more than you and me combined."

"I guess," said McGoon as he stepped aside to let Brigitte pass.

Brigitte moved off to the cargo door, and Bruno followed. McGoon and Coyle watched as Bruno helped her manage the step ladder by putting his hand on her ass and giving her a shove.

"Something tells me they've shared a lot more than a foxhole together," said Coyle.

"I'm amazed he survived," said McGoon.

It was almost 7 a.m. by the time all the paratroopers had arrived at the airfield and climbed into their aircraft. The armada was ready for takeoff. The dual engines on the C-47s wound slowly to life as thumps of black exhaust puffed from their engine exhaust panels. The wheel blocks were pulled by the ground crew, and the tires rolled across the tarmac. One by one, the sixty-five-aircraft taxied down the runway and lifted off into the morning sky. Operation Castor had begun.

The provincial capital of Dien Bien Phu was in the valley of Muong Thanh, an oasis of green rice paddies in the vast tree-covered highlands of North Vietnam. The valley was long and narrow. There were multiple streams flowing from the mountain, like arteries feeding the Nam Yum River, which ran down the center of the valley. The elephant grass was long and green, while the surrounding mountains were steep and shrouded in dense forests. The mountain air was dry, and the temperature cooler than most of Vietnam.

The enclave was the home to the Black Thai clan that lived in dozens of hamlets scattered among the low hills and valley floor. They spoke their own language and built their wooden houses on stilts to hinder venomous snakes and to prevent their homes from flooding during the monsoon season. Both men and women wore blouses with high collars and long skirts. They preferred cloth dyed with dark colors like black or brown. In addition to rice, the Black Thai grew opium for whichever government controlled the valley at the time of harvest. They were mostly peaceful people and were partial to odd numbers over even.

The abandoned airfield sat in the center of the valley and ran along the river. The Viet Minh had dug 1,200 potholes and several 3-foot deep trenches across the runway to prevent its use by the French. Patches of grass with the occasional anthill had sprung up over time, and the locals had stripped the airfield's buildings of their wood siding to build their homes. Still, the airfield wasn't in bad shape. It was a diamond in the rough that could quickly be carved into a jewel worth fighting for. For the French, an airfield meant control of the surrounding area, and control was what they desired most.

On a hill that would soon be called "Elaine" sat a small mansion, the residence of the mayor. It had been built by the French when they previously occupied the valley. The stone structure was French Provincial in style, with windows on the first and second floors and a soft green door between four columns that gave it a boost in prestige. It was meant to make an impression on occupants of the valley who had never seen anything so beautiful when it was built. After the French left, the Viet Minh hung the mayor for collaboration and took over his residence. The Viet Minh didn't believe in such indulgences, while so many of their people were homeless and starving. It now served the dual purpose of party headquarters and administration. Strangely, the Viet Minh had left alone the mansion's interior, which was still filled with elegantly-carved furniture, Persian rugs, and oil paintings of French war heroes on horses.

The French were lucky that morning. The Viet Minh did not know they were coming, and only one of the four expected battalions was in the valley when the paratroopers jumped in. The other three battalions were over thirty kilometers away in mountainous terrain. It would take them several days' march to return to the valley once they received orders.

Corporal Phan Van Ty was eighteen when he joined his local militia. It was the fourth year of the war against the French. The village cadre watched him closely because Ty had been taught to read, write and do mathematics by his father, the village school teacher. Any education, however limited, was a precious commodity in the People's Army of North Vietnam. It meant that Ty could learn to use a compass and find his position on a map. He could write the reports that the bureaucrats so loved. He could read the training manuals that the Chinese advisors translated into Vietnamese and learn how to operate the new weapons that they sent. He had been promoted several times during the first year and was finally transferred to the regular army and assigned to lead a mortar squad as a corporal. But Ty's real dream was to become a sapper, those brave soldiers that planted booby-traps and breached the enemy's defenses. Several times he had requested a transfer to the battalion's engineering company, and several times he was denied by his commander, who did not want to lose one of the few in his battalion that had the potential to become an officer. The battalion was always desperately short of officers, especially junior officers, which had a high mortality rate. Someone else could dig the tunnels and plant mines, but not Ty.

On the morning of November 20, 1953, Ty's mortar squad was training on a low hill overlooking the river and several rice fields in the northwest of the valley of Dien Bien Phu. Ty's squad was part of the heavy weapons company that had been detached from battalion 920, so they could rest and train while the weather was good. Ty's goal was to set up the 81mm mortar and fire the first practice round on target within one minute. It was an ambitious goal that required his five-man team to repeat the drill over and over, setting up the mortar and firing until the action was second nature and didn't require them to think about the order of procedures. Ty didn't own a watch, so he timed the practice drill by counting out the swings of a well-worn metronome that his music teacher had given him when he was a student.

His men had the maneuver down to 92 seconds by the time they heard the low-pitched thrum of plane engines approaching the valley from the eastern mountains. Not many planes passed over the valley, but when they did, the Viet Minh soldiers would often take potshots at them if they were low enough to be within range. The Viet Minh didn't own any aircraft or have any pilots, so anything in the sky was fair game. The odds of hitting a plane were very low, but it was a break in their boring routine and made them feel useful.

The squad picked up their rifles and pointed the muzzles into the air waiting for the aircraft to appear. It was only when Ty's men saw the armada of planes emerge from over the mountain tops that they began to panic. There were a lot of planes, more than any of them had ever seen before. Ty reassured his young squad and ordered them to gather up their gear. They would be receiving new orders shortly, and he wanted to be ready to move.

'Yellow Leader' approached from the south and circled down to 2,500 feet above the main drop zone. 'Natacha,' as it was codenamed by the French, was 350 yards northwest of the village of Muong Thanh and 300 yards east of the old airfield. With two big landmarks, the clearing was easy to spot from the air. The pilot, Colonel Nicot, throttled back to an airspeed of 105 mph in preparation for the paratroopers' jump.

Even at the reduced speed, the wind was biting and cold when the jumpmaster opened the door on the lead aircraft. Bruno stepped to the open door, his parachute's static line already hooked to the wire running the length of the cargo hold. The wind stung his ears as his men gathered in tightly behind him. Bruno was always the first one out of the aircraft. His men thought it foolish that their commander would go first, but God, how they admired him. Bruno, on the other hand, actually thought it was safer to be the first one out because the enemy had less time to prepare, or at least, that is what he told his men. He felt fear just like everyone else; he just chose to ignore it. The red jump light changed to green, and the buzzer sounded. The jumpmaster slapped him on the shoulder and said: "Go!"

"First stick away," said Bruno and jumped out the door. He was followed closely by his men. The empty static lines whipped in the wind and slapped the aircraft's fuselage. It would take a total of two minutes for the C-47 to empty its 'stick' of 24 paratroopers. At 105 mph, that meant the soldiers' canopies would be spread over two miles, and they still needed to land on a drop zone that was only 450 yards across.

Outside the aircraft, Bruno kept his feet together and his hands on his jump harness to prevent any of his limbs from getting tangled in the static line. He dropped twenty feet straight down until the static line pulled his parachute from his pack. The hundred-mile-an-hour wind caught the parachute and swung Bruno sideways, so he was parallel to the ground. His chute filled with air and snapped open. He felt the heavy jerk of his harness against his crotch and chest. With the parachute open, his body swung down like a pendulum until he was once again perpendicular to the ground. He could feel his heart racing, and its heavy thumping inside his chest reassured him that he was alive. He released his rucksack from below his reserve parachute and dropped it on a long line, so it dangled below his feet. As he floated down, he counted his men's chutes. Everyone's chute had opened. He breathed a little easier until he saw the first muzzle flash from the valley below. Then more... a lot more. He was defenseless in the air. Bruno did not carry a personal weapon. He was a natural warrior, and the temptation to fight was too great when he had a weapon by his side. His job was to lead the 651 men dropping with him that day, not fight. Several bullets zipped past him and punctured his parachute's canopy. The bullet holes were too small to have any real effect beyond being a reminder that he was jumping into hostile territory.

There was a thick morning mist still hanging over the valley when Bruno landed. He hit the ground hard with bent knees so as not to break his legs. He tumbled into the long grass on a low sloping hill. The drop zone was alive with enemy machine-gun bursts and mortar shells exploding. He heard the zing of bullets cutting through the grass nearby, but he couldn't see who was shooting at him or from where. That was a good thing, he thought. If he can't see them, they can't see him. His parachute floated down and landed on the top of the grass. He released his parachute harness, gathered his chute, and wadded it up into a bundle. Parachute silk was precious and not to be wasted, even when under fire. He laid the bundled chute down in the grass. He followed the long line through the grass and found his rucksack. He unclipped the long line, slipped the rucksack on his back, and pulled his combat knife from its scabbard on his front combat harness. It wasn't much, but it was something. He hunched low in the grass and waited for the others to land. It was a strange feeling to only see three feet to his front, knowing that there was an enemy out there bent on killing him and his men. He was confident that even with only a knife, he could kill two or maybe even three before they overran his position. His life would buy time for his men, and that was a sacrifice he was willing to make if required. He slipped off his rucksack, opened the top straps, and reached inside. He pulled out a handheld field radio. Its antenna had been smashed when he rolled during his landing. "Merde," said Bruno to himself.

He tried it anyway and heard nothing but static. It was useless. He wanted to throw it on the ground but checked his emotions and put the broken radio back in his pack so as not to leave it for the enemy. He heard the Vietnamese voices heading in his direction. Two more bullets cut the blades of elephant grass around his left shoulder. The enemy had his position and would be coming soon. He heard the grass shifting to his right. He readied his knife, changing the grip, so the blade faced down and away. He decided he would slash with his opening strike. More rustling. His muscles tensed. A face appeared in front of him. It was a Vietnamese in a French sergeant's uniform. "Ah, Major. There you are," said the sergeant.

Bruno relaxed and lowered his knife. Two more faces appeared beside the sergeant, both Vietnamese in French uniforms.

"And the others?" said Bruno.

"We are forming up now."

"Do any of you have a radio?"

"No, sir. Lieutenant Le Page has a radio in his pack. I saw the lieutenant land in a grove of trees to the southeast of the drop zone."

"Okay. Sergeant, you and your men stay here and form a defensive pocket. I'll find your lieutenant."

"Yes, sir," said the sergeant. "The grass is much longer than seen in the recon photos, yes?"

"Sorry to disappoint you, Sergeant. Next time I will be sure to have it cut before you land."

"Yes, sir. Thank you, sir."

"…and for God's sake, don't shoot anything until you are sure it is the enemy… especially me."

"Yes, sir."

Bruno, still only armed with his combat knife, disappeared into the grass.

Bruno reappeared out of the grass on the southeast side of the drop zone. Before him was a grove of trees. He looked for the enemy. With no one in sight, he made a dash for the trees.

Inside the grove of trees, Lieutenant Le Page stood looking up into a tree. Bruno called out in a loud whisper. "Lieutenant?"

"Yes?" said Le Page.

Bruno walked up behind him while scanning the area for the enemy.

"Poor bastard. Bullet caught him under the chin strap," said Le Page.

Bruno looked up to see Captain Raymond, the battalion's medical officer, hanging lifeless with a bullet hole under his chin, his medical bag dangling below.

"It was his first jump. Good man. Brave man," said Le Page.

"Dead man," said Bruno. "There is nothing you can do for him. Tend to your men, Lieutenant. They're still alive."

"Of course. Shouldn't we cut him down?"

"Yes, but later. After the battle is won. Do you have a radio?"

Le Page pulled out his radio. It, too, was heavily damaged and useless. Bruno grunted his displeasure. Luck was not going his way, and he knew luck was an uncontrollable but important factor in battle. "All right. Follow my path through the grass. Your men are waiting," said Bruno. "I've got to find my radioman and report back to headquarters. I'll gather up any stragglers I find and send them your way."

"Yes, Major."

Le Page moved off toward the grass. Bruno glanced up one more time at the dead Captain and said, "You'll be missed, my friend." Bruno used his knife to cut the cord, holding the dangling medical bag, and tied the bag around his chest. He stayed low and ran across the tree line at the edge of the grass, searching for more of his men and a radio that worked.

A Viet Minh weapons squad set up their 75mm recoilless rifle at the edge of the village they were assigned to protect. The tripod legs that supported the weapon had been damaged during a night raid on the French garrison near Lao Cai a few weeks back, and a replacement tripod had not yet arrived from the Chinese border. A short piece of wood tied with bamboo strips reinforced one of the legs that had broken. The loader slid a shell into the breach and closed the hatch at the back of the gun. The gunner took aim through the sight on the barrel at a French machine-gun position in a grove of trees on the opposite end of the village. He fired. A crack and a puff of smoke sent the shell on its way.

The shell landed short and exploded a few yards in the front of the machine position. The French machine gunner quickly readjusted his firing to the new threat.

Bullets hit around the recoilless gun squad, bounced off rocks, pelted the ground, and splintered a nearby tree trunk. It was a familiar race between those that would live and those that were about to die. Like most battles in war, it would come down to training and luck. The Viet Minh loader opened the breech, ejected the empty shell casing, loaded another shell, and slammed the hatch closed. The recoilless gunner adjusted his aim and fired. The vibration from the gun caused the bamboo strips holding the wood on the broken leg to slip, and the gun shifted wildly as the shell left the end of the barrel. The machine gun found its target, and the Viet Minh gunner and loader were both killed by a stream of French bullets.

Bruno had heard the crack of the recoilless rifle in the distance. Moments later, he heard the whoosh of a shell overhead. His training kicked in, and he hit the ground. A thick branch on a nearby tree exploded and showered him with shards of wood and bark. The heavy branch cracked off the tree and crashed to the ground. "They can't be shooting at me," he thought. "They can't see me." A second shell did not follow the first. That was a good sign. It wasn't him that they were targeting.

He felt a stinging sensation in his left thigh and looked down at a small hole in his pants. He was more concerned about the hole in his pants than the potential wound beneath. These were his only pants, and they had to last. He had elected to forgo an extra change of clothes to make room for additional grenades, with tape wrapped around their spoons to keep them from accidentally blowing up. He hated the idea of removing the pants off a dead fellow officer to replace his own. He inserted his little finger into the hole and tore a bigger hole so he could examine the damage. A two-inch wood shard was half-buried in his thigh. He gently but firmly pulled the exposed end and removed the shard. Blood filled the wound. Bleeding was good, he thought. It would clean out some of the remaining splinters that he was sure were still inside the wound. Even with the sulfur powder he poured into the hole, the wound would fester and need to be cleaned and redressed several times a day. One more thing to remember and one more thing to do in a busy commander's schedule. But Bruno knew that gangrene could kill just as sure as a bullet in Vietnam. He stuffed the gauze from a battle dressing packet halfway into the hole in his pants. The gauze would soak up the blood and keep it from staining the rest of his pant leg. That would have to suffice until he could find a medic, he thought. He stood up and again looked around. He put weight on his leg. It was painful, but he could walk. That was good.

Through the morning mist, Bruno saw a soldier at the edge of the trees with his rifle slung over his shoulder and his arms filled with a parachute that he had been gathering. Bruno called to him in hushed French. The soldier stopped collecting the chute and looked over in Bruno's direction. The soldier quickly gathered the rest of the chute and disappeared into the long grass. "Where in the hell are you going?" said Bruno. The soldier's training should have taught him to maneuver back in the direction of the flight path until he found members of his unit. Bruno looked around for enemy soldiers. There were none. He limped over to where the soldier was previously standing and saw a gap in the long grass where the soldier had disappeared. He crouched down as he followed the man's trail, keeping his head down below the top of the grass and out of sight of any enemy snipers. He could hear the soldier moving through the grass up ahead. Again, Bruno called out in hushed French, "Hey, dumbshit. You're going the wrong way. Your company is to the east." Bruno heard the clinking of metal on metal. He was getting closer. He could see the dark outline of the soldier through the grass up ahead. "You're supposed to drop your chute where you land, not carry it." Bruno pulled aside the last of the long grass between him and the soldier. The soldier was squatting on the ground with his rifle and a bayonet now attached to the end of the barrel. Bruno looked at his brown face and up at the little yellow star sewn on his cap. He was Viet Minh.

Both hesitated for a moment, not believing their eyes. Bruno made the first move. His right hand reached up to the hilt of the knife on his chest, and his little finger flicked open the metal button on the leather strap that held the knife in its scabbard. The Viet Minh soldier stood as he thrust with his rifle, and the bayonet hurled forward straight at Bruno's face. Bruno shifted his weight and spun his body to the left. With his left hand, Bruno reached across his body and grabbed the soldier's bayonet and the end of the rifle barrel as it passed inches from his face. Bruno continued to spin with the full weight of his body and pulled the rifle forward as he rolled his weight into the gunstock. The Viet Minh was thrown off balance and forced to lean forward to keep a hold on his weapon. Bruno pulled his knife from its scabbard as he continued his roll toward the soldier. Now close enough to strike, Bruno plunged the blade into the side of the soldier's head just below the ear. He was dead in an instant. It took his leg muscles filled with adrenaline another two seconds to relax and allow his body to collapse into the grass.

Bruno stood over the dead soldier and glanced over at the chute wrapped and tied in a neat bundle on the ground. It occurred to Bruno that the soldier probably wanted to sell the chute for the valuable silk and thought Bruno wanted to steal it from him. The soldier was dead because he had lost focus on his mission. Bruno would not make the same mistake. He quickly searched the soldier's pockets for any maps or documents and disappeared into the long grass to find a radio and report in.

Within the first hour of battle, the Viet Minh commanders recovered from the initial surprise and confusion caused by the French invasion. Orders were issued, and troops deployed to drive the enemy from the valley.

Ty's mortar squad was ordered to protect the retreat of the HQ staff housed in the village. The squad assembled their mortar on the top of a low hill that gave them a good view of the surrounding area.

The 81mm mortar was a simple but lethal weapon. The mortar had a long steel tube that was supported by bipod legs and a heavy steel base-plate that stabilized the weapon and kept the tube from burying itself in the ground after each round was fired. A metal sight and bubble level on the side of the tube helped the gunner set the angle and direction of the tube. The heavy shell was fed by hand into the tube from the top and slid down until it hit a firing pin at the bottom of the tube. The charge in the bottom of the shell exploded, and the escaping gases pushed the shell back up the tube and launched it into the sky. It had an effective range of 3 miles, and the anti-personnel shells were devastating against the unprotected French paratroopers.

Ty estimated that his squad set up their mortar in just under 90 seconds. He was proud of their performance. The field phone rang. Ty picked it up and received his first fire mission as the leader of his squad. He was excited as he plotted the coordinates on his map. Ty called out the coordinates to his gunner. The gunner used the sight and set the tube to the correct angle and direction. The gunner signaled the mortar was ready. Ty ordered his men to commence firing. The first of three loaders dropped the heavy shell into the tube and stepped away. The metal on metal scraping sound indicated that the shell was sliding down the tube as expected. There was a heavy thump as the shell fired and left the tube. The first shell was away. The next loader stepped up with a shell already in his hands, just as the Chinese advisors had trained him. A focused, well-trained mortar squad should be able to fire 22 shells per minute, thought Ty. His squad fired 24 shells per minute that day.

The Viet Minh's Northern Command Headquarters in Cao Bang was nondescript by design. There were no waving red flags with golden stars or communist slogans on hanging banners. There were no guards at the front doors or on the rooftop. There wasn't even a sign to designate the importance of the building and its occupants. It looked like every other building on the street. But it was important. To Ho Chi Minh and the Viet Minh forces that served him, it was everything.

In his bedroom on the second floor of the headquarters, General Giap sat at a wooden table, looking down into a steaming bowl of rice soup. His bedroom was simple, with little adornment beyond a framed photo of Mao. The starchy smell of boiled rice lifted into his nostrils as he inhaled. He cracked a fresh egg and let the contents slide into the hot broth. He watched as a white film formed over the golden yolk. He missed the simple things, like rice soup in the morning. Things that made one's life feel steady and common and sure. His time was filled with troop inspections, writing reports to the Politburo, and meetings with his field commanders. The camp staff always tried to make him comfortable, but it wasn't the same. At night, he would sleep in the back of his sedan as he traveled to the next camp. Any spare time was spent forming strategies that would shorten the war that he both loved and hated. Simple things were a luxury that he could not afford. That the people could not afford. His time was not his own.

But this morning, he stole a bit of time for himself, just a moment, to watch an egg cook in his rice soup. There was a knock on the door. Giap looked up to see a captain enter. It was a familiar face. The captain was his assistant assigned by the politburo. Maybe a spy, maybe not. No matter. Giap had nothing to hide and had long ago given up second-guessing what the directors of the Politburo thought of his performance. The captain snapped to attention.

"Yes, Captain?"

"A report, sir."

"And it couldn't wait until after I had shaved?"

"It's from the highlands, sir. There's been an action."

Giap's interest grew. He waved the captain over and read the report he was handed. "Paratroopers. Do we know which unit?"

"They found a dead medical officer hanging in a tree. He had been shot by our men while descending. His insignia showed that he was from GAP 2, sir."

"Colonel Langlais' outfit?"

"Yes, sir."

"What is Langlais doing in Dien Bien Phu? They already built a garrison there and gave it up last year. Why go back? Why now?"

"We don't know, sir."

Giap thought for a long moment until a realization developed, "The airfield. They want the airfield."

"Sir?"

Giap's mind was racing, grasping. So much to do, and it all had to be done now, while there was still time, while there was still hope. He frantically scribbled a note and handed it to the captain along with the report.

"Get this note and the report to Uncle Ho right away. And tell him that I would like to meet with him as soon as practical."

"Yes, sir."

"I want an updated status report on every unit in the area around Dien Bien Phu, both French and Viet Minh. I want every map of Dien Bien Phu and the surrounding area. And I want aerial photographs."

"Sir, we have no aircraft," said the captain, confused.

"Tell our intelligence operatives in Hanoi to steal the photos from the French. It is to be their top priority. Tell General Thai I want to see him as soon as possible and tell our engineering staff I want a report on the condition of the roads to and from Dien Bien Phu in all directions. Even if it is a goat path, I want to know its current condition. If they don't know its condition, then have them send someone to perform an inspection. It will be about the roads, Captain. It will be all about the roads."

"Yes, sir. Right away, General."

The captain exited.

Giap walked over to a bookshelf stuffed with maps, reports, and paperwork, plus a few well-worn history books such as Sun Tzu's Art of War, Carl von Clausewitz's On War, and Nicolai Machiavelli's The Prince. He pulled out a rolled-up map and walked back to the table, where he pushed his soup aside and unrolled the map. It was a map of the Vietnam highlands and Laos. Dien Bien Phu was only 12 kilometers from the border between the two countries. A strong, mobile French force at Dien Bien Phu could easily cut off the supply lines to any Viet Minh force invading Laos. The French believed that the valley of Dien Bien Phu and its airfield were the keys to any invasion into Laos, he thought. The French Commanding General Navarre would fight to keep Laos, and therefore must fight to keep Dien Bien Phu. By dropping Langlais and his men into the valley, Navarre had made the first move. Now it was Giap's turn.

It was early afternoon and hot. The sky was clear after the morning haze had burned off, but in the distance, dark clouds approached with the promise of rain. A starter motor whined, and a prop slowly turned. With a thump-thump, the Daisy Mae's right engine cranked, and five-foot flames shot out of the exhausts as it roared to life. In the cockpit, McGoon sat in the pilot seat, with Coyle sitting next to him as the co-pilot.

Inside the plane's massive hull sat 66 paratroopers and Brigitte. Her portable typewriter case was in her lap and was tied to her jump harness with a long cord so it could hang below her while she dropped. With a little luck, she wouldn't land on top of it and break it. She was a modern journalist and disliked writing with a pencil and paper. Brigitte looked down at her bouncing knee. It was a familiar sight before any combat jump, but especially when she had been warned that the drop zone would be hot. She put her hand on her knee and pressed down until it was still. She didn't want the others to see that she was nervous. They were nervous, too, and like her, wanted to hide their fear from their fellow soldiers. Everyone knew that fear was just part of the job, but like the emperor with no clothes, some things were best kept a secret. Jumping into a battle was never easy, no matter how many times one did it. It wasn't being unafraid that made a soldier brave. It was being afraid and jumping anyway that made a soldier brave. These men were the bravest of the brave, the best France had to offer, and Brigitte knew it. That's why she jumped with them. They deserved to have their story told, and she was going to tell it, no matter what happened to her. She started to sing "Le Marche" and was quickly joined by the soldiers at her side.

McGoon steered the Daisy Mae onto the far end of the runway and pulled the aircraft to a stop. He locked the wheel brakes. Coyle and McGoon did a cockpit check of props, mixture, throttles, and flaps. A quick wipeout of the controls and the takeoff checklist was complete. An aircraft the size of the C-119 left little room for error during takeoff and landing. With everything in the correct position, Coyle nodded his okay, and McGoon pushed the two throttle levers forward. The Daisy Mae's engines roared, but the aircraft did not move. He needed all the engines at close to full power before the aircraft started down the runway. The wheel brakes strained against the heave of the engines. McGoon focused on the side-by-side tachometers that measured the rotations per minute of the dual engines. If the engines over-revved, they could blow up, potentially sending a prop into the hull where Brigitte and the paratroopers sat. But if they under-revved, the Daisy Mae would not achieve enough speed to take off. It was a delicate balance. Coyle focused on everything else – oil pressure, cylinder head pressure, fuel flow, and exhaust gas temperature. There were other gauges for flight systems and navigation, but those did not matter at the moment. It was all about the power required to lift a 32-ton aircraft and its cargo off the ground before they ran out of runway. When the engines finally hit the required revolutions, McGoon released the smoking wheel brakes and pushed the throttles all the way forward. The Daisy Mae's engine roared even louder as she hit full power. She lunged forward and rolled down the runway, gaining speed.

Brigitte and the paratroopers beside her were surprised by the ear-splitting roar of the engines at full throttle. One by one, they stopped singing as they felt an incredible power vibrating the hull. This beast was not like the smaller C-47s to which they had grown accustomed. Even with its massive wingspan and twin tail booms, the Daisy Mae needed more takeoff speed than the lighter C-47s.

As they reached the end of the runway, McGoon and Coyle both pulled back on their yokes. The Daisy Mae lifted into the sky. McGoon banked the aircraft to the left and joined the formation of aircraft waiting in the sky above the airfield. They would fly in formation to the battlefield. There was safety in numbers. The more targets for the Viet Minh snipers, the better the odds of surviving the journey.

Bruno rejoined Lieutenant Le Page's company with seven stragglers in tow. They had been fighting house to house with the Viet Minh for control of the village. In general, the French soldiers were better armed and better trained than the Viet Minh, but both were brave and believed in their cause. The French paratroopers were especially aggressive and stubborn and feared by the Viet Minh. However, at the moment, the Viet Minh outgunned and outnumbered the lightly-armed paratroopers. Bruno knew that if he didn't turn the tide of battle, his men would be overrun and wiped out. Defeat was one thing Bruno would not accept, and the paratroopers under his command were prepared to fight to the last man if necessary.

Bruno found his executive officer talking on a handheld field radio, communicating with the pilot of the reconnaissance aircraft hovering above the valley. The battalion had lost all their long-range radio sets during the jump and had no way of reporting to their commanding officer in Hanoi. The pilot agreed to act as a relay between the field commanders on the ground in Dien Bien Phu and Colonel Langlais at his headquarters in Hanoi until new radio sets could be dropped.

The XO gave Bruno a quick breakdown of where things currently stood. All six companies in Bruno's battalion had reported in and were engaged with the enemy at different locations around the valley.

Most of the mortars and ammunition parachuted in for Lieutenant Allaire's weapons company were lost in the long grass. His men had only recovered one mortar tube with three shells. Hardly an armory for a weapons company that supported four rifle companies.

Lieutenant Trapp's 2nd Company was busy protecting the battalion's flank on the southern edge of the drop zone when he called in for support fire. Lieutenant Allaire ordered a barrage at the requested fire coordinates, and all three shells were launched from the one mortar tube in less than thirty seconds. It was a very efficient but embarrassingly short barrage.

"Perhaps we should let the tube cool," said a straight-faced assistant gunner.

"And perhaps you should find my fucking mortars and shells, or your supper will be grenades, of which I have plenty," said the unamused Lieutenant Allaire. His men disappeared back into the long grass to continue the search.

Bruno's 3rd Company was commanded by Lieutenant Magnilatt and was tasked with securing the airstrip. The Viet Minh were fighting fiercely to fend off the assault but were outmaneuvered by the paratroopers and forced to pull back. The paratroopers loved taking ground from the enemy. It was better than a cold beer on a hot day.

The 4th Company, commanded by Lieutenant de Wilde, was dropped late and landed several miles to the north of their intended drop zone. They regrouped and headed back in the direction of the aircrafts' flight path as they were trained. It took nearly four hours, and several skirmishes with the Viet

Minh before the 4th Company finally made it back to Natacha.

The French needed to finish the battle quickly and drive the Viet Minh from the battlefield. Bruno's big concern was enemy reinforcements. If the Viet Minh commanders were given the time to send more troops, the odds of victory could very quickly tip against the French. Bruno instructed his XO to call in an airstrike on the Viet Minh recoilless gun and mortar positions protecting the village and the airstrip.

Coyle and McGoon watched the mountains below through the windshield. "Should be coming up... right... about... now," said McGoon.

As the Daisy Mae cleared the last mountain, a valley appeared below. At the far end, the familiar signs of a silent battle. Fire and smoke rose up, forming a grey-brownish haze over the village and airstrip. A mortar shell exploded, and then another.

"The Frenchies and Viet Minh are really slugging it out."

"I'll tell the sergeant," said Coyle as he rose from his co-pilot's chair.

"Let Dominque do it. He's the navigator. I don't need him when I can see where we're going."

"I don't mind. I need to stretch my legs anyway. I'll just be a minute," said Coyle as he slipped through the cockpit door.

"Fine. I'll just fly her by my lonesome," said McGoon to himself.

In the cargo hold, Brigitte looked over at Coyle. There was fear in her eyes. He informed the sergeant in charge of the 'stick' of paratroopers that they were over the valley and that a battle was raging. The sergeant warned his men to perform a last-minute check on their equipment and to be ready to "hook-up" in two minutes. Coyle moved over to Brigitte. "You okay?" said Coyle.

"Yes, yes. Of course. I'm just..."

"Just what?"

"You would think it would get easier."

"Jumping from a plane?"

"No. Dropping into a firefight."

"No, I suppose it don't," said Coyle. "You know, you don't have to do this."

"No. But somebody should... for them," said Brigitte, motioning to the paratroopers. "I'm here now. Don't worry too much, Mr. Coyle. The Viet

Minh don't like to waste their precious bullets on journalists. Our typewriters don't shoot back."

"Good luck and stay safe."

"Merci."

Brigitte shifted her eyes away, releasing him.

Coyle walked back up the cargo hold and into the cockpit. "Everything okeydokey back there?" said McGoon as Coyle sat down.

"Yeah. They're getting ready."

"And your little reporter friend?"

"Yeah. Her, too."

"Okay, then. Let's take her down to twenty-five hundred."

McGoon banked the aircraft into a slow downward spiral over drop zone "Simone," to the southeast of the old airfield.

Inside Daisy Mae's cargo hold, the sergeant motioned for Brigitte to join him in an empty seat near the door. "Mademoiselle Friang, if you please?"

Brigitte tried to stand. Her gear and the parachute were heavy for her small frame. Even with her typewriter and her rucksack tied to her harness below her reserve parachute, the parachute on her back was still much heavier and made her feel unbalanced. She stumbled and sat back down. It was embarrassing, but she couldn't help herself. The men sitting on either side helped her up. She shuffled over to the sergeant and sat down. Normally, a correspondent would be the last to jump, but the sergeant had orders to watch over Brigitte. He wanted to keep her close, and that meant she would jump with him. The red light came on, signaling that the Daisy Mae was approaching the drop zone.

The jumpmaster opened the door, and the cold wind rushed in along with the thunderous thrum of the engines. The jumpmaster barked out orders to "Stand up" and "Hook up." The paratroopers stood and hooked up to the overhead cable. The sergeant helped Brigitte stand up and move to the center. The sergeant grabbed her static parachute line and attached it next to his on the cable. The jump light changed to green, and the buzzer sounded. "Go!" said the Jumpmaster. One by one, the paratroopers and Brigitte jumped.

The jerk of the parachute opening knocked the wind out of Brigitte, and she was caught in the moment. Adrenaline pumped through her body, and she quickly recovered. She gathered her wits and focused on what needed to be done next. She released her rucksack from below her reserve parachute and let it dangle down on a long line. Next, she released her typewriter in its case and let it dangle down just below her rucksack. She decided to swing her typewriter away at the last second before landing so she wouldn't land on top of it. She grabbed the typewriter's cord and wrapped it twice around her hand. She felt the "green rush" of the approaching ground and swung her arm, holding the typewriter cord. The typewriter swung out from underneath her just like she planned, but the weight of the box acted as a pendulum and swung her body sideways. She landed with a thud on her side, almost horizontal. The wind was knocked out of her, and it took a few moments to finally catch her breath. She would have a large bruise on her thigh, but her typewriter was safe. The willing sacrifice of a journalist. The sergeant ran over to her and crouched down, holding his submachine gun. "Are you okay?"

"Yes."

"Can you walk?"

"Yes."

He helped her out of her parachute harness. She gathered up her chute as she had been taught and set it down next to the sergeant's. She found her rucksack, unclipped the long line, and slipped it onto her back. Next, she found her typewriter, unclipped its long line, and opened the case to take a quick peek. No damage. She was relieved. She closed the case, grabbed the handle, and moved to the sergeant's side. "Stay close and keep your head down," said the sergeant.

They moved off through the tall elephant grass in the direction of machine guns firing and mortars exploding in the distance. Somewhere out there, a battle raged, and they were walking into it, thought Brigitte. It seemed like such an insane thing to do and went against all her instincts to run in the opposite direction. She followed the sergeant.

A squadron of eight B-26 Marauders was already en route to the valley when their flight leader received the relayed message. Bruno's men marked their location with smoke grenades, so the Marauders did not inadvertently bomb the wrong positions. The B-26's swooped in low at 1,500 feet, so there was a reduced chance of "friendly fire" killing French troops. They lined up one after the other, dropped their load, and banked hard to allow the next bomber to make its run.

The bombs whistled in on their targets, followed by a series of explosions that shook the ground. The far end of the village erupted in balls of fire. The air was sucked up and away in a heat funnel, making it hard to breathe. The thatched roofs caught fire and burned like torches dipped in oil. Civilians that hadn't left when the fighting started were burned alongside the soldiers. The Viet Minh's back was broken, and their will to fight was gone. The survivors retreated from the village and moved toward the safety of the surrounding hills. The French had won the day, but the battle wasn't over.

The surviving civilians ran for their lives into the long grass. The Viet Minh soldiers regrouped at the edge of the village. Their commanders knew the French would not just stop and let the Viet Minh retreat in peace. The French paratroopers were trained to inflict as much damage as possible to remove their enemy's will to fight back.

Ty's mortar squad was ordered to stay behind and slow the advance of the French forces. His men set up their mortar and launched a barrage of shells from the single tube. As expected. the French forces were exhausted from fighting and hesitated. They had already taken control of the village and the airstrip and were not in the mood to sacrifice more of their lives. Ty's squad kept up the fire until they ran out of shells. Ty and his men had bought time for their comrades. They had done their duty. They gathered their equipment and slipped into the long grass in hopes of escape.

The commander of the main column of retreating Viet Minh expected to eventually meet the reinforcements he had requested on their way to the village. He was not expecting Major Souquet's 1st Colonial Para Battalion on its way to the village from drop zone Simone. The French scouts were the first to spot the approaching Viet Minh. Major Souquet ordered his weapons platoon to set up their recoilless rifles and machine guns just inside the tree line that paralleled the road leading to the mountains.

As the Viet Minh passed, the French opened fire. Brigitte watched and took notes as the new battle progressed. To her surprise, the Viet Minh did not run away in the rout, as the French had expected. Instead, the Viet Minh stood their ground and fought as they retreated. This was new for the Viet Minh - discipline. Brigitte thought about Napoleon's famous line, "You must not fight too often with one enemy, or you will teach him all your art of war." The Viet Minh had learned and learned well. They were no longer a band of guerillas striking, then slinking away into the bush. These men knew how to fight toe-to-toe with the French. Even in defeat, the Viet Minh were dangerous.

A mist had settled over the valley as the sun set. Two paratroopers hammered white crosses at the head of twelve fresh graves. Stepping back, they came to attention and saluted the French Tricolor flag waving above the newly created cemetery on a hillside overlooking the airfield.

The Viet Minh did not attempt to retake the village or the airstrip that night. They had had enough and needed to recover from their brawl with the French. Viet Minh snipers occasionally took shots at French soldiers that strayed from their hastily built foxholes and trenches, but for the most part, it was quiet. Disturbingly quiet and cold.

As night approached the valley, so did the clouds, and the temperature dropped fast. Brigitte made her home on the hilltop of Elaine near the mayor's mansion. Two nearby paratroopers saw her struggling to dig a foxhole with the entrenching spade the sergeant had loaned her. They showed pity and dug the hole for her. She knew that the two men were probably even more exhausted than she was, but she didn't refuse the offer when it came. The air was thinner in the highlands than in the lowlands around Hanoi, and even though she was in pretty good shape, she was feeling the fatigue that often comes with altitude. When they finished, she offered them a can of cassoulet from her jump pack. They were both Vietnamese and didn't like Western food, but accepted her gift out of politeness. Besides, it was better than the combat rations they had been issued before the drop. What they really wanted was some warm rice with a little fish sauce, but that would need to be scrounged from the village over the next few days.

After the two men left, Brigitte carried her gear and her parachute into her newly dug foxhole. It wasn't much of a shelter, but it would keep her safe in the event of a mortar attack. She knew that she only had a few minutes to fix something hot to eat before the bugler signaled "lights out" and she would have to extinguish her portable stove. She lit the can of fuel at the base of the stove and used the tool on her Swiss army knife to open the remaining can of cassoulet from her pack. Inside the can were baked white beans in a thick tomato sauce with slices of sausage and onion. She left part of the lid attached as a handle and set it on the little burner to heat. Her eyes were heavy. She closed them for what she thought was a moment. The bugler woke her a few minutes later. Her can of cassoulet was smoking badly and burned beyond recognition. "Merde," she said.

She blew out the fuel and picked through the smoldering mess that was her dinner in hopes of finding some bits that were less charred. She soon gave up and set everything aside. She would try again in the morning. She used her parachute to keep warm and to protect her typewriter from the morning dew that she knew would come. She watched as a reconnaissance plane slowly circled above and dropped "Firefly" parachute flares that illuminated the rice fields in front of the French positions. She thought about the American flyer that had helped her at the restaurant and was concerned for her safety before the jump. He knew nothing about her or the things she had done. He was arrogant and thought her weak. She wasn't. Still, he had a certain "backwoods" charm and was not bad to look at for an American. The magnesium in the parachute flares burned brightly as they slowly fell to earth. Her eyelids fell with them, and she was asleep.

The finest china, fresh-cut flowers, and his house staff in white formal wear signaled the importance of the visitor at General Navarre's villa in Saigon. Navarre dined with Admiral Cabanier, the assistant general deputy to the National Defense Committee, who had just flown in that afternoon from Paris. They were served in the dining room, away from any prying eyes and ears, even though the patio was cooler. Both general officers wore their best dress uniforms, each decorated with a 'fruit salad' of colorful medals above their left jacket pocket. It was an official visit.

Navarre did not enjoy politics. He was a military man and saw himself a warrior. Few doubted his bravery or his abilities to command. He was aggressive and an excellent strategist. But he did enjoy wearing his dress uniform. There were fewer occasions for it "in country," and he planned on making the most of it. Entertaining dignitaries gave him an opportunity to show his culture and knowledge of wine, a point of personal pride. He believed that good general officers did not get involved in the day-to-day operations of the men under their command. That kind of micromanaging rarely helped improve performance and offered little room for growth in his subordinates. His focus must remain on the whole of Indochina. The big picture. "How do you manage such a fine meal this far from France?" said

Cabanier.

"I have an excellent brigade de cuisine. My chef was originally a saucier at the Grand Hôtel National in Lucerne, and trained under the master chef Georges Auguste Escoffier," said Navarre.

"Remarkable. How did you find such a treasure?"

"I am a general; I have my spies," said Navarre with a smile. "The wine is the biggest problem. It gets tossed about when flown in, and the change in temperature does little to help the vintage. It takes three months of resting in my cellar just to resettle the sediments."

"Impressive," said Cabanier as he shifted uneasily in his chair. "General, I am afraid I do not bring good news."

"Oh?"

"The Defense Committee has reviewed your request for reinforcements…"

"And?"

"We cannot fully oblige at this time."

"Oblige at this time?"

"General, with our new NATO demands, and uprisings in North Africa, our resources are stretched too thin. And the political environment in Paris is not favorable for increasing our commitment in Indochina. Few see the value in wasting more lives for a war we know we will lose in time, even if honor demands it."

"Admiral, when I submitted my plan for a winter offensive to the committee for approval, I was assured I would receive the support I required. I have committed my men to battle based on those promises."

"I understand, General. Believe me, I do. We are not denying the entire request; we just pared it down to an acceptable level."

"How acceptable?"

"One third."

Navarre was stunned.

"You, of course, are free to recruit from regional resources to make up the difference," said Cabanier. "The good news is that the Americans have agreed to supply your full list of additional weapons and replacement aircraft."

"Now, if we can just find the pilots," said Navarre.

The conversation was more subdued the rest of the evening as they drank their coffee and sipped brandy. They talked of little things. Navarre's mind was preoccupied and distant. He knew there was little hope of changing the committee's mind. He and his men would once again have to make do with the resources available. Operation Castor needed more, and he knew it, but it was too late to turn back now, he thought. Or was it?

THE GARRISON

The first day of the French occupation of Dien Bien Phu was quiet, except for the occasional Viet Minh mortar attack and the sniper fire from the surrounding forest. As usual, a thick mist hung over the valley, and it smelled of damp earth. The hills were green and covered with thick grass, bushes, and trees. The two enemies could not see each other, except for the occasional glimpse as soldiers moved across an open area. The Viet Minh occupied the surrounding mountains and most of the villages in the valley. They took up firing positions along the earthen dikes that hemmed the rice paddies with their muddy ponds and in the few small groves of trees that had not been cut down by the villagers for their farms. The French had occupied several hills and sent out patrols to keep the Viet Minh from getting too close to their positions. The French still had no artillery beyond their mortars, but they could call in airstrikes if the enemy consolidated. Both sides would pick at each other with sniper fire and the occasional mortar barrage. Neither side was ready for a major conflict and kept to themselves whenever possible, like a match that nobody wanted to light.

The civilians that had left during the first day of fighting were now returning. They had no choice. They had to tend their farms and feed their animals, or they would starve. They would hide when a battle broke out between the two antagonists and then return to work as soon as the fighting died down. Like most wars, civilians and soldiers shared in death equally, and this war was no different.

The early morning fog of Vietnam was a two-edged sword for the French and Viet Minh. It kept their soldiers cool, but it hid their enemy. The fog would remain until the sun burned it off sometime in the late morning or early afternoon. The French paratroopers wasted little time and went to work. Rudimentary foxholes dug into the hills were the beginnings of the garrison that would protect them from the Viet Minh assaults they knew would come. The highest priority was the repair of the airfield. The airfield was their lifeline, and without it, all supplies, ammunition, and reinforcements would need to be airdropped, a painstakingly slow and dangerous process. It was not uncommon for a soldier not paying attention to be crushed by a one-ton pallet of ammunition floating down silently from the sky.

Two platoons of paratroopers used their mobile entrenching tools to fill in the potholes and trenches dug by the Viet Minh. The Viet Minh had hidden anti-personnel mines at the bottom of some of the potholes, which forced the French to inspect each hole thoroughly before filling it in. It slowed the work, which was exactly what the Viet Minh wanted. Once a hole or trench was filled in with dirt, soldiers used homemade soil tampers borrowed from the villagers to compress the dirt. They could not compress the runway enough to carry the weight of the cargo aircraft, but it would withstand the landing of smaller scout planes. Bruno supervised the work and kept tabs on the patrols that protected the perimeter of the airfield.

"This is why I joined the paratroopers? To fill in potholes?" said a French corporal.

"I should have stayed in Lyon and worked on a road crew," said another paratrooper.

"Yes, but girls' panties would not get wet when you walked by in your red beret," said Bruno.

"Good point," said the corporal.

"The sooner you finish, the better we eat," said Bruno.

The mention of better food picked up the pace of the work. The French field kitchens were known for their cuisine, and the chefs took great pride in the quality of the food they served to the soldiers. The men were already tired of the field rations they had carried into battle in their rucksacks. Bruno always knew how to motivate the troops under his command.

On the hilltop called "Dominique" that overlooked the airfield, Brigitte took photos with her camera and interviewed some of the Legionnaires as they worked. A Legionnaire sergeant and private set up a recoilless rifle on a dirt platform built in the side of a trench. The firing position had a two-foot notch for the barrel and was reinforced by double-thick stacks of sandbags, with a compacted dirt slope in front. It could easily take hundreds of hits from a heavy machine gun and even withstand a couple of shots from another recoilless rifle before the defensive barrier gave way.

"You're from Romania?" said Brigitte, taking notes.

"Yes. I'm from Brasov in Transylvania, just below the Carpathian Mountains," said the private.

"Land of vampires," said the sergeant with a smirk.

"And you, Sergeant?" asked Brigitte.

"Bucharest, the capital. My family owns a restaurant," said the sergeant. "My father is the chef. Best sarmale and mamaliga in all of Romania."

"That's a matter of opinion," said the private.

"What would you know? You only suck blood," said the sergeant.

"And how did you end up in the Legion?" asked Brigitte.

"The movie Beau Geste," said the sergeant. "I wanted to be Gary Cooper."

"Private?" said Brigitte.

"I killed a man," said the private. "It was an accident. I was repairing the facade on the front of the town's movie theatre, and a hammer fell off the top of my ladder. He was walking underneath, and it hit him on the top of the head. What kind of idiot walks under a ladder while a man is working? Anyway, he never woke up. Judge gave me three years for negligence. I ran from the courtroom before they could haul me away. I ended up in Algiers and joined the Legion."

"Did the recruiting officer know of your crime?" asked Brigitte.

"He didn't ask a lot of questions," said the private.

"They don't, you know?" said the sergeant. "It's a fair trade. Ambivalence for loyalty."

"And a chance for a new life in France when my three years are up," said the private. "Things could be worse, yes?"

It was still morning and hot, but the sky was clear at the Bach Mai airfield outside of Hanoi. A Vietnamese ground crew loaded a small bulldozer and its heavy steel blade--each strapped separately to reinforced wooden pallets--into the back of the Daisy Mae. The entire process was supervised by the Daisy Mae's loadmaster, Kim-ly, whose name meant "Golden Lion." Nothing was loaded into the aircraft's hold without Kim-ly knowing what it was and how much it weighed. It was his responsibility to keep the load balanced and he took it seriously. Like many Vietnamese, Kim-ly had joined the French because of the money. The French Air Force paid well. He didn't really care who ruled his country as long as he had enough money to feed his family and to buy the two beers that he drank after each shift. He worked hard and learned enough French to understand the commands he was given, and even joke with the French aircrews. He was proud of his promotion to loadmaster and thankful for the additional money accompanying the new rank.

Each of the jump packages had a large cargo parachute mounted on top and attached to the pallets. Under Kim-ly's watchful eye, the ground crew secured the pallets to the cargo deck with steel cables so the load wouldn't shift during flight.

One of the ground crew squatted down out of sight as if checking a deck cable. He waited until the French lapdog Kim-ly exited the back of the aircraft with the rest of the ground crew. He used a small pair of bolt cutters to cut a nick in one of the parachute's steel cables on the bulldozer's pallet. He was careful not to cut all the way through, which might be seen on closer inspection by Kim-ly or his assistant loadmaster. Instead, he would let the weight of the load help his little sabotage. He was careful to leave the aircraft's cargo hold without Kim-ly seeing him.

Inside the cockpit, Coyle sat in the engineer's seat and watched as McGoon supervised the removal of the Daisy Mae's pilot's chair and the installation of an oversized wicker chair in its place.

"Not exactly military issue, is it?" said Coyle.

"We ain't military. 'Sides, I believe in comfort," said McGoon.

"Can't argue with that," said Coyle. "So, did you keep tabs on any of the other guys from our training squadron?"

"Nah. My letter writing kinda tapered off after I got captured. The Japs weren't big believers in free speech."

"How did you finally escape?"

"I didn't. They were marching a bunch of us to a new prison camp up in the hills. They weren't feeding us nothing but a little rice with a fish head now and then. I got to the point where I was so weak I couldn't walk anymore, so I sat down on the trail and refused to get up. They waited for a few minutes, then left me with a squad and kept the other prisoners moving up the hill. After about an hour, the corporal in charge of the squad had his guys build me a kinda hammock attached to two poles and started carrying me up the hill. They got so tired, they had to trade off every ten or fifteen minutes. Finally, they got in a big fight over whose turn it was, and they just left me there in the middle of the trail."

"Why didn't they just shoot ya?"

"Never did figure that part out. I guess I was kinda famous for shooting down all those Jap Zeroes. I imagine they had orders not to shoot me cuz the mucky-mucks in Tokyo wanted to have a big public trial and hang me."

"Are you yanking my chain, McGoon?"

"I swear on a stack of bibles."

With his new chair in place, McGoon sat down to give it a try. "Oh yeah, that's much better," he said, trying the different controls. "Look, Coyle. I can pull the yoke all the way back without hitting my belly. That's gonna make takeoffs a lot easier."

Lieutenant Colonel Langlais jumped out of the C-47's rear door, and his chute snapped open with an all too familiar jolt against his harness. He could see the valley clearly. He made mental notes of the major landmarks and their positions in relation to the airfield. It would be all about the airfield. That was the prize. That's why they were here. That's why some of his men would die.

There was little enemy fire from below. Bruno had led two platoons around the perimeter of the landing zone and cleared away any snipers. It would not do to have his commander killed while under his watch. Besides, he liked and respected Langlais. Langlais loved the men under his command but understood the need to sacrifice. Their lives would not be wasted if Langlais was in charge. That was all a paratrooper could ask of his commander. It was good to have him in the valley.

Colonel Langlais could not see the tree stump hidden below the long grass. A farmer had long ago cut down the tree so he could build his family a house of wood, and a colony of carpenter ants had hollowed out the rotting insides of the stump. Langlais' left boot plunged deep into the decomposing stump. He fell backward and landed on his ass. He was unharmed. He pulled at his boot. It was stuck. "Merde." He saw his chute flutter on the top of the grass. There was a slight crosswind. He realized what was coming. "No, no. You behave." He pulled harder to free his boot. It wouldn't budge. He struggled to free himself from his gear and his parachute harness, but it was too late. The wind was light but enough to re-inflate his chute and pull him like a puppet. He heard his ankle snap. He fought down a scream, not wanting to give away his position to the enemy. He pulled out his knife and cut the two straps between his harness and the parachute. Without tension, the parachute collapsed. Langlais fell back in pain, helpless. It was one of Bruno's platoons that found him.

Langlais sat outside a thatched hut as a medic examined his swollen ankle. Brigitte used her typewriter to put the finishing touches on her story.

"Colonel, may I use your radio to publish my story?" said Brigitte.

"Yes, as long as it doesn't interfere with operations," said Langlais.

The medic probed the fracture with his fingers. Langlais winced. His temper was short. "You don't need to poke it to know that it's broken, Sergeant."

"Yes, sir. It's definitely broken. Shall I arrange for your evacuation?"

"No. Get my boot back on before my ankle is too swollen, then wrap it up as best you can. Tight."

"It's gonna hurt."

"Really, Sergeant?"

"Sorry, sir."

"And find me a walking stick."

Brigitte pulled a small flask from her backpack and offered it to Langlais. "Cognac to kill the pain?" said Brigitte.

Langlais took a long pull from the small flask. Bruno approached with a white mountain pony in tow.

"Your stallion awaits, Colonel," said Bruno.

"You can't be serious," said Langlais.

"It's a big valley."

The medic pushed Langlais' boot back on. Langlais swallowed his scream and drained the rest of the flask of its Cognac.

Brigitte took a photo of Langlais riding on the little white pony. It was now a moment in history.

Cogny sat at his desk in his Hanoi headquarters and updated Navarre in Saigon by phone. "Our troop strength after the initial assault is twenty-six hundred and fifty. There were fifteen killed in action and thirty-five wounded," said Cogny.

"That's good. Lighter than our estimates," said Navarre.

"Yes, General. We got lucky."

"And the enemy?"

"One hundred fifteen bodies were recovered. I imagine many more were carried away. We captured four prisoners. All were wounded. And as expected, there were some civilian casualties from the crossfire."

"And enemy strength?"

"We know Battalion 910 is there and putting up resistance, but as for the others... we're unsure of their location and strength."

"Our priority should be determining the location of the other three battalions."

"Colonel Langlais reports that his men are in high spirits and ready to fight."

"They're paratroopers. They're always ready to fight. Instruct Langlais to probe the enemy defenses. We must know what we are facing."

"Yes, sir."

"I think it's time to consolidate our other forces in the area. Close the garrison at Lai Chau and have air transport pick up Lieutenant Colonel Trancart and his battalion and transport them to Dien Bien Phu."

"And the villagers?"

"Those that can make the trek should join with the Thai auxiliaries and travel by land."

"And those that can't make it?"

"We're not the Red Cross, Rene. They must fend for themselves."

"Yes, sir."

Navarre hung up the phone.

The Daisy Mae appeared over the mountain rim and immediately started its descent toward drop zone Octavie to the south of the airstrip.

Inside the cockpit, McGoon sat in his new pilot's chair. "Good chair always takes a bit of adjustment," said McGoon.

"Like a pair of cowboy boots?" said Coyle.

"Something like that. You really ought to get you one of these when your plane arrives."

"I'll make do with what I'm issued."

"Suit yourself. It's your butt."

The rear cargo door on the Daisy Mae opened. Kim-ly and his assistant loadmaster, each wearing a safety harness attached to a cable, rolled the two pallets to the edge of the ramp and attached the parachute static lines.

Inside the cockpit, Coyle flipped the switch on the cargo launch indicator as McGoon goosed the throttle a bit and pulled back on the yoke to kick up the nose of the Daisy Mae.

Inside the hold, Kim-ly and his assistant loadmaster watched the red light switch to green and felt the familiar upward tilt of the aircraft that allowed them to easily shove the packages out of the back end one after the other.

The parachutes on top of the two pallets were the heavy-duty triple canopy-type, designed to float the largest of loads. Both popped open when the packages holding the bulldozer, and its blade left the cargo hold, and their static lines snapped tight.

Coyle watched out of the side window as the Daisy Mae banked hard to the right. "Looking good on both loads," said Coyle.

"Good. First time I ever dropped a bulldozer. I'd hate to screw the pooch," said McGoon.

The sabotaged parachute harness on the bulldozer held for the first hundred feet, then the weight finally took its toll on the nick in the harness cable and broke through. One end of the pallet dropped a foot. That was enough to shift the load, and the bulldozer tore free of its pallet and the parachutes. It dropped toward the earth like a 6-ton bomb.

"Oh shit," said Coyle as he watched.

"I know what I mean when I say, 'Oh shit,' and it ain't never good," said McGoon.

"Harness failure. Bulldozer is off its pallet and in freefall," said Coyle.

"Oh shit," said McGoon. "We screwed the pooch."

"Better warn your buddies on the ground we got a hot load coming down," said Coyle to the navigator and the engineer. Neither understood. Coyle made hand motions to describe what happened. The navigator switched his radio set and called the units on the ground to warn them. It was already too late.

A farmer with a bundle of rice saplings hanging from a sling on his shoulder was replanting his field in knee-deep mud covered with a layer of water. He heard a loud thud and what felt like an earthquake. He looked over to see a fifteen-foot-deep crater in the center of the field. At the bottom of the crater sat the 6-ton bulldozer. He had never seen anything like it. Maybe he could sell whatever it is, he thought. A cascade poured down from the sky, soaking the farmer in fertilized water and mud. The water from the field drained into the hole and filled in the crater. The machine was gone.

Coyle listened to the radio on his headset. "Yep. They're pissed. They want us to go back to Hanoi and pick up a replacement," said Coyle.

"So much for dinner," said McGoon as he turned the Daisy Mae back to Hanoi.

Brigitte walked along the French foxholes. Several of the men were packing their rucksacks with grenades and rations. She hurried along until she found Bruno just finishing a briefing. "You are going on patrol?" said Brigitte.

"Yes. The brass wants to know what's lurking in those mountains," said Bruno.

"How long will you be gone?"

"Three, maybe four days. Depends on how well the Viet Minh are at playing cache-cache."

"May I join you?"

"Of course, but no typewriter. I don't want to end up carrying it."

"That only happened one time because I twisted my knee."

"I still ended up carrying it," said Bruno. "Seriously, Brigitte. Pack light. There is going to be a fight if we are lucky, and we don't know what we'll be facing or how many. We have to be able to move fast if there is trouble."

"Okay, my little Bruno," said Brigitte. "No typewriter."

Brigitte moved off to get her gear.

Under the cover of darkness, Bruno led his battalion out of the French perimeter and toward the mountains surrounding the valley. Paratrooper recon squads scouted ahead and covered the flanks of the column. The recon squad on the left flank crossed a field and entered the thick underbrush on the edge of the forest. As they moved through the darkness, they strained to see the silhouettes and shadows and listen for any sounds that might announce the enemy's location.

They entered the forest. The light from the parachute flares was mostly blocked out by the tree canopy, and what little light did get through turned into moving patches of glowing green as the flares descended into the valley. The animals and birds that normally filled the forest with sound were long gone. The paratroopers only heard their own footsteps, which seemed amplified every time one of them stepped on a crunching leaf or snapped a twig. The more they tried to be silent, the more they knew the enemy could hear them and would be ready when they finally met somewhere in the night.

The air felt heavy and hard to breathe as they climbed up the mountainside. A French corporal almost tripped over a Viet Minh light machine gun position just three hundred yards into the forest. He was ripped in two when the machine opened fire on him at close range. What should have been a light skirmish turned into a full-fledged pitched battle when the

Viet Minh hit the recon squad with a hidden recoilless rifle. It was a Viet Minh heavy weapons platoon, already dug in like a tick and ready to scrap.

The paratroopers took multiple casualties early in the battle, surprised by the enemy's strength and determination. The flashes from guns and explosions lit up the mountainside. Brigitte was on the ground behind a tree. She kept her head down and stayed out of the way. The flashes of light from the explosions were blinding, and the air was pungent with the stench of cordite and nitroglycerin.

When the Viet Minh were finally overpowered by the French battalion, they abandoned their heavy weapons and fled deeper into the forest. Bruno moved up and examined the recoilless rifle position, which overlooked the valley below and, more importantly, the French airfield. The 75mm recoilless rifle was a direct-fire-only artillery piece and could only target an enemy in line-of-sight. Even so, once the airfield became operational, a well-placed shot could easily have taken out a plane taking off or landing. Bruno knew that it did not bode well that the French had no idea it was even here. He immediately radioed the information to his commander.

Langlais was sitting in his newly-built command bunker with his broken ankle, still in his boot, propped up on an empty ammunition case to relieve the swelling and slow the constant throbbing. He listened to the radio and was deeply concerned by Bruno's report. He ordered Bruno to send his wounded and dead back to the garrison and to continue his sweep of the mountainside.

It was early evening when Cogny called Navarre to give him an update on the garrison. "We were surprised to see a recoilless rifle hidden so close to the airfield. It had a clear line of sight on any aircraft landing or taking off," said Cogny.

"And the position was taken and the gun destroyed, I assume?" said Navarre.

"Yes. By Colonel Langlais and his paratroopers."

"Good. It seems the Viet Minh are taking the bait and surrounding the garrison."

"Yes. But much quicker than we expected."

"We cannot hope to foresee everything, Rene. We both understand that war requires flexibility."

"But if they cut off the airfield…"

"Then, we resupply and reinforce by airdrop until we retake the airfield."

"And our wounded?"

"We will do what we can for them. Honestly, Rene, did you think we could be victorious without sacrifice?"

"No, of course not. I just worry about the men."

"As do I, but only to a point. We cannot let our emotions cloud our judgment."

"With enemy positions surrounding the garrison, it will be difficult to carry out offensive operations."

"It may not matter. The point of the offensive maneuvers was to draw the Viet Minh to battle. If they surround and attack the garrison, we will achieve our objective. Let the Viet Minh come to us. We will crush them with our Air Force and artillery. We can finally end this war with honor."

It was raining, and the street was starting to flood when a car pulled up to General Giap's HQ. Two men got out and entered the building.

General Giap sat in his headquarters, poring over maps of Dien Bien Phu. An elderly university professor was escorted into the room by a Viet Minh lieutenant. "The professor you requested, General," said the lieutenant.

"Thank you, Lieutenant," said Giap.

The lieutenant took up a position by the door. The geologist looked around the room at the maps and models. He had never been inside a military building, much less met the great General Giap. "Would you like some tea?" said Giap

"No, thank you, sir," said the professor.

"You teach at the university?"

"Yes, sir. Geology. Twenty-two years."

"Are you familiar with the highlands near the Laotian border?"

"Yes, sir. It is part of the South China plate, one of my fields of study. I have taken several trips over my career to take soil and rock samples there."

"Any samples from Dien Bien Phu?"

"Of course. It is an important rice-growing region."

"I am more interested in the mountains around the valley."

"They date back to the early Paleozoic era. They are mostly made up of strata and igneous rock mixed with soil and sand."

"Can they be mined without the use of explosives?"

"Perhaps. I would need to take more samples of the exact area you have in mind."

"I need you to travel to the valley and take the samples you require to determine the viability of mining without explosives, especially near the airfield."

"When?"

"Now. I have a car waiting."

"But my classes," said the professor. "It will take several weeks to travel to the valley and back."

"I have already spoken to the head of the university and informed him that you are required elsewhere. Your students will be tended to, and your position will be waiting when you return. You have fifteen days to report back to me with your conclusions. And only me. Do you understand?"

"Yes, sir."

"Good journey, Professor," Giap said, motioning to the lieutenant standing by the door. "The people thank you for your service."

The professor was escorted out by the lieutenant and placed in the waiting car in front of the building. The car sped off in the rain.

It was early morning. A light mist hung over the airfield at Dien Bien Phu. The sound of a heavy engine straining pierced the fog. A newly assembled replacement bulldozer used its steel blade to fill in the potholes and trenches that remained in the old airfield. The paratroopers watched as the bulldozer made short order of the work they had done. A small but heavy steam-powered roller leveled and compressed the loose soil on the runway.
French engineers laid PSP - perforated steel plates - over the newly leveled ground, and the simple dirt runway became a steel-reinforced landing platform capable of handling the heaviest aircraft. The perforated holes in the grid allowed the rainwater to quickly drain off and kept the runway operational during the monsoon season. It was a shining example of modern engineering and was a key component of Navarre's air-bridge strategy. The airfield must stay open to receive supplies and reinforcements, even during severe weather.

In the skies above, C-47s continued to drop cases of ammunition and smaller supplies by parachute through their side cargo doors. The C-119s, with their rear doors and increased cargo capacity, were used for larger loads.

Inside the Daisy Mae's cockpit, McGoon and Coyle watched as the last mountain ridge swept below, and the valley appeared. "Coyle, you wanna take this one in?" said McGoon.

"Sure," said Coy.le.

Coyle took control of the aircraft. "Three hundred feet?" said Coyle.

"Roger that," said McGoon.

The Daisy Mae swooped down into the valley and aligned its flight path to run the length of drop zone Simone. The two doors that formed the back of the cargo hold opened between the twin tail booms.

"All right, boys. Let her rip," said Coyle over the intercom. The green light illuminated, and McGoon pulled back on the control wheel to kick up the plane's nose. Kim-ly and his assistant loadmaster pushed out twelve wooden pallets without parachutes, each carrying a ton-weight spool of barbed wire.

The pallets slid out of the back of the Daisy Mae's cargo ramp like a freight train falling off a cliff, plunging toward the drop zone below. The wooden pallets crashed into the ground and shattered into splinters. The barbed wire spools bounded like giant springs, unaffected by the drop.

Inside the Daisy Mae's cockpit, the side window cracked, revealing a bullet hole. It surprised the flight crew. Coyle heard a high-pitched whistle, like a bad note on a flute. He looked down at the floor and saw the bullet's entry point just two inches from his left foot. "Shit. We're taking fire," said McGoon. "Get us outta here, Coyle."

Coyle banked the Daisy Mae hard to the left and up. He pushed the throttles forward. The engines groaned under the strain. He flattened the ailerons, the wings leveled, and the Daisy Mae gained altitude. "Frenchies are supposed to patrol our flight path to clear out the snipers. That was the deal," said McGoon.

"It was a lucky shot," said Coyle.

"Lucky it didn't kill ya. Contract says no combat runs. They gonna keep us doing these low-level drops, we're gonna ask for hazard pay."

"For one bullet?"

"It's the principle. 'Sides, an extra 25 bucks a week ain't gonna break the French treasury."

"Each?" said Coyle.

"Each," said McGoon.

The Daisy Mae leveled off at a higher altitude and flew back over the mountain top on its way back to Hanoi.

Vietnamese and French paratroopers strung chest-high walls of triple concertina wire, consisting of two parallel lines of two-foot barbed-wire loops joined by twists of wire and topped by a third barbed wire loop. The concertina wire had been coated with oil to make cutting it with wire cutters more difficult. To make the concertina stacks even more effective, the French drove upright iron posts into the ground below the center of the stacks and tied them off with wire. Every three feet, the soldiers hung a couple of tin cans on the wire as alarms. This made going under the wire undetected almost impossible without tunneling, a dangerous and time-consuming process that was usually detected this close to the French lines.

Miles of barbed wire was strung in front of the trenches they protected. They wove back and forth across the hillsides and formed the perimeters of the garrison's strongpoints. Every section of wire had a gateway guarded by a squad of riflemen with a machine gun or flamethrower. The gateway's path through the wire doubled back several times and allowed French patrols to safely enter the strongpoint without setting off mines or getting entangled. It was a deadly labyrinth that only the French knew how to navigate and was kept secret until the dirt compacted by the soldier's boots revealed the path to the enemy. To stifle the enemy, the French built false gateways with compacted paths that led nowhere and were often mined.

Bruno and his executive officer, a young captain, inspected the men's work. It was standard procedure for field fighting positions, but hardly the fortress Navarre had envisioned. "Not exactly a Maginot Line, is it?" said the captain.

Bruno was unamused. "What about more wood and concrete? We need wood and concrete to build blockhouses," said Bruno.

"Nothing yet. Ammunition and troop transport still have priority. We stripped the wood from the houses in the villages. It's not thick enough for blockhouse headers or tunnels, but we have been able to use it to reinforce trench walls."

"How are we supposed to build a garrison without supplies?"

"Things should improve once the airfield is operational," said the captain.

"Let's hope the Viet Minh don't know that," said Bruno.

Coyle still wore his flight suit as he stood on the patio at the back of McGoon's bungalow overlooking the multi-colored Red River. He used a pen knife to carve the finishing touches on the leopard-shaped whistle he had worked on the night before. He gave it a try and played a simple tune. Below the patio on the riverbank, a five-year-old boy holding a bamboo fishing pole heard the whistle and looked up. Coyle, satisfied with his work, tossed the whistle down to the boy. The excited boy grinned at Coyle and blew a high-pitched shrill before running off. "Your parents are gonna love me," said Coyle.

Coyle, reflective, looked out at the dozens of sampans tied up along the river, selling fresh fish, rice, and vegetables to city-dwellers. It was a floating market, simple and efficient. McGoon walked out onto the patio.

"I figure we got time for a couple of beers and a beefsteak before we head over to Mama Sing's. Is that what you're wearing?" said McGoon.

"You suppose any of those people down there really gives a damn who is running their country? French, communists or otherwise?" said Coyle.

"Don't go getting philosophical on me when I'm hungry. You know it makes me cranky. Now get dressed and let's get something to eat. Mama Sing's is waiting."

"You go ahead. I'm not in the mood."

"You don't have to be in the mood. That's their job. And let me tell you, Mama Sing's girls take pride in their work."

Coyle considers for a moment, "Well, I am a bit hungry."

"Thataboy," said McGoon, slapping him on the shoulder a little too hard.

TERRA ROUGE

It was morning, and the November sky was a familiar bluish-grey. Three Morane scout planes were the first aircraft to land on the newly-built airstrip with its steel runway. The French now had eyes in the sky that could hunt down enemy positions and call in artillery strikes. The scout plane pilots stayed in the air as long as their fuel lasted and wasted little time on the ground once they refueled.

Eight 120mm mortars roared to life when one of the pilots spotted a Viet Minh machine gun position firing on French paratrooper foxholes on a nearby hill. The ground around the machine gun squad churned from explosions. It only took five rounds before the Viet Minh were blown to bloody pieces and the machine gun permanently destroyed.

The French paratroopers watching from a hillside cheered. In addition to their training and esprit de corps, artillery and aircraft gave the French an edge over the Viet Minh forces. A very sharp and powerful edge. Now that the airfield was operational, the French Air Force and artillery were truly dangerous, and the Viet Minh knew it. The airfield was code-named "Terra Rouge." Red earth.

It was late afternoon following many delays when Lieutenant Colonel Trancart led his battalion of Vietnamese Colonials and the leaders of the Thai federation onto the transport aircraft waiting on Lai Chau's airfield. The villagers wept as they prayed to their ancient stone gods for the last time. Thai partisans and French commandos walked through the village, setting fire to the thatched roofs on the long pole houses and throwing thermite grenades into storehouses to burn remaining food stocks. Nothing would be left for the Viet Minh.

As the planes took off, a large group of villagers gathered at the far end of the village to watch. Many cried, wondering if they would ever see their leaders again. They were to be escorted by the Thai auxiliary and gorilla units to their new home at Dien Bien Phu, some 50 miles to the south through heavy forests and steep mountain trails. It was not a good day to be sick or old.

The villagers, all wearing conical hats to shield against the rain and sun, loaded up their carts and headed out of the village perimeter that had protected their families for so many years. They traveled along the dirt mule trail that wound its way up into the hills. It would be a long haul and slow going, with most of the villagers on foot and carrying their belongings. It felt like the villagers were chum in shark-infested waters, just begging for a Viet Minh attack. The Thai commander knew his men would protect the people no matter the cost. The Viet Minh knew it, too. And so, he walked and waited and watched.

The first attack came shortly after sundown, barely a mile out of the abandoned garrison. The Viet Minh had waited until the villagers had been separated from the French. They laid in an ambush on the uphill side of the trail, using the long grass for camouflage. It didn't take much to break up the column. With the first mortar rounds exploding around them, the frightened villagers scattered into the hills, and the Thai Auxiliary units ran to protect them. Small groups of villagers and soldiers formed in the long grass under the cover of darkness. The Viet Minh would hunt them down, surround them, and exterminate them. It would be over a week before a handful of survivors stumbled into Dien Bien Phu and told their horror stories. Few survivors followed. Of the 2,100 Thai Auxiliary soldiers that left Lai Chau, only 185 made it back to Dien Bien Phu. It was a blow to the morale of the Vietnamese soldiers in the garrison, who wondered why they were fighting for the French if they could not protect their families from the Viet Minh. It was not long after that some of the Vietnamese soldiers deserted their posts and disappeared into the hills.

A lone C-47 landed on the airfield. General Cogny and the new garrison commander, Colonel De Castries, exited the aircraft and were met by Colonel Langlais, General Giles, and Lieutenant Colonel Piroth, the artillery commander. An experienced veteran of WWII, Piroth had a face like a gnome and was missing his left arm, which he'd lost during a Viet Minh ambush on his third tour in Indochina. The group of commanders was escorted by a squad of paratroopers to the command bunker near the airfield.

Inside the rudimentary bunker, the officers were served light refreshments and briefed on the current disposition of forces. De Castries listened intently and studied the map showing the position of French units. It would all be his responsibility as he took over command of the garrison. "We are currently receiving around eighty tons of supplies per day. We hope to increase that number. In the meantime, priority will be given to ammunition and construction supplies for the building of the garrison," reported the major in charge of the supply depots.

"And our artillery?" said De Castries.

"It will start arriving today," said Lieutenant Colonel Piroth. "Once operational, the new artillery will drive back the Viet Minh units that we encountered in the mountains near the airfield. We only need to identify their location to destroy them. The new squadron of scout planes will help with that."

"Do we have any idea on the Viet Minh artillery?" said De Castries.

"A mix of field mortars and recoilless rifles, as we projected."

"No indirect fire capability?"

"None. There are over three hundred miles of mountainous terrain between Dien Bien Phu and their major supply bases at Viet Bac. The roads, if you can even call them that, are in poor shape after years of neglect, heavy rains, and landslides. And let's not forget our air force. Our bombers would surely destroy any weapons and ammunition en route. General Giap does not have the ability to transport his heavy artillery to the valley or the logistics to keep it resupplied once they get here. Not even Hannibal would attempt such a feat. A few pieces may get through the mountains, but even if they do, I assure you our counter-batteries will destroy their guns within three volleys," said Piroth.

"And how many pieces will we be supplied?" said De Castries.

"As promised, you will be given everything you need to annihilate the enemy, Colonel," said Cogny.

The Daisy Mae landed on the steel runway and taxied to the unloading area. Her rear doors opened, exposing two 155mm artillery guns in her belly. The new heavy artillery pieces were rolled out one by one. In all, the French would have eight 155mm guns at Dien Bien Phu. The 155s were the heaviest artillery pieces in all of Indochina, and once deployed to the various fighting positions, were capable of hitting anything within the valley and its surrounding hills. Each shell weighed over 100 lbs. and required a separate propellant charge, which slowed loading. Its firepower was truly ominous and gave the French a decisive advantage over the Viet Minh. Only the American C-119s could carry the 155s because of their weight and size.

Coyle exited the rear of the aircraft and jumped down to the tarmac. He crossed to a chow line set up on the edge of the airfield and got in line for coffee with the other soldiers. While standing in line, he thumbed through a well-worn French dictionary. Brigitte approached. "You are learning French?" said Brigitte.

"I thought I'd give it a whirl," said Coyle.

"Most tourists do not bother learning a country's language when they visit."

Coyle poured himself some coffee and offered some to Brigitte. She declined. "Well, first of all, I'm not a tourist," said Coyle. "And second, if I were gonna learn this country's language, it'd be Vietnamese, not French."

"Vietnam is a French colony."

"That may be, but most of the people still speak Vietnamese."

"For now."

"You think you're here to stay?"

"You don't believe we should be here?"

"A question to answer a question."

"I am a reporter. It is my job to ask questions."

"Fair enough. I believe people should determine their own fate."

"You Americans believe democracy is the solution to everything."

"It hasn't hurt us."

"Would the Vietnamese be better off without the French hospitals and schools? Without French roads and airports? France has been here for over eighty years, building, teaching, protecting. Without us, the people of Indochina would still be living in the Stone Age."

"They pay for your civilization with their freedom."

"Freedom? Before France was Portugal, and before Portugal, China. The Vietnamese have not known freedom for over two thousand years. They have no idea how to govern themselves."

"They can learn if given the chance. We did."

"And who will teach them. Mao and the communists?"

"That should be up to the Vietnamese to decide."

"If you do not believe in our cause, why do you fight? Money?"

"I ain't fighting. I'm flying. And yes, I do it for the money. Money paid by the French," said Coyle.

"Capitalists," said Brigitte with a condescending tone.

"Ya know, when I first saw you, I thought it might be nice to get to know ya and maybe steal a kiss or two," said Coyle. "But you are by far the orneriest person I've ever met. Now, if you will excuse me, my coffee is getting cold."

Brigitte was at a loss for words as Coyle walked away. Men walking away was not something she had often experienced. Coyle was an enigma. A puzzle to be solved.

French and Vietnamese legionaries strung barbed wire and dug defensive trenches along the edge of the airfield. Brigitte interviewed De Castries as he inspected the airfield. His assistant, Paule Bourgeade, a brave and cheerful 28-year-old with an uncanny ability to organize, trailed behind, taking notes when asked by her boss. Paule had been in Indochina for over 5 years and knew how to get things done. "Colonel Langlais says you are to be trusted," said De Castries. "But so we are clear, Brigitte, nothing is printed in your magazine unless first cleared by our headquarters in Hanoi."

"Of course. I am well aware of the rules, and I have no wish to endanger our troops, Colonel," said Brigitte.

"Very well. The garrison is made up of nine strongpoints protecting the airfield and our artillery positions on the surrounding hills—Gabrielle, Beatrice, Elaine, Claudine, Anne-Marie, Francoise, Huguette, Dominique and, seven kilometers to the south, Isabelle," said De Castries.

"The names of your former mistresses?"

"One does not reveal such confidence, Mademoiselle."

De Castries looked out over the rice fields and homes with thatched roofs near the airfield. He didn't like what he saw. "Paule, make a note to have our men clear the perimeter around the airfield another two hundred meters. Tear down the homes if need be and compensate the owners. I want clean lanes of fire for our machine guns and recoilless rifles."

"Yes, Colonel," said Paule.

Major Andre Sudrat, commander of the engineer battalion, approached with his clipboard in hand. He looked worried.

"Major, you look like you swallowed a cat," said De Castries.

"Yes, sir. I have completed my evaluation of the engineering resources needed for the garrison. Perhaps we should talk in private?" said Sudrat.

"Brigitte, may we resume our conversation later?"

"Of course, Colonel. I'll get some coffee."

Brigitte walked away toward the mess tent.

"So, Major?" said De Castries.

"Including the PSP for the airfield, barbed wire for the perimeter of each strongpoint, lumber to support the trench walls, concrete and elephant iron for the command bunker and hospital, and the sawed lumber for the blockhouse support beams… thirty-four thousand tons."

De Castries was stunned. "Major, how is that possible?"

"As you requested, we need fighting positions, command bunkers, and support structures for twelve battalions, plus gun pits for our artillery. It's a massive garrison, Colonel. The largest ever built in Indochina."

"How long will it take to fly in that amount of supplies?"

"Assuming eighty aircraft loads per day, five months."

"I doubt the Viet Minh forces will allow us that amount of time before they attack. What can we build in the next sixty days?"

"Perhaps the hospital and your command post."

"And the blockhouses?"

"No, sir. Each requires a large amount of wood for the support beams and headers over the firing holes. I suppose we could forgo the roof and build open-air blockhouses, but our men would not be protected from an artillery or mortar attack."

"I am less concerned about the enemy's artillery than frontal assault by human wave."

"We can scavenge some wood from the villages in the valley, and we might be able to harvest some timber from the surrounding forests, but it will take a large amount of labor and slow our construction."

"Can we hire men from the villages?"

"Some, yes. But most are farmers and do not understand even basic construction. Training them may take more time than they save us."

"But we can try, yes?"

"Of course, Colonel."

"See to it, Major."

Each day, more and more aircraft landed on the airstrip. As the supplies were unloaded from the aircraft, they were transported by truck to the various strongpoints, and the engineers went to work building the garrison while the Legionnaires and paratroopers kept watch for the enemy. Bulldozers cleared away brush around the French firing positions, giving the soldiers clear lanes of fire. Soldiers used old railroad ties as headers above the doorways in the command bunkers and firing ports in blockhouses. Foreign Legionaries and Vietnamese colonial troops strung mile after mile of barbed wire, creating a maze of steel, and dug trenches in circles around each hillside. Engineers laid thousands of anti-personnel mines around the suspected enemy approaches to each of the French fighting positions and around the outer rim of the airfield. Open firing pits, with high mounds of dirt as the surrounding walls, were dug for the artillery, along with reinforced ammunition bunkers with steel doors.

Jeeps, trucks, half-tracks, and ambulances were flown in the holds of the C119s. Ten US-built M24 Chaffee tanks, nicknamed "Bisons", were disassembled in Hanoi and flown into Dien Bien Phu, where they were reassembled in an open-air factory. The tank squadron was commanded by Captain Yves Hervouet, young and aggressive, yet calm and controlled in combat. He wore owl-style glasses and kept his blond hair hidden under his beret so the enemy snipers wouldn't target him from a distance. Each M24 tank in his squadron had a 75mm cannon, a .50 caliber machine gun, and two .30 caliber machine guns, giving its crew of five plenty of firepower. They would be used to support the infantry by targeting enemy machine guns and recoilless rifle emplacements.

Building the garrison was a massive effort that seemed never-ending. It was mind-numbing work for the paratroopers and Legionnaires. The paratroopers especially hated to prepare fixed fighting positions because they believed the best defense was to take the fight to the enemy where- and whenever they could be located. Day after day, week after week, the garrison took shape. Low-lying hills, with their nine strongpoints, formed the backbone of the garrison. There was a field hospital, nine battalion command bunkers, eight sandbag bunkers for the aircraft stationed at the airfield, dozens of artillery and heavy mortar firing pits, firing dugouts for 10 tanks, a transportation and repair depot for the fleet of vehicles, dozens of dugouts for the field kitchens to feed the thousands of soldiers within the garrison, and fifteen ammunition and supply depots. It was the largest fighting position ever built in Indochina.

Every day, more French troops were flown or parachuted into the valley. Over 10,800 soldiers from around the world were sent to the valley to fight for the French, including Moroccans, Senegalese, Congolese, Germans, Italians, Spanish, Algerians, Tunisians, Polynesians, Laotians, Cambodians,

Indonesians, Malaysians, Thai, and of course, Vietnamese.

Thousands of pallets of supplies, food, and ammunition were flown in, unloaded onto the airfield, and trucked off to different parts of the garrison to be stored in supply and ammunition depots until they were needed. When the pallets were unloaded, the wood was cannibalized by the French engineers to create blockhouses and reinforce trench and tunnel walls. Nothing was wasted.

There was a mobile water purification facility run by a portable generator and supplied by the stream paralleling the airfield. It supplied fresh drinking water for the entire garrison and dramatically reduced the odds of a dysentery outbreak that could cripple a fighting force.

The French garrison grew stronger, and Colonel De Castries grew more confident with every shipment airlifted into the valley. And the Viet Minh grew stronger and more confident as their battalions returned to the valley, and their combined forces grew in numbers. Every day, there were skirmishes between the French and Viet Minh forces. It was a never-ending battle as they mangled each other and tested their enemy's strength. It was the only way to be sure about what they were facing.

The Daisy Mae lifted off from the airfield outside of Hanoi. Coyle and McGoon sat in the cockpit with Geneviève de Galard, a 29-year-old flight nurse, sitting in the navigator's seat. "You're from Toulouse?" said Coyle.

"Yes, in southern France, near the Garonne River," said Geneviève.

"Yeah, I got a chance to visit it before heading home after the war. The buildings were a kind of a pink color if I recall," said Coyle.

"Yes, many of the bricks are made from terracotta. The French call it 'The Pink City'."

"You're a flight nurse?" said McGoon.

"Yes."

"That's gotta be a tough job, with the change in altitude and the pressure and all."

"Yes, at times, very tough. We lose too many."

"Why ya heading to Dien Bien Phu?"

"My Red Cross plane is meeting me there. They are flying in from Saigon."

"You been on vacation?"

"No. A funeral. One of my patients. I cared for him for three days before he died of his wounds. You get to know people when you care for them, and they you. It was the least I could do."

"Sorry to hear it."

"Yes. Me, too."

The Daisy Mae touched down on the steel grid and taxied off the runway. Coyle climbed out of the lower cockpit door and helped Geneviève down.

Off to the side of the airfield, Brigitte poured herself a cup of coffee from the airfield's mess tent and sat down on a stack of empty supply crates serving as tables while they waited to be scavenged. She watched with interest and a tinge of jealousy as Geneviève picked up her flight bag and kissed Coyle on both cheeks, as was the French custom to say goodbye. Geneviève walked toward Brigitte. "Do you know the way to the hospital?" said Geneviève.

"Yes, just up there on the hill," said Brigitte, pointing. "Are you a new nurse?"

"Yes, but I won't be staying."

"Oh, that's too bad. It would have been nice to have another French woman to talk with."

"I will be coming back when troops are to be evacuated. I am a flight nurse."

"Oh, great. You fly with the Americans?"

"At times, yes. Perhaps we can share a coffee together on my next trip?"

"That would be nice," said Brigitte as Geneviève walked toward the hospital. Brigitte turned back to watch Coyle, who still hadn't noticed her. She had a job to do and didn't need a distraction like Coyle. After all, she was not a schoolgirl with a crush. She picked up her coffee and walked away.

This type of set battle was new to the Viet Minh. The People's Army had never successfully assaulted a French fortified position with more than two companies guarding it and only rarely fought more than one night. A set battle was a style of fighting all too familiar to the French, having fought the Germans in two world wars. They understood the logistics required to fight a sustained conflict, and they understood the brutality of fighting an enemy face-to-face. It was all so new to the Viet Minh commanders and their soldiers. But they learned fast and learned well.

Both sides wanted to get at the other. The French, to thrash the Viet Minh and show them what a real army could do with modern-day weaponry and logistics. To prove to the Viet Minh that the French were not beaten. And the Viet Minh, to prove they were more than just a band of guerillas unable to fight toe-to-toe with a western army. They wanted the French gone from their country once and for all, and the only way to do that was to show the French that they could not win, that the Viet Minh were resolved to fight on forever if need be. Both sides wanted and needed this battle.

Inside his command center bedroom, General Giap was awakened by a lieutenant. He slipped on his pants and followed the lieutenant into the map room. The professor he had sent had returned and was seated slumped over with his hands holding his head. He looked exhausted and suffered from a head cold. He looked up at Giap, cleaned his runny-nose with a handkerchief, and said, "It can be done."

A Viet Minh engineer led his surveying team up a mountain trail. The mountainside was covered with tall trees, and the ground was thick with underbrush. The group came to a slight break in the forest canopy and looked out over the valley. They could clearly see the French airfield and several fighting positions in the distance. Their position was well hidden by the trees overhead. The engineer studied his map carefully. Satisfied, he walked over to the mountain slope and pounded a surveying stake about chest-high into the loose soil. He nodded to the team of surveyors. They went to work using a well-worn Wye level on sticks to calculate their exact altitude. It was far from the latest technology, but it got the job done. Next came the transit, used to calculate their exact position on the mountainside. The engineer noted the coordinates on a small pad of paper. He had them double-check their calculations. The coordinates had to absolutely correct to accomplish his mission.

The engineer and his surveying team climbed up the backside of the mountain. There was no trail, and the climb was difficult. The soil was loose, and the vegetation thick. Again, they took their measurements and carefully rechecked the calculations. The head surveyor motioned to a spot on the slope and guided the engineer, using his transit to find the exact spot and angle on the slope. The engineer pounded in a surveying stake. The two surveying stakes marketed the opposite ends of the shallowest point in the mountain at that elevation.

Two groups of villagers, each with picks and shovels, went to work. One carved a 6-foot-wide trail into the mountain slope. The other began digging into the mountainside next to the surveying stake, stripping away the soil and loose rocks. It was the beginnings of a tunnel from the backside of the mountain to the front. One of many that the Viet Minh would carve into the mountains surrounding the valley.

Sergeant Rouzic, a French Legionnaire, was interviewed by Brigitte as he supervised his platoon digging trenches and stringing barbed wire in front of their fighting position on the hillside of strongpoint Beatrice.

"Colonel De Castries said you were a getaway driver for the bank robber Pierrot-le-Fou," said Brigitte.

"Yes. Crazy Pierre. We'd knock over a bank in the morning, then spend all the money on wine and women before sunset. But that was all before the legion, of course… my new life, no?"

"With honor?" said Brigitte.

"Some say yes. And when I die, perhaps a better place in the history books, no?"

He walked past a German Legionnaire digging a trench in the stifling heat. "One and a half meters deep, Corporal, and not a millimeter less," said Sergeant Rouzic.

"Oh, my god," said the German Legionnaire. "Look, Sergeant, an Englishmen. I've dug all the way through to London."

"Make jokes now, Corporal. But you'll be wishing it was so once the enemy starts charging the wire."

Lieutenant Colonel Gaucher, a seasoned battalion commander, moved up behind Brigitte and Sergeant Rouzic.

"Na-San all over again, eh, Sergeant?" said Gaucher.

"Let's hope so, Colonel," said Sergeant Rouzic.

"Are your men getting enough to drink, Sergeant? They look a bit drained."

"Just this damned heat, Colonel."

"We could do with a little rain."

"A little rain…" mumbled the German Legionnaire to himself. "You can bet he won't be sleeping in the mud."

It was late afternoon. Coyle kept low as he walked along a trench leading up the side of a hill on strongpoint Elaine. Viet Minh snipers had been taking potshots at anything that moved within their range, and two Legionnaires had already been killed. Reaching the top of the hill, Coyle climbed out of the trench and walked to Brigitte's foxhole. She was gone. He was disappointed. He heard the clack-clack of a typewriter and followed the sound to the mayor's mansion. The French Legionnaires had been disassembling the mansion for badly needed building material. The stone and wood were invaluable. Most of the roof was gone, and only a couple of interior walls remained. Coyle found Brigitte in what looked like the former living room. She was typing a story and did not notice him enter. Her laundry hung on a rope strung between the fireplace mantel and a crystal chandelier. He knocked on an empty door frame. The door had already been scavenged by the hospital for use as an operating table. She looked up from the typewriter. "Monsieur Coyle," said Brigitte.

"Are you busy?" said Coyle.

"No. Please come in. I would offer you a chair, but it seems they have already been pilfered."

"That's okay. I've been sitting for the last couple of hours. I need to stretch my legs. 'Sides, I came by to apologize. I kinda lost my temper the other day, and I said some things that I wish I hadn't."

"No, no. It is not necessary. I understand passion, and I like a good argument. It keeps the mind sharp, no?"

"I suppose."

Brigitte grabbed an open bottle of wine and a glass. "Would you like some wine?"

"No, thanks. Gotta keep my wits. I still have to fly back to Hanoi tonight."

"So soon?"

"They work us pretty hard. So, new digs?"

"Digs?"

"New place. Where you live now?"

"Yes. It's cleaner and a bit more comfortable. At least until our engineers carry away what remains. It was the Communist Party headquarters. They decided to leave when they saw French parachutes."

"And you moved in?"

"Yes. Until the battle starts, then it's back to the mud where it is safe."

"So, you're planning on staying even after the shooting starts?"

"Of course. I fought like hell to get here. Besides, I am type A."

"Type A?"

"My blood. It is type A. You know you are driven by your blood type. During World War II, the Japanese commanders would only pick type A pilots to fly Kamikaze missions. They were single-minded and dedicated to their cause, even unto death."

"Kamikazes. Just seems the waste of a good aircraft."

"You love flying, no?"

"It's something I got a knack for."

"A knack?"

"Something I'm good at."

"Ah, yes. Then I have a knack for writing. It's what I love. May I ask a favor?"

"Sure. What's up?"

"General Cogny has granted me an interview, and I need a lift back to Hanoi. I was wondering if could… how you say…hitch a ride?"

"Yeah, sure. I mean, I'd have to ask McGoon because it's his plane, but I don't see why not."

"Thank you. You are very kind."

Coyle stood in front of McGoon, who was seated on an empty ammunition crate in the airfield's mess dugout. McGoon was finishing the last of three perfectly cooked two-egg omelets, a baguette, and a very pungent slice of Époisses de Bourgogne, a cow-milk cheese washed in brandy and banned from public transportation in eastern France.

"No," said McGoon.

"What do you mean 'no'?" said Coyle.

"It's the opposite of 'yes,' Coyle. Our contract with the Frenchies says cargo and soldiers only. We ain't a taxi service for civilians."

"Wait a minute. First, you said, 'we're not military,' now you say we ain't civilians. Which is it?"

"It's a grey area. And one where we don't need a reporter snooping around."

"She's not going to report anything bad about us."

"And you know that… how?"

"Okay. I admit I haven't known her for long."

"Two weeks, Coyle. You've known her two weeks."

"Yeah, but…"

"What is with you and this girl? You are in the land of beautiful women, and you choose her? She's trouble, Coyle. And not the kind of trouble we need, seeing we're supposed to be undercover and all. We gotta a good thing going, Coyle. Don't screw it up."

"You don't think she's beautiful?"

"Well… I mean… I admit she's got a little something about her, but come on. All she does is argue, and she's sneaky and manipulative."

"Wait a minute…"

"She's already got you wrapped around her little finger."

"That's it. I saved your ass. I'm calling in my chit."

"What? You're gonna use your chit for her?"

"Yep. It's my chit. I can do what I want with it."

"Fine. She can go. Just let me finish my meal in peace."

Coyle snatched the chunk of cheese from McGoon's plate, popped it into his mouth, and walked away.

"Hey, hey! I was gonna eat that," said McGoon. "Good way to get your hand stabbed by a fork, mister."

It was early morning, and the mist was already burning off as the sun rose into the grey sky. Twelve Viet Minh porters pushed and pulled at the ropes that held the two-and-a-half-ton howitzer. The artillery gun was American-made and captured by the Chinese during the Korean War. The Chinese did not make a 105mm shell, and therefore, the American 105s were not considered part of their army's standard inventory. They became hand-me-downs to the Viet Minh, who were only too happy to accept them, especially since they used the same shells as the French, which could be captured.

The porters were moving the gun around a landslide that had occurred the previous night. The ground had not yet stabilized, and the road crews had been unable to fix the mountain road to the point that the heavy Russian trucks could pass. It was now daylight, and risky to be on the road, but it had to be done to stay on schedule. One of the trucks had dropped the gun off along with the rest of its cargo, and the porters were now moving the gun by hand across the broken ground to another Russian truck waiting in a grove of trees on the opposite side of the slide. They had worked all night unloading and loading dozens of trucks and were exhausted. This was the last truckload that needed to be transferred. Once the gun was across the landslide and hitched to the waiting truck, the porters could eat and sleep. The porters heard the high-pitched thrum of an aircraft engine. They quickened their pace. It was only a few more yards to the safety of the trees.

A French reconnaissance plane passed over the mountains, following the road the Viet Minh had been rebuilding. Looking down through the side windshield, the pilot saw the porters moving the artillery gun along the road and toward a grove of trees. The pilot waited until his aircraft was directly over the artillery gun before pressing the trigger on the camera mounted on the bottom of the fuselage. He almost missed the shot as the porters rolled the gun under the cover of the trees and disappeared. Almost.

It was late afternoon, and it had been raining all day at Navarre's villa. The ground was saturated to the point that the rainwater had nowhere to go and just gathered in great pools on the lawn, turning the flower beds into muddy swamps. General Cogny sat with General Navarre in a conference room. Cogny had thought the photo was important enough that he flew down to Saigon and met with Navarre personally. Navarre examined the photo using a jeweler's loupe to study the blurry image. "It's a mountain howitzer. So, what?" said Navarre.

"Intelligence believes it is a 105," said Cogny.

"We both know that's not possible."

"But what if it is possible?"

"Rene, I do not have the time or the inclination to play games."

"I understand, sir. Neither do I. But the entire operation was predicated on our having superiority in artillery."

"Your point?"

"If the enemy were to have 105s, and they were to overrun even one of our hillside strongpoints, they could shell any of our firing positions in the garrison."

"It's one photo of one gun. It's hardly an armada, Rene."

"Sir, if the enemy can transport one gun, they can transport more."

"And what would you have us do? Pull up stakes and run? I am tired of running, and so are the men."

"As am I. But we might consider reducing the size of our commitment. Reassigning some of the men to protect Hanoi and the Red River Delta."

"Giap and his army will not be in Hanoi or the Red River Delta. They will be in Dien Bien Phu. That is where the battle will take place. That is where we will destroy him."

"Or he us."

"Have you lost that much faith in our ability to fight, Rene?"

"No, sir. But I believe we should take precautions."

"Fine. Take whatever precautions you deem necessary to protect the garrison. But our men stay."

"Yes, sir. I shall inform Colonel De Castries of the threat."

"No. Not yet."

"He must have time to prepare."

"Yes. But not until our intelligence group confirms the type of artillery in the photo. De Castries has enough to worry about without chasing 'maybes.'"

"Colonel De Castries is under my command."

"And you are under mine," said Navarre sharply. "That will be all, General."

Cogny reached to pick up the photo. "Why don't you leave that here, Rene. I'd like to have another look later."

"Of course."

Cogny stood at attention, saluted, and left the room.

It was early morning. A mist hung over the valley. It was unusually cool, even a bit nippy. The villagers had already started their fires to boil their morning rice. The fences around the gardens and animal pens were made of horizontal sticks woven together with bark and tied to poles dug into the ground. Laundry hung on slender ropes strung between the trees. Chickens roamed the street pecking at anything that looked edible, while children played a Vietnamese version of petanque with rocks instead of steel balls.

The opium harvest had begun, and even at this early hour, farmers squatted among the opium poppies in a nearby field. They used small knives to cut slits in the unripened opium seed pods hanging on the plants. The thick opium liquid oozed out of the slits and was allowed to dry into a gum. The gum was collected with a curved spatula and dried further in well-guarded wooden boxes, then rolled into dark balls for sale to the French or Viet Minh, depending on who was in control of the valley. The treasured little balls were sold to opium dens in Saigon, Paris, and Beijing to be smoked in long pipes held by pretty ladies. Patrons forgot about the war, and all worries vanished as long as the opium flowed. It was a lucrative business, and the money collected by the villagers was used to buy medicine, fertilizer for the rice fields, and hard candy that rotted their teeth.

Coyle searched through the wood piles, looking for a stick to carve. He found a branch that he liked and offered a coin to the woman cooking over a fire. She smiled, took the coin, and bowed. Coyle bowed back and continued his stroll through the village. He pulled out his pocket knife and went to work, carving away the knots. Coyle's uncle had taught him how to carve. He believed that the wood spoke to him as he whittled and told him what it should become. Coyle knew it was hokum, but he liked the memory of sitting with his uncle.

A young Black Thai girl played in front of her home. She had a live blue and green dragonfly tied to a string and flying in circles above her head.

"What's his name?" said Coyle.

The little girl ignored him. He needed to say it in a simpler way if she was to understand. He tried again.

"Your pet. Name?"

"It's not a pet. It's her breakfast." Coyle turned to see Bruno at the head of a company of paratroopers returning from patrol. Bruno's uniform was caked with mud, and the hole in his pants was getting bigger. "She is like a cat playing with a…how you say… souris?" said Bruno.

"Mouse?" said Coyle.

"Yes, a cat playing with a mouse," said Bruno. "Do you have children?"

"Me? No."

"But you wish to, yes?"

"Someday, I suppose."

"Ah, yes. But this is not a good life for one that wants a family. A good father and mother stay home with their children. A soldier must go where he is ordered," said Bruno, motioning to the passing paratroopers. "They understand this. Brigitte understands this."

"Look, I don't know what you're thinking, but— "

"No, of course not. But Brigitte is unique, no? Like a beautiful dragonfly. Not to be kept as a pet."

Coyle looked over at the dragonfly, now exhausted and hanging limply on the end of the string. The little girl lost interest and tossed the dragonfly into the fire, and ran off. Bruno slapped Coyle on the back, "Have a good flight back, Coyle."

"Stay safe, Major," said Coyle.

"Safe is not part of my job," said Bruno, and walked off to rejoin his men.

It was early afternoon, and the blue sky was sprinkled with clouds shaped like gobs of cotton balls. A good day for flying. The Daisy Mae climbed over a tree-covered plateau. Inside the cockpit, Brigitte sat in the navigator seat, watching Coyle and McGoon fly. Brigitte was excited about getting back to her apartment in Hanoi, taking a hot shower, and changing into some clean clothes. "I appreciate the lift," said Brigitte.

"Seat was empty. They took away our navigator. Just as well. I fly by dead reckoning anyways," said McGoon.

"McGoon's like a homing pigeon," said Coyle. "Just point him in the right direction and let 'em go. He'll find his way."

"Why do they call you 'McGoon'? It's a nickname, yes?" said Brigitte.

"Yeah, a nickname. I was the largest pilot in flight school. One of my instructors was reading the funny papers in the New York Times, and he said I looked like Earthquake McGoon in Li'l Abner. You know Li'l Abner?"

"Ah, yes. Li'l Abner… hillbillies, yes?"

"Yeah, hillbillies. Earthquake McGoon is the big guy."

"Ah, yes. Very big… but not too smart, no?"

Coyle laughed. "She's got ya pegged, McGoon."

"Just keep your lips buttoned and fly the plane, Coyle. Can't ya see the lady and I are having a conversation?" McGoon turned back to Brigitte. "He may not be too smart, but when he sets his mind to something, he's determined. And at times, that's all ya need."

"And you, Coyle," said Brigitte, "are you determined?"

"I've been known to lock and load when I get my sights set on something I really want."

Coyle and Brigitte's eyes met for a long moment. She turned away.

The Daisy Mae touched down at the airfield outside of Hanoi, taxied to the apron, and parked alongside four C-47's. Brigitte thanked Coyle and McGoon again and climbed out the doorway below the cockpit. Coyle thought for a moment and jumped up from his co-pilot's seat. "McGoon, you mind wrapping things up on your own?"

"Why should I mind? I'm just the pilot," said McGoon.

"Thanks, McGoon. I'll catch up with you later, and I'll buy you a beer."

"Big of you."

Coyle exited the aircraft and ran to catch up with Brigitte. "Have you eaten?" said Coyle.

"Yes, before we left. Why?" said Brigitte.

"I know this barbeque place down by the lake. Chicken and pork mostly."

"No, hotdog?"

"McGoon told you?"

"Yes. He thought it was very funny. I think he was right."

"So, you wanna grab a bite?"

"Mousier Coyle, are you asking me out on a date?"

"I suppose I am."

"Very well, then I accept," said Brigitte, wrapping her arm inside his. "Do you mind if we stop at my apartment? It's close to the park, and I promise I'll only be a few minutes. I could really use a shower and a change of clothes before the interview."

"Okay, but I think you look fine."

"You are blind as a mole, but thank you."

They walked toward the main gate and the street in front of the airfield. Coyle flagged down a trishaw, and they climbed in. Brigitte gave the driver instructions in Vietnamese.

"I didn't know you spoke Vietnamese," said Coyle.

"Not really. Just enough to get by," said Brigitte.

Coyle and Brigitte sat on a park bench overlooking Hoan Kiem Lake on the edge of Hanoi's colonial district. The lake was surrounded by Loc vung trees, with their branches drooping down as if to take a sip of the cool green water. Vietnamese couples strolled around the lake holding hands. The women wore their long black hair down past their breasts and wore their best Ao Dai, the traditional Vietnamese dress, embroidered on the front with exquisite flowers or birds and split up the sides to reveal white silk pants. Sidewalk vendors displayed their goods on blankets spread out on the sidewalk that bordered the lake.

Brigitte was wearing Western-style slacks and a blouse that gave her a business-like appearance. She carried a small bag with a clean jumpsuit that she would change into after the interview before she returned to the valley. Her hair was curled and hung down on her shoulders. It was the first-time Coyle had seen her hair long, and he liked it. A pile of barbeque chicken and pork satays sat between them on a napkin, and each had a half-finished bottle of Coke. "According to the legend, there was this emperor paddling around on the lake when this golden turtle god stuck his head out of the water and asked for his magical sword, called "Heaven's Will." I guess the turtle had loaned the sword to the emperor so he could fight off a Chinese invasion," said Coyle.

"And did the emperor give the sword back?" said Brigitte.

"Well, yeah. You don't want to aggravate a turtle god."

"Of course not."

"Anyway, the emperor built a tower in the middle of the lake to honor the little guy and renamed the place "Tháp Rùa" which means "Lake of the restored sword.""

"And the other tower?" said Brigitte, pointing to a tall tower built on a little island on the edge of the lake.

"That's "Ngoc Son" or "Temple of the Jade Mountain." It was built to honor the supreme commander Tran Hung Dao, who fought against the Yuan Dynasty somewhere around the thirteenth century. It's got a nice bridge called "The Morning Sunlight Bridge" that connects the island to the shore if you want to go see it."

"I already have," said Brigitte. "I've lived here for two years, Coyle. It's hard to miss."

"Yeah, I guess I forgot that about you. Why did you let me ramble on?"

"I like to hear you ramble. Where did you learn all these names and legends?"

"I don't know. I guess I just kinda picked 'em up along the way. I like history. What do you like?"

"Sleeping in my own bed."

"Yeah, I suppose it's pretty hard keeping up with a bunch of paratroopers."

"Yes. They are fond of sleeping in the mud. It makes them look tough."

"So, why do you do it?"

"I ask myself the same thing every morning when I am out in the field. I don't know. I like the excitement. It makes me feel alive. And I really do believe their story should be told. They fight and die for my country. I admire them."

"Do you need to get to your interview?"

"Not yet. I still have a couple of hours. Have you been to the Thang Long Theatre?"

"No. Where's that?"

"Not far. You bought lunch. It will be my treat."

"No, no. I'll buy the tickets."

"Monsieur Coyle, you should know by now, I am a modern woman. I do not need to be pampered."

"Fair enough."

They got up from the bench. Coyle picked up the remaining satays and wrapped them in the napkin. "They're for McGoon on the flight back. He gets ornery when he gets hungry," said Coyle.

Brigitte laughed.

Brigitte and Coyle sat in the Thang Long Theatre, watching a water puppet performance. A six-piece band used traditional Vietnamese instruments to accompany two women singing and talking to the puppets. A male narrator told the story of each vignette. The stage was a pool-sized lake of green water in front of a red-tiled pagoda. The pagoda had thin bamboo screens that hid the puppeteers, who used long bamboo poles to operate the floating puppets.

The puppets were dancing water dragons spewing water and sparks, a stork fishing with its beak, a child playing the flute riding a water buffalo, rice farmers plowing their paddies, and sowing rice seeds, fishermen using bamboo cages to catch jumping fish, and dragon boats racing each other. It was a child-like performance steeped in ancient culture.

Brigitte explained the history behind the water puppet theatre and the legends behind each story being told. She liked Coyle and wanted to impress the American. And he was impressed. She was smart, beautiful, and brave. He wanted to kiss her but thought better of it. He would take his time and hopefully make her want him as much as he wanted her. She was worth the effort and wait.

Brigitte was escorted by a lieutenant through Cogny's headquarters. "General Cogny is running a little late. He asked if you would mind waiting in his office?" said the lieutenant.

"Of course not," said Brigitte.

The lieutenant led her into the office. "I am sure he will only be a few minutes," he said.

He offered her a seat in front of Cogny's desk and left, shutting the door behind him. Brigitte looked around the room. It was neat and orderly. Everything had its place. There were framed photos of comrades and of

Cogny, when he was young and still had both his eyes, on the wall and on the credenza behind the desk. There was a French flag in the corner. And then there was the general's desk. Not a scrap of paper on it, except for a black and white aerial photo in the middle of the desk pad. She thought it strange that he would leave what was obviously a reconnaissance photo out. It was a breach of security. It was not like the Cogny she knew. She looked back at the closed door and stood up. She dared not touch the photo, but it was out on the desk for anyone to see. She was anyone. She leaned over and looked closer. She recognized the fuzzy outline of the artillery gun. It was a 105. She was sure of it. She had done a story on a French artillery squad that had fought bravely at Na San. They'd had a 105, and even let her fire it once. It looked like it was being pushed by Vietnamese peasants, with a Viet Minh soldier keeping watch nearby. She heard Cogny open the door and sat back down in the chair. "I'm sorry to keep you waiting, Brigitte," said Cogny.

"It's quite all right, General. I know you are a busy man, and I appreciate you taking the time," said Brigitte.

Cogny walked to his desk and noticed the photograph. He looked at her and smiled as he picked it up and placed it in his top desk drawer. He shut the drawer, locked it, and placed the key in his pocket. It was as if he was showing her it was something of value and should be protected. She simply smiled and said, "May we begin?"

"Please," said Cogny, and sat down behind his desk.

Brigitte walked out of the office, followed by Cogny. "Thank you for your time, General Cogny," said Brigitte.

"The honor is mine. Do you have time for dinner?" said Cogny.

"Unfortunately, no. I am flying back to the garrison tonight."

"Brigitte, you must make time for yourself. Life is not all about work."

"I try."

"Hmmm. Next time try harder."

"Of course, General. I will."

Cogny personally escorted her out of his headquarters and put her into a waiting taxi, something generals do not usually do for reporters. But Brigitte was different. Cogny admired her and, more importantly, he needed her. Generals' careers do not advance without good press of their victories. And there was also the business of the photograph he had left out on his desk for her to see. He was not completely sure what he hoped to accomplish. Would she try to piece together the story and warn Colonel De Castries? Probably not, he thought. She was a reporter but also a patriot. But still, if there was a chance…

Brigitte rode in the backseat of the taxi. She was deep in thought. She knew that the French believed the Viet Minh were incapable of moving artillery into the valley. The roads were too badly damaged by years of neglect to be utilized by truck or even car. And yet, that photo showed them moving a 105 by hand. Was it possible that they could move their artillery all the way to the valley? Why did Cogny leave the photo out on his desk? He wasn't a careless man. She hated to be played, even by a general.

The sun had set at the airfield. The orange twilight created silhouettes of the aircraft parked on the apron. Ground crews were busy loading up the last pallets of cargo into the aircraft, getting them ready for their night flights back into the valley.

The Legionnaires manning the quad-50s anti-aircraft gun at the far side of the airfield smoked cigarettes and joked about their wives. They didn't notice the two Viet Minh sappers wearing dark blue pajamas and carrying bows on their backs as they belly-crawled toward the gun position. The two sappers nocked their arrows and stood up behind the two Legionnaires. Both arrows found their target and pierced the Legionnaires' throats. The sappers dropped their bows and pulled out their knives as they ran toward the gun position. The dying Legionnaires could not scream or fight back. The sappers finished them off with their knives.

Coyle sat in the open doorway of the Daisy Mae while McGoon paced. "You told her five-thirty, right?" said McGoon.

"She'll be here. I'm sure she's just running a little late," said Coyle.

"We got a schedule, ya know."

"I know. Why are you getting your panties in a bunch?"

"I ain't getting my panties in a bunch. Like I said before, the Daisy Mae is not a taxi service, Coyle."

"Never said she was. We're just helping a friend."

"Your friend."

"You don't like Brigitte?"

"She's fine for a reporter, but that ain't saying a lot."

"Be nice, McGoon. She'll write good things about you. Maybe make you out to be a hero."

"Ya think?" said McGoon, reconsidering.

Coyle watched as a taxi pulled up in front of the main gate, and Brigitte got out. "There she is now," said Coyle, walking toward her.

Brigitte showed her credentials to the guards and passed through the main gate. She saw Coyle approaching from a distance and waved. Coyle waved back and walked toward her across the tarmac.

"I thought you weren't coming," said Coyle as he came closer.

"No, no. There was an accident on the road. A trishaw hit a water buffalo sitting in the middle of the road. The water buffalo won the argument."

"I'm sure it did."

The thundering kak-kak-kak of the quad-50s interrupted their conversation. Orange tracer rounds flew behind Brigitte and hit the guards at the main gate, tearing them to pieces. Brigitte instinctively hit the ground. Coyle ran toward her.

"Get down, you fool!" said Brigitte.

The gunner of the quad-50s redirected its fire on the guard towers around the perimeter of the airbase. A jeep smashed through the lowered main gate and raced past Brigitte toward the line of aircraft. A sapper in the passenger seat opened fire with a submachine gun on Coyle, still running toward Brigitte. Coyle dove to the ground and rolled out of the jeep's path. Brigitte jumped up and ran to his side. "Are you okay?" said Brigitte.

"Yeah, I think so," said Coyle.

"What the hell did you think you were doing?"

"Saving you."

"Americans," said Brigitte. "I don't need saving."

The jeep sped toward the first aircraft, a C-47. A sapper in the back of the jeep pulled the cord on a satchel charge and flung it under the aircraft as they passed. The satchel charge exploded and engulfed the C-47 in flames, destroying it. The jeep kept moving down the line of aircraft, the sapper in back throwing more satchel charges and obliterating the cargo planes one by one. At the end of the line was the Daisy Mae. Her engines started to crank. McGoon was in the cockpit, determined to move his aircraft to safety before the sappers reached it.

Coyle could see that McGoon would never make it in time. "Come on," said Coyle and grabbed Brigitte's hand, pulling her to what remained of the guardhouse. Coyle picked up one of the guards' weapons, a submachine gun.

"Stay here and keep your head down. I'll be back in a jiffy."

Coyle ran off before Brigitte could argue. He ran toward the anti-aircraft gun taken over by the Viet Minh sappers, still firing on the guard towers, ripping them to shreds and killing the guards inside. The two sappers did not see him coming until it was too late. Coyle stooped down and moved forward until he was sure he would not miss. He opened fire, killing the two sappers and silencing the anti-aircraft gun. In the distance, another C-47 exploded. The Daisy Mae was next.

McGoon throttled the engines. The Daisy Mae's wheels began to move slowly. "Come on, baby. You can do it," said McGoon. He could see it wouldn't be enough before the sappers were in range.

Coyle pushed the dead sapper from behind the anti-aircraft gun and climbed to the seat. He wheeled the gun around and leveled it at the jeep. He fired. The tracer rounds were short. He tilted the gun up and shot ahead of the jeep. Once he had the gun firing at the same level as the jeep, he stopped wheeling the gun. Hundreds of hot shell casings ejected from the four machine guns gathered at his feet and blistered his ankles. He didn't flinch and kept firing.

The jeep drove right into his line of tracers. The sappers and their remaining satchel charges were torn to shreds, and the jeep exploded in a huge ball of flame.

Inside the cockpit, McGoon, wiping the sweat from his forehead with his sleeve, throttled down the engines. He and the Daisy Mae were safe. "I ain't never gonna hear the end of this," said McGoon to himself.

Brigitte got up from behind the guardhouse and ran to Coyle as he climbed out of the gun's firing position. "That was amazing," she said, wrapping her arms around him and kissing him on the cheeks. "You are such a fool."

Coyle smiled, put his hands on her face, and kissed her full on the lips. She was taken aback. She had daydreamed of her first kiss with Coyle, and it wasn't with the burning wreckage of three French planes in the background and surrounded by dead men. Still, it was a nice kiss. He had soft lips. She smiled and gave him a quick peck on the lips as if to say, "Thanks." It was not exactly the reaction Coyle was hoping for. His confused expression pleased her. She was back in control.

It was late in the afternoon at Giap's HQ. A light rain fell. Uncle Ho's Russian sedan was parked on the side and covered with a tarp to keep any passersby from knowing of his presence. Ho's bodyguard, Phung, stood in the rain, keeping watch with his submachine gun tucked under his arm.

Uncle Ho and Giap were alone in the HQ's conference room. "It is a well-thought-out plan," said Uncle Ho, studying the maps and reports Giap and his staff had prepared for their meeting. "I want the French gone from our country. I want our people to be free."

"As do I," said Giap. "They will leave when they finally realize that they cannot win and that they will never control us again."

"You believe Navarre intends to defend Dien Bien Phu?"

"I think he must. He knows that if his forces leave, we will invade Laos. If his forces stay, he can counter any move we make on Laos or against his other garrisons in the highlands. It's the smart move, and he is a smart man. He is preparing for a fight."

"He prepared for a fight in Na San. He thrashed our best soldiers and then left as if it was nothing."

"This is not Na San. Dien Bien Phu is far more strategic. It keeps the French in control of the upper Mekong River and its supply lines. To lose the Mekong would be catastrophic to the French. Our forces could reach all the way down into southern Vietnam and even threaten Cambodia. The French would never let this happen."

"If the French stay, we fight?"

"That is the hope."

"We will be gambling a great deal."

"It is a risk, I know. But we must fight and beat the French decisively if this war is to end. It is the only way."

"If we commit the bulk of our resources to this battle that deep in the highlands and the French leave, it could take us years to recover. We will not be able to launch a spring offensive, and that will give the French the time they need to build their army of South Vietnamese puppets."

"You are correct."

"And yet, you would risk all?"

"Yes. The French have given us an opportunity that may not come again.

We must risk all and win."

Uncle Ho grew silent, deep in thought. Giap was patient as always and gave his commander the space to think. It was probably the most important decision of Uncle Ho's career. A true test of the Viet Minh forces. The final tipping point, one way or another.

"If we fight and lose, you will not survive the wrath of the politburo and the Chinese. Not even I can protect you."

"I understand. If we lose, I do not plan on returning from the battlefield."

"Then we truly do risk all, my friend."

"Yes."

"How long before our forces are in place?"

"We must march our men and transport our artillery over three hundred miles to the battlefield, and the roads are still in great disrepair. The French aircraft will pick at us the entire way. It is hard to imagine we would be ready to fight before early March."

"Very well. When you are that far away, do you worry about leadership across the entire battlefield of Vietnam?" said Ho.

"The deputy chiefs of staff and the deputy head of the Political Department will all be there with me. We will organize a vanguard staff at our field headquarters in Dien Bien Phu to direct battlefields across the country, including the volunteer soldiers in Laos and Cambodia. Nguyen Chi Thanh and Van Tien Dung will remain behind at general headquarters and oversee the fighting in the Northern Delta. But I do have one worry while at a distance; if there's an urgent problem, I won't be able to ask for guidance from you and the Politburo," said Giap.

"When you reach the front, remember this: you are the commanding general, and you have absolute decision power! Delegate all lesser decisions. If there is a problem, discuss it and reach unity within the Party Committee, and reach unity with our Chinese advisors. Then, you have your decision. You can report to us later."

"I understand."

"One last thing," said Ho. "This is a crucial battle. You must fight to victory. Fight only if you are sure of victory. If you're not sure, don't fight."

Giap nodded in agreement.

"There is no better man for this task. Go with your people's blessing, General."

"And yours?"

Ho smiled. "And mine."

They shook hands, perhaps for the last time.

THE BATTLE OF THE ROADS

Giap stood in his bedroom alone, staring at the empty table where he once ate his rice soup. "What have I done?" he thought. It was one of the few times he would allow himself to doubt. He knew he must be strong. His men would find confidence in his resolve. Pity and self-doubt were not something he would allow himself. He gathered the last of the books, two books on poetry and one on the history of Hannibal. He placed them in a leather satchel and tightened the straps. It was time.

He walked out of the room and down the stairs. Seeing him, a lieutenant on his staff stopped working and began to applaud. He was quickly joined by the other staff members clapping their hands and cheering their general. This was the man that would bring them to a final victory over the French. They believed in him more than themselves, and that was enough. Giap, moved by his staff's confidence in him, walked through the building and out the front door.

Giap set his satchel on the passenger side of a jeep already loaded with map cases, boxes of paperwork, and rucksacks. Three of his staff officers were already waiting in the back of the jeep. His bodyguard, Phung, sat behind the steering wheel. It was a very tight fit. The jeep was American and had been captured from the French. It was reliable. A red square with a gold star had been painted on each side and on the back of the jeep, so his soldiers did not mistake it for a French patrol. However, they left the American white star on the hood so any French aircraft passing overhead might think twice about strafing it. Giap climbed into the front passenger seat, and Phung cranked the engine to life and put the vehicle into gear. It would be a long and dangerous ride to Dien Bien Phu. The jeep pulled away from the building and sped down the street.

There was a light drizzle as the sun set over the mountains. The forest was quiet. A village commissar, with four militiamen armed with rifles, led a group of two hundred coolies carrying picks and shovels up a badly maintained mountain road. Large sections of the road had been washed out by the rains and avalanches. Other sections had been taken over by vegetation as if the dirt road was slowly being swallowed by green vines and ferns.

The commissar stopped and barked out orders to the group. The coolies dispersed along the road and got to work. They worked without complaint, grateful for the bowls of warm rice and the dried fish they were given at the beginning of each shift to give them energy. They were mostly peasant farmers, accustomed to this kind of back-breaking labor. They worked like a colony of ants, a collective mind that needed little guidance, instinctively knowing when to help their fellow workers remove a large boulder or shovel away a pile of debris.

The commissar and militiamen kept watch with their weapons in their arms, protecting the work party. It was the sky that worried them most. The French scout planes and the bombers that would surely follow if they were spotted were their biggest danger. A single B-26 with a rack of anti-personnel bombs, which spread lethal clouds of steel splinters when they exploded, could kill them all if it hit its target.

As the path through the mountains was repaired, coolies with ropes wrapped around their chests climbed up the trees on each side of the road. They lashed the ropes to the top of the trees and pulled the treetops together to form a living tunnel that obscured the road and the vehicles that would travel on it from the aircraft above. The French could not effectively bomb what they could not see.

The Viet Minh had been given 600 Russian-made Molotova trucks to transport their troops and supplies to the battlefield. They were well-worn hand-me-downs from WWII with bullet holes in the doors, blood-stains on the seats, and large rips in the canvas cargo tops, but their engines were still good, and they were reliable. The Viet Minh were grateful to have them. Each 2 ½ ton truck had a hitch on the back that allowed it to pull an additional trailer of ammunition or a piece of artillery. They were heavily camouflaged with local foliage, which was replaced with new, matching foliage whenever the trucks passed into new terrain. The trucks were divided into caravans of 30-40 vehicles each and dispersed along the entire length of road between Viet Bac and Dien Bien Phu. Road gangs of women with palm fronds brushed away the tire marks once each convoy passed, leaving no trace for the French scout planes to follow.

The heaviest artillery pieces were wheeled up the mountains and through the forest with ropes and pulleys fastened to trees and heaved by dozens of porters. They would travel by night and hide during the day. Every thirty miles of road, the work parties carved a hidden truck park into the forest for the drivers and the troops to rest and sleep in safety during the day. Nets strung from the trees were combined with the local vegetation to create a camouflaged canopy. Mobile kitchens were set up to feed the drivers, passengers, and work crews. Hammocks were strung from the trees, and straw mats laid across the ground. Fuel depots refueled the trucks, and mechanics checked the engines for loose fan belts, cracked hoses, and proper levels of oil and water while the drivers slept.

In addition to the trucks, the Viet Minh had over 20,000 porters using two-person bamboo slings and reinforced bicycles. A single reinforced bicycle could carry 300 pounds of supplies or ammunition, and two bicycles lashed together could carry the heavy barrel of a mountain howitzer. With few exceptions, the porters were mostly women from the surrounding villages. The villagers along the road were only too happy to help the Viet Minh, who promised land reform and food to the masses. It was something the French never offered: the simple hope of a better life for their families.

The human supply chain stretched over 300 miles and transported thousands of tons of food and ammunition to the valley. Even when the human chain was broken by French fighters or bombers, it was quickly repaired and resumed its mission. There were always more coolies and porters to take the place of the dead and dying. It was an unstoppable force of human will.

The last of the day's light was waning when the commissar heard an airplane's engine in the distance. He blew his whistle, signaling the danger. The work party and militiamen dove into the elephant grass and ran below the tree tunnel to hide. Two hundred workers and the four militiamen disappeared within a matter of seconds. The commissar didn't move from the middle of the road and watched as an unarmed French scout plane passed overhead. He wanted to take a potshot with his rifle but knew better than to attract attention. The aircraft passed without incident. The commissar blew his whistle again, signaling the "all clear." The militiamen resumed their guard duties, and the coolies climbed from their hiding places and returned to their work.

Giap and his staff continued their journey along the route through the mountains, passing the coolies repairing the road and porters carrying equipment and supplies. Some of the soldiers could not believe their eyes on seeing the leader of their army and the man that determined life or death for many of their countrymen. Many of the soldiers carried small photos of both Giap and Ho Chi Minh in their pockets for luck. They clapped and cheered as the jeep passed. Giap did not like the attention. He was just a man, after all, and capable of mistakes. Besides, he didn't want the French spies that he knew were among his ranks to know he was heading to the valley. The road was dangerous enough without the French sending aircraft and patrols to hunt him down. He wasn't afraid to die. That fear had left him long ago. He had an important mission to accomplish and didn't want anything to hinder its success, including his death.

At times, the jeep sputtered and stalled as it climbed the steepest parts of the road, its four wheels spinning for traction in the soft dirt. During these times, Giap and his staff dismounted and walked to lighten the jeep's load. Porters along the road set their loads aside and helped the vehicle with a push. They were not well-educated but understood the importance of getting their general and his staff to the front lines as soon as possible. Once past the difficult part, Giap and his staff would climb back into the jeep and resume their journey, as the porters would resume theirs. They all had a job to do and were critical to the success of their army. Giap was proud of these simple villagers, their strength, and their willingness to serve the greater cause. They were the factor that the French most underestimated and gave the Viet Minh a crucial advantage. He did not possess the machines or technology to move mountains like the French, but he had the people, and the people were enough.

Dozens of women gathered rocks along a riverbank and carried them in bamboo baskets held on their backs with cloth straps. Many had babies that they would carry in a blanket wrapped around their chests. The loads were heavy, but they were strong. The women would carry their cargo of rocks to a shallow part of the river and toss the rocks into the water. Giap's jeep crossed the river on one of these "hasty bridges" made of thousands of rocks just below the surface of the rushing water. The French aircraft could not spot these fords and, therefore, could not bomb them like a normal bridge.

The jeep continued day and night. It only stopped when Phung was too tired to continue without endangering the general. These pauses were welcome by the jeep's passengers, who used the time to stretch and rest their backs from the relentless pounding of the road. They were always presented with the best food available, which oftentimes was no more than some hot tea, dried pork, and a bowl of rice. Giap knew that someone would go without in order to feed him and his men. It was a sacrifice that he accepted reluctantly. He used this downtime to find a radio and hopefully get a report from his field commanders on the French progress on the garrison. Giap so wanted the French to build their garrison, to make it big and strong, to fill it with troops and supplies. To make them feel secure so they would stay until he and his army arrived.

It was early evening in the forest truck park. Small oil lamps with overhead shields were lit to illuminate the tables in the dining area. The kitchen staff prepared the evening meal to be consumed by the porters and coolies before they started the long night of work. A troop of entertainers played instruments and sang songs for the troops as they waited to continue their march. Giap was sitting with his staff when they heard a single-engine plane overhead. The oil lamps were extinguished.

Firefly flares were dropped from a French scout plane and lit up the early evening sky. The flares marked the road below. A few moments later, the sound of heavier aircraft filled the air, a squadron of B-26 bombers flying overhead. Bombs whistled against the air as they dropped.

The road and the truck park exploded into balls of fire that lit up the mountainside like the noonday sun. Porters and coolies scattered for cover. Deep craters were blown into the road. The bombs destroyed their hard work and blocked any escape. Several bombs landed on the mountain slope and created an avalanche that buried porters running for their lives.

Giap and his officers stayed still and kept low to the ground, knowing that one place was as good as another during a bombing raid. The explosions were earsplitting and the air concussed against their bodies, making it hard to breathe. When the last bomb exploded, the empty aircraft left, and there was silence once again, except for the moans and screams of the wounded and dying.

Porters ran to help their comrades caught in the avalanche. Others helped the wounded to the makeshift field hospital next to the kitchen. Still, others picked up their picks and shovels and went to work repairing the damage to the road.

Giap watched with amazement as his ant army of coolies and porters made short work of the craters in the road. They sang patriotic songs in defiance to the French. Within two hours, the road was repaired, as if the French bombers had never been there. The people would not despair or even slow down. Giap drew strength from their example. The coolies and porters were not soldiers, but this was their way of fighting the French.

The caravan was like a 300-mile-long snake. The soldiers wore new long-sleeved cotton shirts, and each carried a rifle, ammunition, a backpack, and a "sausage sack" of rice as they marched briskly past. Women chatted and joked along the way and used shoulder yokes slung over their shoulders to haul rice and ammunition. The engineers constructed bamboo footbridges across streams. Thai and Dao sympathizers wearing colorful dresses used woven back baskets to haul rice and supplies. Reinforced pack-bicycles, nicknamed "elephants," carried hundreds of kilos of ammunition and supplies.

A new squadron of Bearcat fighters based at the French airfield in Dien Bien Phu used heavy machine guns and rockets to cut through the forest and attack the road crews. The French killed hundreds, but the work rarely stopped for more than a few minutes. The workers carried away the wounded and dead, then filled in the craters like it was just part of their daily life. Even the French, with all their technology and war machines, could not stop a willful people. The laborers broke out in chants as they worked to repair the road, demonstrating their united spirit to beat the French once and for all. They wanted their country back.

In the valley of Dien Bien Phu, Viet Minh road crews cut 18 miles of new roads on the surrounding mountain slopes and through the forests. Night by night, the road network continued to make its way through the forests, allowing the Viet Minh forces more freedom of movement. With the roads hidden under the forest canopy, the Viet Minh could attack one end of the French garrison, then move to the opposite end of the valley and attack another part of the garrison within a few hours.

It was morning, and the sun was already out. The garrison was beginning to look more and more like a fortress, with multiple layers of concertina wire, miles of six-foot-deep trenches with firing steps, and hundreds of blockhouses. Walls of sandbags surrounded artillery pits and the entrances to battalion command centers. Field hospitals and aid stations were dug down into the earth on the hillsides of each strongpoint. The airfield had a respectable perimeter, with layers of barbed wire and sentry towers.

A squad of engineers used small canisters of TNT to blow up the remaining tree stumps that blocked the fields of fire in front of the French machine guns and recoilless rifles. An engineer would cut the tree roots with an ax, dig a hole beneath the stump, then place the TNT canister directly below the thickest part of the stump. He would attach the bridgewire leads to the end of the charge's blasting cap, then run the bridgewire to the squad leader 100 feet away. The squad leader would attach the other end of the bridgewire leads to an electric detonator, then call "Fire in the hole!" before pressing the plunger to ignite the explosives and send a three-hundred-pound tree stump hurling through the air. Engineers loved to "blow shit up." It was always a nice break from building the garrison's blockhouses, artillery pits and command posts.

Legionnaires and paratroopers lined up in one of the field kitchens for a hot breakfast with coffee or tea. Colonel De Castries joined them. He used this time to check on the men's morale and show his face to the garrison. Each day he made a point to visit a different field kitchen and dine with a different group of men.

Brigitte was already seated when De Castries showed up. She had been waiting and made sure the seat across from her was empty. She had put on some makeup and combed her hair. She hoped that the Colonel, a well-known womanizer, would take the bait. It didn't take long. "May I join you, Mademoiselle?" said De Castries.

"Of course," said Brigitte.

De Castries sat down across from her and said, "I take it your accommodations are adequate?"

"When it's not raining," said Brigitte. "I'm fine, Colonel, but thank you for asking."

"You will let my staff know if you have any special requirements that we might accommodate?"

"Of course. You might help me with one thing."

"What's that?" said De Castries, sipping his coffee in between bites of an omelet.

"I'm writing a piece on one of your artillery officers. Lieutenant Brunbrouck?"

"I don't believe I know him. There are so many new faces."

"He is in charge of a battery of howitzers. 105's, I believe. Anyway, I remember you mentioning something in our interview, and I was hoping to get a little clarification."

"What's that?"

"You said that the Viet Minh were not capable of transporting their heavy artillery to the valley because the roads were too damaged."

"Yes, that is true. Because of the ongoing war, our maintenance crews have been unable to repair the roads, so they are now useless for us and the Viet Minh. A good thing in this particular case."

"What if they found a way to repair the roads and transport their heavy guns?"

"Impossible. It is a matter of logistics. Our engineers estimate that it would take over thirty thousand workers three months to repair the roads. It would take another fifteen thousand porters to supply the tools, supplies, and food necessary to support a workforce of that size. The Viet Minh just don't have the manpower available for that size of a project."

"And if they found a way to bring their guns to the valley?"

"Then we would simply destroy them with our counter batteries and aircraft. You see, it really just gets down to math, Brigitte. We have more artillery than they do. Not to mention our aircraft, of which they have none. You can sleep easy. There will be no enemy artillery bombardments in Dien Bien Phu."

Brigitte considered telling De Castries about the photograph she had seen in General Cogny's office. She knew it would betray the confidence that Cogny had shown in her, and the confidence of a general officer was not something to be wasted lightly. Besides, she wasn't sure what the photograph really showed or what it meant. She was a reporter and, while not completely neutral, it was not her responsibility to affect command decisions. She would leave it alone for now. "Thank you, Colonel," she said.

The sun was out, and the sky was clear in Hanoi. The streets were full of trishaws and bicycles. Coyle and McGoon sat on the patio of a coffee house, enjoying the cool air after an early morning supply run to Dien Bien Phu. "You're gonna love this. It takes a little longer, but it's worth it," said McGoon.

"As long as it ain't some kinda trick."

"Don't be a sourpuss, Coyle. It's my job to keep things lively. You don't wanna get stuck in a rut, do ya?"

"I suppose not."

A waiter poured sweet condensed milk into the bottom of each of their cups, then placed a metal drip-filter filled with coffee grinds on top. He poured hot water over the coffee grinds inside the metal filter. The water dripped down through the grinds and mixed with the sweet condensed milk. The waiter moved off.

While they waited for the last of their coffee to drip, McGoon leaned in closer. "Ya know how I told ya we should get in and make some real money?" said McGoon.

"Yeah."

"Apparently, the Viet Minh are making much faster progress on their roads to Dien Bien Phu than the Frenchies thought possible. It's got the French generals a little worried. They want us to slow the Viet Minh's progress, and they're willing to pay a big bonus if we do."

"How are we gonna slow 'em down? We're flying cargo planes."

"Well, that's the thing. The C-47's don't have big enough doors for a clean drop, and 'sides, they're limited on weight."

"Doors for what?"

"Napalm."

"What?"

"The Frenchies want us to drop napalm canisters outta the Daisy Mae. We can carry ninety fifty-five-gallon drums in our hold and drop them from the cargo ramp. The Frenchies wanna make a big impression on the Viet Minh. Make 'em think twice. Slow 'em down."

"You said no combat, McGoon."

"I know what I said, but we're talking a big bonus here. 'Sides, if we don't slow down the Viet Minh, this whole thing could be over sooner than we planned, and we're out of a job."

"You're saying the Viet Minh could attack the garrison."

"Damn right they could. And that's what the Frenchies want, but they need more time to get ready and finish their defenses. We can give them that time. The Frenchies still hold a couple of the key mountain passes along the highway, but they can't hold them without our help. The Viet Minh will overrun them soon enough, and then it's a clear shot to Dien Bien Phu. Troops and supplies will flood in, and sure as shooting they'll attack as soon as they have enough to overrun the garrison. Look, you're gonna get your own plane in a few more days. They're flying it in from the Philippines on Tuesday. Napalm is tricky stuff, as we both know. I don't wanna be dropping it with a new co-pilot. I say we do this together, or we don't do it at all."

"We're talking napalm, McGoon. You know what that'll do to the people we drop it on."

"Yeah. I know. But it's the Frenchies' decision. And Coyle, we need to be making as much money as possible before this whole thing blows up in the Frenchies' faces."

"That's a sorry excuse."

"They'll try dropping it from the C-47s if we turn 'em down. And you know someone's gonna flub it up and die if that happens. Our planes are the safest way."

"For us, maybe, but what about people that we bomb?"

"They're damn Commies, Coyle. They made their choice. Ain't our fault they chose wrong. The Frenchies want us to make three runs at night when the crews are working on the roads. Scout planes will light up the road with firefly flares before we make our runs. If we're lucky, we might catch some of the Russian trucks on the road."

"I won't call it 'luck,' McGoon."

"It's war, Coyle. We didn't start it, but we can help end it. If the Frenchies win at Dien Bien Phu, they think they can negotiate a peace agreement with Ho Chi Minh and the Chinese. Then all this killing stops."

Coyle liked the French, and he didn't want to see them get hurt or killed, but he didn't agree with their war on the Vietnamese people. It was colonialism, pure, and simple. He was an American that believed in people's freedom to choose their own destiny. Plus, the thought of killing anyone with napalm turned his stomach. The images of people burning would continue to fill his dreams. And then there was Brigitte. She was determined to stay, and there was nothing he could do about it. He would do what he needed to protect her.

"All right."

"All right?"

"Yeah. I'll do it."

"Great. I'll tell the captain," said McGoon, taking a peek under the filter on his cup, "Coffee's ready. Ya gotta stir in the milk."

They each pulled off their cup filters and set them aside, then stirred the thick condensed milk at the bottom of their cups into the coffee. McGoon took a sip.

"Oh yeah. Like milk from your momma's tit."

"McGoon, ya gotta a colorful way of describin' things."

"It's a talent," said McGoon with a smile.

It was late afternoon at Cat Bi airfield outside of Hanoi, and the sun was getting low in the cloudless sky. Coyle and McGoon watched as ground crews with forklifts loaded pallets, each carrying four 55-gallon drums of napalm, into the hold of the Daisy Mae.

"A stray bullet hits just one of those drums, and we both become barbeque," said Coyle.

"Best not to think about it. 'Sides, I hired a Buddhist monk to give the Daisy Mae a blessing before each mission. We're gonna be fine," said McGoon.

It was still dark with predawn approaching when Giap and his staff rode up a treeless mountainside in the American jeep. After a long and perilous ten-day journey, they had come to the last pass before the valley of Dien Bien Phu. It was by far the most dangerous stretch of road because of its proximity to the French garrison and the fighters stationed on the airfield. It was only one day since the French battalion of Legionnaires guarding the pass had finally given up their position and retreated back into the valley. Hellcat fighters with rockets from the aircraft carrier Arromanches pounded the pass, cratering the roadway, smashing Russian trucks, and killing porters with bicycles as they waited their turn to enter the narrow pass.

The driver of the jeep pulled to a stop behind a long line of Russian trucks blocking the road. This is a bad spot, Giap thought. No cover, and the sun will be coming up soon. And with it, French aircraft. He turned to a nearby commissar, walking past the jeep. "What is the holdup?" said Giap.

"The French bombers dropped anti-personnel mines all through the pass and surrounding mountainside. There is no way to continue until the mines are cleared."

"We must go around."

"Impossible."

"Have you radioed the engineers?"

"They're on their way."

Giap was the first to hear the thrum of the single engine of a scout plane. He looked up. It was one of the Crickets from the valley's airfield. Three firefly flares were ejected one after another from the side door of the little plane and ignited as their parachutes opened. The three flares floated down, illuminating the pass and the roadway. Why three? he thought. And then he realized what was about to happen. The flares were marking an approach path, but of what he did not know. "Get out of the jeep," he told his men. "Everyone out and grab the maps." Giap grabbed his satchel and an armful of maps. He looked around for cover. There was nothing nearby. He jogged back down the mountainside along the road. His men followed.

The Daisy Mae swooped over a mountaintop. McGoon and Coyle sat behind the controls in the cockpit. The mountain pass came into view through the windshield. It was lit up by the flares.

"There it is," said Coyle.

"Looks like they got themselves a little traffic jam," said McGoon. "Tell the boys to open the doors and arm the napalm canisters. I wanna drop twelve on our first pass."

Coyle radioed back to Kim-ly. Kim-ly released the rear door latch, and the heavy door swung open and locked into place on the side of the aircraft. He pushed the first three pallets into position with his assistant loadmaster's help. Kim-ly armed the fuses of the four drums on each pallet.

"Ya know, there are probably civilians driving those trucks," said Coyle.

"They ain't civilians if they're transporting war supplies," said McGoon. "Don't be going soft on me, Coyle. Let's just get the job done and get our asses back to Hanoi."

"All right, McGoon. I'm with you."

"Tell 'em they can let her rip when we pull up."

Coyle radioed Kim-ly with the instructions.

"On my mark," said McGoon. "Mark."

Coyle and McGoon both pulled back on the yoke's wheel, and McGoon pushed the throttles forward. The Daisy Mae's engines strained.

Giap saw the Daisy Mae roll in toward the line of trucks and then pull up. He saw a pallet fall out of the tail of the aircraft, and four drums fall free, tumbling through the air. "Get down!" he told his men. Giap, his staff, and the driver dove behind a grouping of rocks.

When the canisters hit the ground, the lid on each canister popped open. The magnesium fuse ignited in a bright burst of light. The napalm, a gelatin mixture of gasoline and Styrofoam, burst into flames as it was flung from the tumbling barrels. The flaming gel stuck to whatever it touched and was almost impossible to extinguish. The mountainside erupted in a giant ball of flame, and people screamed in pain and horror. Ten of the trucks were splashed with the gel and caught fire. Dozens of porters with bicycles, troops on the march, and coolies working on the road crew were engulfed. They dropped their loads and rolled on the ground. Their comrades threw tarps and blankets on them. It mattered little. The napalm, deprived of oxygen, would go out, only to reignite once it found air again.

One of the trucks carrying ammunition exploded, killing even more men and women. Giap and his men watched, helpless. Even Hell knew not such fury, thought Giap. The French will pay dearly for this. I swear.

Once the Daisy Mae leveled off, Coyle jumped up from his seat and ran back into the cargo hold. "Where the hell are you going?" said McGoon.

Coyle ran to the back of the aircraft and looked out the open cargo doors at the scene below. He saw men and women aflame running helplessly down the road until they dropped, while others were torn to pieces by explosions from the burning trucks. "Shall we arm the next load?" said Kim-ly.

Coyle vomited in response.

The sun rose in the morning sky, revealing burned-out trucks and blackened artillery guns with melted tires. The aftermath of the napalm attack was shocking. The entire mountainside had burned, and charred bodies lay everywhere. Those that survived were carried to the Viet Minh aid stations. There was little the medical students assigned to care for the porters, coolies, and troops could do with the burn wounds. They quickly ran out of medical supplies. Skin and clothes were fused together on the victims, and any attempt to separate the two resulted in incredible pain and death from shock. The best they could do was hope the patient died quickly. Some patients begged their comrades to shoot or smother them. It was difficult not to comply.

The sun was up, and the engineers understood the need to reopen the road as fast as possible before another French air attack. As the sun rose, the morning fog would burn off, and the entire convoy would be exposed, at the mercy of the French fighters and bombers. Viet Minh engineers used Russian mine detectors to find the French mines dropped by the bombers. Once they found a mine, they used long bamboo poles to trigger it. It was dangerous, but triggering the mines was faster than disarming them.

The American butterfly mine used by the French was a copy of the original German mine design used in WWII. Aircraft dropped large canisters, each of which held 90 mines. The four-pound mines deployed their wings after being released from the canister. The wings whirled around, slowing the mine's descent and arming the mine. It was the first cluster-type munition designed to spread over a large area. It was small but powerful.

The engineers moved with caution as they cleared the road. It was slow work, requiring complete focus. When an engineer with a mine detector found a mine, another engineer would touch the mine with his pole. The mine would explode and trigger other mines in the area. With a little luck, the mine explosions would move away from the engineers and not toward them. There was no way to know if all the mines had exploded. Once things settled down, the engineer with the mine detector would again walk forward, looking for more.

Giap and his staff climbed into the jeep they had abandoned and started up the road, moving past the smoldering remains of the Russian trucks and the burned bodies still being cleared from the mountainside. It was a sobering reminder of the terrible cost of war. The jeep was flagged down by the chief of the engineers and pulled to a stop. "General, we cannot guarantee the safety of you and your staff. We have cleared away the mines that we have found, but there is no way to know for certain. Some mines may be below the surface of the soil and could be triggered by the weight of your jeep," said the chief of engineers.

"We understand the risks, but we must get through. Besides, sitting here waiting has its own risks, as we have seen," said Giap.

"Yes, sir. Keep to the right of the road and go slow. My engineers will escort you."

"Thank you, Chief. Good luck."

The jeep moved forward on the road. The top of the pass was only three hundred yards away, but the soil around it was heavily scarred by explosions and napalm. Four engineers, each holding a shield made of steel, walked alongside the jeep as it inched forward, its four wheels grinding against the dirt as it climbed.

One of the engineers signaled the jeep to stop. He set down his shield and lay down on his stomach. He belly-crawled toward an unexploded mine partially exposed in a dirt berm on the edge of the road. The engineer disarmed the mine with his exposed face just inches away, knowing that if he accidentally triggered the mine, he would most likely be decapitated. He gently turned the mine on its side and used the small screwdriver on his knife to remove the three screws on the detonator cap. Drops of sweat fell from his brow as he removed the detonator cap to expose the arming mechanism. He tried to place the end of a twig into a threaded hole on the detonator arm. It didn't fit. He used the blade on his knife to trim the end of the twig to the correct size. He again placed the end of the twig in the hole, and this time it fit. The detonator was temporarily locked in place. It was a quick fix and still very dangerous. He carefully removed the mine from the road and motioned the jeep's driver to continue. The jeep rolled forward.

It was still early in the morning when the jeep reached the top of the pass. The sky was grey, and the sun was hidden behind a wall of white gauze. Giap could see the valley below covered in a thin mist. It was green and still. On the far end of the valley, he could see the French garrison and airfield still under construction. The earth was torn and scratched, where the French had cleared away the vegetation and dug their trenches on the hillsides. The garrison was like cancer in the valley and growing. With luck, we will fight here and win, he thought.

The jeep continued down the steep road until it came to a village at the base of the mountain. The morning fog was beginning to burn off. They needed to get off the road and out of sight of the French aircraft. Giap and his men were exhausted and needed to rest. The jeep's driver was flagged to stop by the local commissar. He told Giap and his staff there was food and tea waiting for them at the house of a Thai family at the edge of a forest. They dismounted the jeep and followed the commissar on foot.

The family that owned the house stood in front, bowing as Giap approached. "No, no. It is I that should bow to your hospitality," said Giap. Giap and his staff sat down at a table on the patio and were served hot tea, rice, and a thick stew made of rabbit and vegetables. It was delicious. After the meal, Giap was escorted to the house's only bedroom. The wife carried in a large bowl of water and set it at the foot of the bed. She pulled off Giap's dirty boots and cleaned his feet with a soft cloth. It was such a simple thing, but it made his mind and body relax. He was safe for the moment. Unable to keep his eyes open any longer, Giap lay back and fell asleep on the bed.

It was late afternoon when Giap finally awoke to the smell of burning tobacco. His eyes opened to see a man sitting on a chair in the corner of the room, smoking a cigarette and staring at him. It was General Thai, his unflappable operational commander and trusted friend.

"How long have you been there?" said Giap.

"Not long. It's been a long journey. I didn't want to wake you," said Thai.

"The French, will they withdraw?"

"I doubt it. The French are still flying in supplies and troops. They are busy building their defenses. If they leave now, even by airlift, we will inflict heavy losses on them as they withdraw."

"And the size of the garrison?"

"Nine thousand, give or take. Mostly legionaries and colonials, with a couple of battalions of paratroopers."

"And our men?"

"The 320th is in position, and the 312th is just arriving now. They will need to rest. In all, we have about forty thousand soldiers and thirty thousand support personnel. It's going to be one hell of a battle."

"If the French stay. I've been thinking about reminding them of why they came in the first place."

"An attack on Laos?"

"Seven battalions should be enough. Can we afford that many?"

"As long as they return before the final battle, yes. It will do them good to stretch their legs."

"Make it so."

General Thai nodded and continued his report, "There is something strange about the French this time. So far, they are only building field combat entrenchments. Some sides of their defenses remain open to attack by mortar and artillery."

"Their commander, Colonel De Castries, is not experienced at building fortified positions. As a cavalry officer, it is his nature to always think about an offensive position that allows his men to get at the enemy quickly, never defensive," said Giap. "They still don't believe we can transport our artillery through the mountains and are not threatened."

"That is a mistake."

"And an opportunity."

"When you are ready, I will take you to your front command base so you can meet with your field commanders."

"I am ready."

"Very well, but you might want to put on your boots first."

Giap glanced around the sparsely decorated bedroom.

"Where are my boots?"

The woman appeared in the bedroom doorway, holding his freshly cleaned and polished boots. She was proud that the great General Giap had slept in her house.

"The commander must look good for his men," said General Thai with a smile.

The jeep carried Giap, Thai, and the staff through a mountainous area covered by forest, streams, and waterfalls. It reminded Giap of Quang Uyen in Cao Bang Province, a place he and his family had often visited in his youth.

The driver stopped the jeep at the head of a trail on Thai's command. The group continued on foot and crossed a wide stream on a bridge made of huge logs lashed together with vines.

The forward command base was set at the bottom of a waterfall. Some of his staff had arrived a few weeks before and were busy preparing maps and models of the valley and the French positions. They were excited to see their commander and wanted everything to be ready for his review. They wanted to attack as soon as practical and didn't want to waste General Giap's time.

Giap and his staff were greeted by the field commanders and political commissars. Several Chinese advisors were also there and offered their opinions on the best way to fight a modern Western army. The Chinese advisors were, of course, also spies and would report back to their superiors in Beijing on the Viet Minh's adherence to Mao's philosophy and directives.

The Chinese knew that the Viet Minh were using them to win their war of independence. What they didn't know was what the Viet Minh leaders would do once the war was won. The Chinese would do whatever was required to ensure a friendly Communist neighbor on their southern border. Like an older, more experienced brother, the Chinese were patient with the Viet Minh leaders, but only to a point, and would threaten to reduce aid if things did not go their way.

A detailed model of the valley sat on a table beneath a camouflage net. Giap and his staff gathered around and studied the French positions as they listened to the commanders, commissars, and advisors offering their opinions on the best strategy to defeat the French. The overwhelming opinion was that the Viet Minh forces should 'strike fast and win fast' before the French were able to consolidate their position and add more troops from other highland garrisons. His officers were worried that if the conflict went beyond a few weeks, the French would bring up reinforcements and use their aircraft to cut off the Viet Minh supply lines. It was a valid concern. The Viet Minh rarely fought battles beyond a few days and were inexperienced at the logistics required to keep such a large force in the field for an extended period. General Thai agreed with the field commanders and commissars and thought they should strike at the soonest possible moment.

Giap took it all into consideration before announcing his decision. While a fast victory was certainly preferable, Giap knew the price his men would pay if they attacked the French before they were ready, as they had at Na San. He wanted his artillery and anti-aircraft in place before such an attack. He wanted to isolate the French and cut off their supplies and reinforcements. He wanted to wear down the French defenses until they could be overrun without heavy losses. He wanted to destroy the French airfield and to use his anti-aircraft guns to destroy the French aircraft that attacked his men.

His field commanders wanted to get at the French and grew impatient. He, too, wanted to fight the French, but on his terms. He set offensive operations to begin in late January, well before the beginning of the rainy season. In the meantime, his men would attack Laos in hopes of drawing the French into a battle that would reduce their numbers. His hope was to keep the French engaged and believing the airfield and garrison at Dien Bien Phu were critical to saving Laos from a full-on invasion. He would use the lives of his men to buy the time he needed and keep the French in place.

General Giap's plan was not popular, but it was respected. His commanders had fought for their general before, and they knew he was their best hope for victory. Giap was a brilliant strategist, and his commanders were professionals and carried out his orders to the letter, no matter the cost. The political commissars would not challenge Giap's plan. They knew better than to go against Ho Chi Minh's favorite general if they wanted to continue in their positions.

The Chinese advisors listened and watched. They studied different commanders and their popularity with the other leaders. Defeat, while costly, was not always the least desirable option when pursuing a covert agenda. If the Viet Minh were facing imminent annihilation because of their missteps, and the Chinese were forced to intervene, it would forever bind Vietnam to China, as it had with North Korea.

It was morning and humid. Clouds rimmed the top of the dark mountains. Lieutenant Paul Brunbrouck looked sick when he climbed down the side of the hill called "Dominique." He wasn't sick; that's just the way he always looked, with his sunken eyes and pale complexion. He was 27 and mostly kept to himself. He spent his spare time reading military history. He loved studying the famous battles and the tactics used by the great generals like Rommel and Patton, with their tank battles in North Africa, Lee and McClellan during the Seven Days Battles, and Napoleon and Wellington at Waterloo.

His artillery battery was being repositioned for the third time since he and his men, mostly West African colonials from Morocco and Tunisia, had arrived in the valley. He could see the issue right away when he arrived at the bottom of the hill. There was a six-foot-deep gully carved into the meadow that divided the two strongpoints of Dominique and Elaine. It was perfect cover for a Viet Minh assault force. The artillery stationed on the two hilltops were howitzers and could not effectively fire down into the gully. He wondered about the wisdom of placing an artillery battery at the bottom of the hill until the morning mist cleared when he saw a flat plane of rice fields directly in front of the two hills. His guns could fire on them freely and destroy any troops massing for an attack on either of the hills. It was like he could see the battle unfolding before his eyes. His position would be protected on both flanks by the two hills. There was a river behind his position that protected his rear and a Baily Bridge across the river that gave him and his men an escape route if their position was overrun. Smart, he thought.

The first order of business was gun placement. Once he knew the location of the guns, his men could build up the defenses around them. He was assigned a rifle company to take up positions on his flanks and protect his guns from ground attacks. It's good ground, he thought and went to work.

It was raining hard on the day De Castries inspected the field hospital. The hospital was dug below ground to protect the patients from enemy shelling and gunfire. The clay walls insulated the hospital from the heat and kept the patients cool. Sandbags around the hospital entrance kept most of the rain out, but there was always some water that trickled in, making the tunnels muddy and damp. A clay ramp at the entrance was built to help medical assistants carry the wounded on stretchers down into the hospital tunnels. The tunnels and rooms were carved in the clay and reinforced with ceiling beams, and the walls were lined with scavenged wood from parachute pallets.

The hospital had a large triage room to examine and prep the incoming patients. There were medical supply closets, a small nursing station, and exam rooms. The operating theatres had their walls covered with clean bedsheets over rattan mats to give visitors and patients the appearance of cleanliness, but it was far from a sterile environment, and secondary infections were common. There was an x-ray machine in one of the theatres that would dim the lights in the entire garrison when switched on.

There were dozens of patient rooms, three-foot by six-foot cells carved into the tunnel walls, which gave the place the look of a crypt. Patients' were covered with flat sheets from head to toe. The sheets cut down on the smell and kept bugs and worms from falling into the patients' mouths, nostrils, and wounds from the ceiling of the cell.

Flies constantly pestered the patients, but maggots were welcome because they cleaned the patients' wounds of rotting flesh and infection. There were ventilation shafts built throughout the facility, but without a strong breeze, they offered little relief. The smell was well beyond pungent and left the uninitiated weak in the knees.

De Castries and his assistant Paule were escorted through the facility by Major Grauwin. Paule took notes whenever instructed by De Castries. She covered her nose and mouth with the handkerchief offered by De Castries when they entered the tunnel complex and caught wind of the smell. It was all she could do to keep from gagging.

"And your medical supplies?" said De Castries.

"We only keep seven days of supplies on hand, but we are resupplied daily by air," said Major Grauwin.

"Seven days hardly seems adequate."

"I agree, especially if there is heavy fighting. However, many of the medicines and our blood supply must be kept cool, and we only have one portable refrigeration unit."

"Paule, see to it that another refrigeration unit is ordered, and double the hospital's supplies," said De Castries.

"Thank you, Colonel," said Major Grauwin.

"Do not thank me, Major. It is for the men. They deserve the best care we can offer if they are wounded in the service of their country."

"Of course."

"What is your current capacity?"

"We have forty beds available, which is adequate under our current load and with daily air evacuations."

"Paule, have the engineers increase the size of the facility to two hundred fifty beds and an additional operating theatre."

"You expect that number of casualties?" said Major Grauwin with concern.

"I expect the unexpected. If we get into a scrape, you could quickly be overwhelmed. We must be prepared."

The tour continued down a side tunnel of patient rooms. A little stream of water ran down the tunnel, making the clay floor muddy and slippery. In one of the coffin-sized cells lay Guinevere, curled up and asleep.

"She sleeps here?" asked De Castries quietly.

"When she sleeps. She is the only real nurse we have. She works tirelessly until she is too exhausted to stand. Even then, I have to order her to lie down and rest."

"Paule, see to it that the engineers build Nurse Guinevere proper quarters… and for the major, too."

"Thank you, Colonel."

"You must take care of yourself and your staff, Major. If all goes well, I believe we are in for a long and bloody battle."

It was dark, and rain was coming down in sheets. A convoy of Russian trucks twisted its way through the mountains, staying beneath the forest canopy whenever possible. The trucks had metal shields over their headlights, which were turned off when they were warned of French patrol planes passing overhead. In addition to a load of supplies carried in the truck's bed, each truck towed an anti-aircraft gun, artillery gun, or ammunition trailer. The heavy load made for slow going, especially around tight curves, where the wheels of their towed load barely fit on the road.

The first anti-aircraft gun arrived in the valley of Dien Bien Phu and was unhitched from its truck. The artillery commander did not want to risk exposure of the weapon to French mortars and bombers that might spot the truck driving through the valley. Porters and gun crews wheeled the gun by brute force down a three-mile-long trail to a hidden artillery depot, where each gun was checked for damage and proper operation. Once cleared, each gun was assigned a fighting position overlooking the airfield or strongpoints in the garrison.

It was late afternoon. The sky was cloudy and growing darker by the minute. It would rain soon. A captain entered the field command post and snapped to attention upon seeing General Giap and General Thai discussing potential gun positions on the model of the valley and the surrounding mountains.

"What is it, Captain?" said General Thai.

"Our scouts have spotted multiple fires around the airfield," said the Captain.

"Fires? What are the French burning?" said General Thai.

"We don't know, general. The smoke is shielding our view."

"They could be preparing to pull out, as they did in Na San. Burning their supplies to keep us from using them once they leave," said General Giap.

"Or they could just be clearing their fields of fire," said General Thai. "Have your best scout get a closer look, Captain. We want to know what they are burning and why."

"Yes, sir," said the captain. He saluted and the left. General Thai saw the strain on Giap's face.

"You are worried the French will leave before offering battle?" said Thai.

"We sacrificed so much to get this far. It would all be a waste," said Giap.

"I doubt French pride will let them leave. They, too, have sacrificed," said General Thai.

"Let's hope you are right, General," said General Giap.

The sun was setting, and rain clouds were moving in with the promise of relief from the heat of the day. After a hard week, Brunbrouck's defenses were almost complete. His artillery was in place. The howitzers formed a shallow V, with one gun in the bottom of the gully and the others spread out on the meadow's low slopes leading to the base of the two hills. Each gun was surrounded by a wall of dirt and two-layers of sandbags, with a U-shaped portal in front. This was unusual for a howitzer battery, which was normally positioned several yards back from the blast wall. Fifteen meters in front of his firing position was a line of triple concertina wire and a thick layer of mines.

The rifle company assigned to his position had a 30-cal machine gun stationed to the side, which gave it a clear firing lane of the strip of land between his guns and the wire. In addition, each of the two hillside strongpoints had quad-50s that could support his position in case of attack. The "Meat Grinders" were a powerful deterrent against any enemy assault.

Brunbrouck called over the sergeant in charge of the battery's construction. "Sergeant, I want you to take some of the empty shell crates and fill them with dirt, then place them upright ten meters in front of each gun," said Brunbrouck.

"Sir?" said the sergeant.

"Three for each gun should do the trick. Space them five meters apart from each other in a line perpendicular to the guns," said Brunbrouck, offering no further explanation. "Oh, and Sergeant, make sure the men give their infantry weapons a good cleaning and keep them close at hand."

"Yes, sir."

As always, the sergeant followed his orders to the letter, even though he didn't understand their purpose. Brunbrouck was satisfied with the results and felt ready for the battle he knew would come. He would let his men rest. They will need it, he thought.

Sixty-five foreign Legionnaires filed out of the Daisy Mae's cargo doors at the Dien Bien Phu airfield. Coyle stood at the doorway and saw Brigitte and Bruno at the edge of the airfield. Bruno was wearing his rucksack. He was leaving with his battalion of paratroopers. Brigitte was saying good-bye. "I am going to miss you, Little Bruno," said Brigitte.

"You know, I have never been fond of the 'Little' part of my nickname," said Bruno.

"Yes, but I am," said Brigitte.

"Then I guess I keep it. You will be careful?"

"Yes, if possible. And you?"

"Yes… if possible."

She kissed him twice on the cheeks, and he walked over to lead his men on board the waiting aircraft. He walked up the ramp and past Coyle.

"Heading to Hanoi for some R&R?" said Coyle.

"Yes, until our next assignment. And you?"

"Guess I'll just have to keep coming back here. Don't worry, Little Bruno. I'll make sure she's okay."

"Do Americans always gloat this much?"

"Only when we win."

"I do not think you have won," said Bruno.

"Yet," said Coyle.

Bruno boarded the plane. Coyle waved to Brigitte and closed the cargo doors.

LAOS

It was the morning of Christmas Eve. The fog lifted early, and the sky was clear and blue. A group of German Legionnaires decorated a huge skeletal tree outside Lieutenant Colonel De Castries's command post using paper garlands painted with mercurochrome, vehicle lights, and bits of multicolored parachute cloth. They sang traditional German Christmas carols and smoked cigars given to them by the commander.

The Moroccan and Algerian Legionnaires made a meshwi feast with several spit-roasted lambs purchased from a nearby village, dressed by their company cooks with seasonings from their home country. Several pots of couscous were cooked on the portable stove, along with harissa sauce and gallons of mint tea. They were mostly Muslim and did not believe in the Christian traditions, but they never missed an opportunity to celebrate any holiday. It was a welcome break from the monotony of digging trenches and building blockhouses.

The Vietnamese Legionnaires had grown accustomed to the French celebration near the end of each year. They welcomed servings of pork, sticky rice, noodles, and their infamous nuoc mam, fermented fish sauce. And then there was the beer. As much as they could drink that one night unless they had guard duty. It was a gift from their commanders to show their gratitude for their service in the French army and a time to enjoy the friendship of their comrades in arms.

The more the men celebrated, the more they remembered their homes and families far away, and the more melancholia they felt. Holidays were never easy for soldiers under the French flag but were always celebrated, and traditions maintained, no matter where they were.

The hospital was also decorated with strings of paper snowflakes and Christmas trees down each of the tunnels. Guinevere was tending to an Algerian Legionnaire that had had part of his foot blown off by a Viet Minh mine hidden in a rice paddy he was patrolling. Major Grauwin entered the exam room. "When you are finished, Guinevere, I'd like to see you," said

Grauwin.

"I'm just wrapping up, Doctor. I'll be right there."

Guinevere followed Grauwin out the entrance to the hospital and over to a set of steps that led down into a small bunker with several rooms. Grauwin opened the curtain on the doorway of one of the rooms. The bedroom walls and ceiling were covered with silk parachutes, and the floor was covered with rattan mats. There was a portable cot with clean sheets, a blanket, and even a pillow. A mirror and hairbrush, along with a small water basin with a pitcher, sat on two empty ammunition cases in the corner.

"Your new room, Guinevere," said Grauwin.

"I don't know what to say," said Guinevere, tearing up. "It's beautiful."

The Daisy Mae touched down on Dien Bien Phu airfield and taxied to the edge of the tarmac. The cargo doors opened, revealing General Navarre and dozens of pallets filled with boxes of wine, frozen beef roasts, blocks of cheese, and crates of fresh vegetables. There were even boxes of gateaux, baked, and decorated with chocolate in the Hanoi bakeries that morning. It was Christmas Eve.

The chess player Navarre was more sophisticated than Montgomery or Patton, but he still understood the need to win his men's hearts and that one of the best ways to do that was through their stomachs. Navarre was greeted by Generals Cogny and Gilles, who had flown in earlier from Hanoi, along with Colonels De Castries and Langlais. "You bring gifts," said Cogny.

"Always," said Navarre. "No man should go without a respectable meal on Christmas, especially a Frenchman."

"I am sure the men will agree," said Cogny.

"And how are our men?" said Navarre to De Castries.

"Full of good cheer and anxious to celebrate with their commander and chief," said De Castries.

"Of course, they know he always brings good wine," said Langlais.

"And champagne," said Navarre.

The commanders moved off as the airfield's ground crew unloaded the bounty. Coyle, a bottle of brandy in his hand, and McGoon stepped down from the crew door just under the left side of the cockpit. "One thing about working for the Frenchies during the holidays, you can always count on a good meal and lots of wine," said McGoon.

"Save me a plate, will ya?" said Coyle.

"Where are you going?"

"To spread good cheer," said Coyle. "It's Christmas."

Coyle walked toward the hillside where Brigitte was living. "Bet he's gonna spread a lot more than good cheer," said McGoon to himself.

Coyle reached the top of the hillside and entered what was left of the governor's mansion. He saw Brigitte wearing a freshly ironed jumpsuit and using a cracked mirror to put on makeup. Coyle knocked before entering the room. "Are you decent?" said Coyle.

"That is a matter of opinion, but I am dressed," said Brigitte. "Please come in."

Coyle entered. She put down her makeup, walked over, and kissed him on both cheeks. "Joyeux Noël, Monsieur Coyle."

Coyle handed her the bottle of brandy. "Merry Christmas, Mademoiselle Friang."

"We should drink, yes?"

"Yes."

"If you do not mind?" said Brigitte handing the bottle back to Coyle to open.

She went back to putting on her makeup and brushing her hair. Coyle opened the bottle.

"Glasses?" said Coyle.

"No glasses. We drink like French peasants."

Coyle handed her the bottle. She took a drink straight from the bottle and handed it back to Coyle. He took a long pull from the bottle.

"You look very nice," said Coyle.

"Thank you. I have been invited to join Colonel Gaucher and the men of the Foreign Legionnaires of the 13th Demi-Brigade."

"Oh, I thought maybe we could… Ah, nevermind," said Coyle. "I should have phoned."

Brigitte laughed. "You should join me. But I must warn you, Colonel Gaucher is a hard drinker."

"That's nice of you, but I told McGoon I'd join him for drinks. I gotta keep him sober, you know, for the flight back."

"Ah, McGoon. A hillbilly Christmas?"

"I suppose."

"Will I see you before you go back to Hanoi?"

"If you want."

"Of course. We are friends, yes?"

"Yeah. Friends," said Coyle, confused and frustrated. "I hope you enjoy the brandy," said Coyle.

"I will if I keep it away from the colonel and his men."

"I'll let you finish getting ready. Merry Christmas, Brigitte."

"Merry Christmas, Tom."

She again kissed him on both cheeks. He could smell her perfume. It was subtle, unlike the woman that wore it. He left.

A company quartermaster and his supply sergeants set up a huge tent next to the command post. He had requested the tent from the regional supply depot in Hanoi but was surprised when it actually showed up on one of the C-119 loads. Empty ammunition crates were stacked and used as tables, complete with white bedsheets that were borrowed from the field hospital and used as tablecloths. The French would celebrate in style no matter how imprudent it seemed. Their commanders knew the importance of tradition and did everything possible to boost morale.

It was Continental tradition to celebrate on Christmas Eve rather than Christmas Day. Colonel De Castries was honored to host a feast for his commander and chief. The cooks in his command mess dugout were only too happy to use the food and wine Navarre had brought with him to make a meal worthy of the holiday. Two dozen bottles of champagne were put on ice made in the garrison's mobile refrigerator.

The interior of the tent was decorated with several strings of small light bulbs and white candles on six silver-plated candelabras flown in from Saigon. A pastry table with several gateaux and other pastries was set up at one end of the tent. Dinner was served on real plates with real silverware rented from a Hanoi hotel. There were cold cuts, roast beef with sautéed potatoes and gravy, fresh carrots in honey, long beans sliced French-style at an angle and, of course, wine, brandy, and champagne for the many toasts that night. It wasn't France, but it was as close as they could make it, rustic but charming.

De Castries' assistant, Paule, somehow had managed to put on makeup, high heels, a cocktail dress, and a string of pearls. Later in the evening, after one too many glasses of champagne, and the air thick with blue smoke from cigarettes, she would sing French Christmas carols slightly out of tune. The men didn't care. She was a welcome distraction from the mundane work of building the garrison and patrolling the perimeter.

Navarre sat at a table with his field commanders and executive officers, enjoying the evening and sharing his best wine. He would open each bottle of wine with an explanation of its origin and vintage. They told stories of Christmases past in foreign countries with strange traditions. As usual, the conversation shifted to individual experiences in the battles they had fought. The telling of war stories was a warrior's therapy and memorialized their fallen friends and the sacrifices made to achieve victory.

The aroma in the tent was a sharp mix of cheese, unwashed uniforms, brandy, herbs de Provence, wet leather boots, chocolate ganache, body odor, and sautéed butter. Which combination of smells filled the nostrils depended on where one was standing at the moment. Fortunately, the cigarette and cigar smoke combined with liberal amounts of alcohol made it all somewhat bearable.

After dinner was served and the men were appreciating the brandy and cigars, General Navarre stood and lightly tapped his brandy glass with a spoon, seizing the room's attention and silence. "Gentlemen and Lady, I do not wish to interrupt your celebration, but I would like to make a short presentation," said Navarre. "Colonel De Castries, if you would stand?"

De Castries rose. Navarre's assistant, Captain Pouget, handed him two boxes, one small and the other large. He opened the large box to reveal a general's kepi, with its ornate golden stitching around the crown, flat top, and polished visor. He opened the small box to reveal the two general's insignia, each with two stars, to be worn on the shoulders. "The general staff of the Army of France has deemed you qualified and worthy of promotion to General de Brigade," said Navarre. "Congratulations, General Christian De Castries."

The room burst into applause as General Navarre handed De Castries his symbols of rank. Paule began singing "Le Marche," and her voice was quickly drowned out by the entire tent of men singing. As was tradition, General Cogny was about to make a toast when the major in charge of the garrison's communications walked briskly into the tent and searched the occupants. He spotted General Navarre and rushed over to his table.

"General, I am sorry to interrupt, but this message just came in. It was coded 'urgent,'" said the major as he handed Navarre the typed message.

Navarre expression turned grim as he read in silence. The field commanders and executive officers waited to hear the news. "Gentlemen, it seems several of our garrisons near the border have been overrun, and the Viet Minh have invaded Laos," said Navarre in a low and controlled voice.

"My god," said Cogny. "How far did they get?"

"Two Viet Minh battalions joined forces with the Pathet Lao and captured the city of Thakhek on the upper Mekong River. Our intelligence estimates that another five battalions are just two days' march from Luang Prabang," said Navarre. "We must act quickly if Laos is to be saved."

"Major Bigeard and the 6th Colonial are in Hanoi," said General Gilles. "They should be deployed immediately to reinforce Luang Prabang."

"I agree," said Cogny. "The Viet Minh are far from their bases. We should use all our scout planes in the area to find their supply routes, then attack with our fighter-bombers to disrupt their supply chain. They cannot continue their attack if they lack ammunition and food."

"Good," said Navarre. "We should move our conversations to the garrison's command post. There is no need to interrupt the men's celebration until we have solidified our plans."

On a nearby mountainside, under the safety of the forest canopy, the Viet Minh watched and listened to the French celebrate. The French took so much but shared so little with the people. Soon, the Viet Minh would no longer need to watch from a distance but would enjoy the fruits of their country when the French were driven from their land.

It was dark and raining. A Viet Minh lieutenant walked through a reinforced passage lit by oil lamps. He approached the end of the passage, where a dozen coolies with picks and shovels stood waiting with their commissar. In the wall in front of him was a small hole. It was the end of the tunnel, and the coolies had punched through the wall of dirt and rock to the outside mountain slope facing the valley. The lieutenant took a quick look through the hole. He could see a firefly flare parachuting down from a passing aircraft. The lieutenant picked up a shovel and ordered the commissar to extinguish all the lamps. The tunnel went black. The lieutenant used the shovel to carefully widen the opening until it was large enough to walk through. He stepped out of the tunnel and looked through the trees on the mountain slope. He could clearly see the airfield and the garrison below illuminated by the flare. He smiled knowingly.

The lieutenant congratulated the commissar and his men. He ordered the commissar to finish the opening, compact the dirt on the floor near the opening, and reinforce the tunnel's ceiling and walls with heavy timber. The commissar and his men were to use camouflage from the surrounding foliage to keep the opening hidden while they worked.

A gun crew of five, along with six porters, used ropes to pull a mountain howitzer through the tunnel. They reached the end of the tunnel, now an encasement made of timber and a concrete slab large enough to hold the base of the gun. They wheeled the gun into place and aligned the barrel toward the airfield. A dozen coolies used wooden sleds to haul cases of shells into a reinforced room carved in the side of the tunnel near the encasement. The shells were unloaded and stacked vertically on wooden pallets to keep them dry during the rains. The squad leader reported to the lieutenant that the gun's hidden fighting position was now ready and waiting. It was the first of many.

It was early morning. Coyle sat on a stack of ammunition cases drinking his morning coffee. In between sips, he whittled the finishing touches on an alligator-shaped whistle. Brigitte, with her rucksack on her back, walked on to the airfield. "Scuttlebutt said you might be heading this way," said Coyle.

"Yes. I follow the 6th Colonial to Laos," said Brigitte.

"Bruno's battalion?"

"Yes. He and his men are flying in from Hanoi."

"He didn't get much of a rest."

"No. He rarely does. But he likes to fight. It's in his blood."

"How long are you gonna be gone?"

"I am not sure. A week, maybe two."

"Not enough action around here?"

"It's a story that should be told."

"And you must tell it?"

"I am here, and it is my job."

"I am beginning to see that."

"Who is that little monster for?" said Brigitte motioning to the whistle.

"You," said Coyle handing her the alligator whistle. "Give you something to do when you're not writing."

"I think I will have little time but thank you."

"Do you know how to whistle?"

She pursed her lips and blew the whistle, producing an ungodly shrill.

"Takes a bit of practice," said Coyle. "You'll get the hang of it."

Brigitte saw a pilot waiting by his scout plane. "I have to leave, Coyle."

"Stay safe, Brigitte."

She kissed him twice on the cheeks and boarded the plane. Coyle watched as the little plane took off and disappeared over the mountains.

Medics and nurses loaded the last of the wounded into the Daisy Mae. Coyle climbed aboard and sat down in the co-pilot's chair. McGoon was already going through the pre-flight check.

"Couldn't talk her out of it, huh?" said McGoon.

"I didn't try."

"Why not? She might have stayed if ya had."

"It wasn't my place. Let's go."

"A please won't kill ya."

"Right now, it just might."

"Lord O'Mighty. Looks like someone got whupped with the ornery-stick this morning," said McGoon as he flipped the switch to feed fuel to the engines.

Having flown in the scout plane from Dien Bien Phu, Brigitte waited at the airfield in Luang Prabang. The Royal Lao Army numbered 15,000 but was lightly armed and poorly trained. The Laotian commanders had formed a defensive perimeter around the airfield, their only lifeline with the French, in hopes of staving off an attack until the French paratroopers arrived. All eyes were focused on the surrounding mountains and the sky. Except for the digging of combat trenches, it was quiet and still.

Brigitte wondered about the wisdom of arriving before the French forces. She could see the fear in the Laotian troops. If their position was overrun by the Viet Minh, there was little hope that she could escape. The silence was broken by the sound of aircraft engines. Nine C-47s and two C-119s, including the Daisy Mae, appeared over the mountaintop. The French had arrived. Brigitte's eyes teared up. She was proud of her countrymen and grateful.

The planes landed one after another on the airfield. Bruno and his men stepped from the aircraft. He ordered his men to immediately take up positions between the Laotian troops on the perimeter.

Coyle watched from the cockpit of the Daisy Mae as Brigitte ran up and gave Bruno a big hug.

"You shouldn't have come, Brigitte. There will be a fight here," said Bruno.

"Why else would I come if not to report on another French victory?" said Brigitte.

"Let's hope so. But you should fly back to Hanoi with the Americans. It's not safe here."

"You know I won't do that. My job is here with the French."

"We will not be staying long."

"Oh?" said Brigitte.

"I do not plan on waiting for the Viet Minh to attack. We will take the battle to them."

"May I go with you?"

"No, Brigitte. Not this time."

"Bruno, please. I am safer with you and your men."

Bruno thought for a moment then nodded in agreement.

A morning mist hung over the mountains. A caravan of porters carrying baskets of supplies on their backs and bundles slung between two-man bamboo poles climbed up a mountain trail only a few feet wide, the trail flanked by elephant grass and the occasional tree. The main Viet Minh force was moving quickly to reach its objectives in Laos. The porters had little choice but to continue their march during daylight if they were to keep their troops resupplied with food and ammunition. The mist was burning off, and soon they would be exposed to the French scout planes they knew were hunting for them. They needed to find cover, fix a meal, and sleep. But every mile they marched that morning brought them closer to their comrades and their purpose. They could bear the risk a little longer, or so the commissar leading the caravan thought.

The squadron of single-engine Bearcat fighters from Dien Bien Phu was returning from an attack on the main force of Viet Minh near the royal capital of Luang Prabang when they spotted the caravan below the thinning mist.

The rocket and bomb rails under their wings were empty, and their fuel was dangerously low, but they still had ammunition in each aircraft's four Browning M2 machine guns, two in each wing. They swooped down and opened fire.

Porters dropped their loads and ran for cover in the elephant grass. It gave little protection from the rain of .50-cal bullets. Dozens of porters were torn to bits by the huge bullets meant to takedown other aircraft. A stray bullet found an ammunition box abandoned on the ground and ignited one of the grenades inside. The box exploded, killing several porters hiding under the canopy of a nearby tree. Bullets ripped into sacks of rice, spilling the precious contents on the ground.

The French aircraft did not have the fuel for a second run at the caravan, but one was enough to inflict death and terror on the porters. There would be no more marching that day. The Bearcats headed for home.

It was early morning when a Viet Minh advanced scout walked into a large meadow on a slope covered in mist. He found a small mountain spring feeding a gentle stream near the center of the meadow. It was quiet and still except for a slight breeze floating over the elephant grass. There was a dense forest on the far side of the meadow that would provide his comrades with good cover from the French aircraft patrolling the area. His battalion needed to eat and sleep after their long night march. This was a good resting place, with fresh running water.

He walked across the meadow and into the forest. It was silent and still. He did not see the French paratroopers hiding behind the trees or their machine gun squads hidden under camouflaged nets in hastily dug foxholes and behind fallen logs. They would leave the scout unharmed if he did not raise the alarm.

Brigitte, squatting next to Bruno behind a broken and rotting tree trunk, watched silently as the scout left the forest back the way he came. There was no question now. There was going to be a fight, and many would die on both sides. She wanted to be here and tell the story of what was about to happen, but she didn't want to die or be captured, either. Her mouth was dry with fear and felt full of cotton. She tried to swallow what little saliva she could muster, but it was no help. She didn't dare reach for the canteen in her rucksack.

It was another hour before the Viet Minh scout returned at the head of the battalion. A line of Viet Minh skirmishers walked across the meadow and edge of the woods, checking for enemy troops, mines, and booby-traps, while the rest of the battalion waited on the trail covered by a few trees and flanked with elephant grass. They were exhausted and impatient after the long march. It would be another hour before they could eat as the cooks still had to set up their gear, cook the rice, and prepare the evening meal. After they ate, they would sleep for four hours and then march again for another eight hours during the night.

The first skirmisher entered the forest on the far side of the meadow, where Bruno and his men were hidden. He looked around at the fallen trees and ferns that covered the ground and the trees that towered above. It was still and quiet. Strange. No birds calling, he thought. He didn't give it much more than a thought; he was hungry and tired, too. He moved back out of the forest and reported to his sergeant. Convinced the meadow and forest were clear, the skirmishers waved the battalion into the meadow and towards the forest on the far-side.

The French paratroopers had placed their machine guns in the shape of an L, with the shortest line across the edge of the woods where Bruno and Brigitte were hidden. The Viet Minh battalion crossed the meadow, unaware. Some of the troops stopped for a drink from the stream. Others continued toward the woods.

Bruno needed all the Viet Minh to come farther into the meadow before his men attacked, or he would risk a counterattack when the survivors regrouped. Brigitte reached out and grabbed a broken stub of a branch on the fallen tree to steady herself on the soggy and uneven ground. The branch broke with a snap. Bruno's eyes filled with anger. Brigitte knew her little mishap could endanger the mission, but now was not the time for an apology.

The skirmisher that had entered the forest heard the snap and turned back to the woods.

Bruno pushed Brigitte down behind the log and motioned for her to be silent. He gently unsnapped the button on the strap that held his knife.

The skirmisher walked into the forest again and looked around. He walked over to where he thought he'd heard the noise and looked around. He was standing on the opposite side of the fallen tree and right above Bruno and Brigitte. If he looked down, he would see them. He didn't leave as Bruno had hoped. Instead, he just stood there watching the forest. Bruno reached down and picked up a small rock and cradled it in his index finger. He flicked it with his thumb, and it landed five feet away next to a fern. Bruno waited until the skirmisher turned. Brigitte watched wide-eyed as Bruno rose, unsheathed his knife, and plunged the blade into the skirmisher's temple, killing him instantly and squirting blood onto Brigitte. Bruno helped the dead skirmisher collapse into the ferns, so there was little sound beyond a rustle. Brigitte looked down at the splatter of blood across her breasts and wanted to scream. Bruno saw her and put his blood-soaked hand over her mouth to muffle the sound. Brigitte was terrified but kept quiet.

The rest of the Viet Minh entered the meadow and walked toward the forest on the far side where the skirmishers were waiting. The French continued to stay hidden and silent until a Viet Minh soldier moved behind a tree to urinate. What he found on the opposite side of the tree was a French paratrooper with his submachine gun leveled at the soldier's chest. A short burst killed the surprised soldier instantly. Bruno's paratroopers on the edge of the forest opened fire and quickly dispatched the Viet Minh that had entered the trees, while the machine guns tore into the Viet Minh in the meadow.

Bruno released Brigitte and told her to stay low and out of the crossfire. The mountain stream ran red. French mortar squads fired on the Viet Minh troops, still coming down the trail. Sandwiched between the machine guns and mortars, the confused Viet Minh troops ran down the meadow slope toward another tree line looking for cover. Instead, they found the long leg of the "L," with more French machine gun positions and paratroopers firing into them with their submachines guns and throwing grenades. Disorganized and confused, the Viet Minh fled back up the mountain slope and into the safety of the tall elephant grass. The French rose from their hidden positions and fired as they walked in a staggered line. The French paratroopers, who were so often outnumbered and outgunned when they fought, knew they must continue to slaughter the fleeing Viet Minh, or they could overrun the French once they regrouped. War was sometimes just simple math that the paratroopers knew all too well. The carnage continued until the French ran out of targets. The Viet Minh battalion had taken such a heavy toll in dead and wounded, they ceased to be an effective fighting unit and disappeared into the mountains. Their spirit was broken. The paratroopers had carried the day, and the meadow was once again quiet. It was a massacre.

Brigitte, her face and chest streaked with Viet Minh blood, walked out of the forest. She knew Bruno had killed men. She had watched him do it but from afar. This time she saw his expression as he took another human's life. He had no fear and no remorse once the deed was done. The Little Bruno she had loved, and perhaps still loved, was a killing machine. She looked out over the battlefield at the dead, which were almost all young Viet Minh men. Where is the glory in this? she thought. Whatever innocence remained in Brigitte left at that moment. Her eyes teared up at the loss.

She saw Bruno and his men returning from their hunt. The paratroopers were in high spirits, joking and laughing as they walked across the meadow. Brigitte looked at Bruno, and their eyes met. He could see that she was emotional. He felt ashamed, even though he understood the necessity of what he and his men had done. He knew she understood, too, but she couldn't hide her feelings on seeing so much brutality and human suffering. There was nothing he could say that would ease her pain. Not now. It was too soon. He walked away silently.

PIROTH

It was early morning when Bruno and his paratroopers returned to the garrison at Dien Bien Phu. Word of their victory in Laos had preceded their arrival, and the paratroopers were once again heroes. The Legionnaires and colonials in the garrison cheered and shouted as the exhausted paratroopers climbed down from their aircraft. It had been decided to station the para battalions at the garrison in case the attack on Laos again flared up. In addition, Bruno and his men would be able to carry out offensive maneuvers while the Legionnaires and colonials protected the garrison.

Brigitte climbed down from the doorway of a C-47. She was dog-tired and just wanted to post her stories on the radio, eat some hot chow, and sleep for a week. In which order she could not decide. She saw Bruno on the edge of the airfield. She wanted to apologize for her reaction after the battle--he was a man of violence, a hunter, and a killer, doing the job he was ordered to do-- she just didn't know what to say. Everything that rolled through her mind sounded trite and naïve. Perhaps it was better to wait until she had slept and could think better.

In between congratulations from the ground crew and the Legionnaires guarding the perimeter, Bruno turned to see Brigitte walk from the airfield at a distance. She saw the killer beneath the warrior, and I've lost her again, he thought.

Bruno didn't like to lose, especially when it came to a woman that he still loved. He remembered the first time she had rejected him. They had been lovers for almost a year while fighting in the resistance together. They were both young and inexperienced. She was captured by the Gestapo, tortured, and thrown in prison. There was nothing he could do to save her. He felt helpless. When the Germans were finally defeated, she was released and returned to Paris. He hoped they could pick up where they left off, but of course, that was impossible. Things were different. She was different. She needed time to recover, and Bruno was never known for his patience. She was broken, and he left her when she needed him most. He told himself she was just another woman, and there would be others. And he was right, there were others, but none were like Brigitte. None had her spirit. He realized his mistake and asked her to forgive him. She said their relationship was over. Once trust was broken, sorry meant little. He swore to himself that one day he would win her back, and once he had her, he would never let her go. That day looked very far off from where he was standing, even as his men cheered his name.

It was early morning when a C-47 landed in Dien Bien Phu and pulled to a stop in front of a wooden control tower. A group of Legionnaires and colonials gathered and watched with keen interest as the tail door opened, and twenty-six Indonesian and Algerian prostitutes stepped out of the aircraft's hold. The mobile brothel was an important addition to the garrison and kept morale high, even though most of the men manning the far-off strongpoints would never have the time to visit the ladies. Just the thought that they were near seemed to lighten spirits.

Major Grauwin, the surgeon in charge of the field hospital, was placed in charge of the brothel. Grauwin and two orderlies stepped forward to greet the prostitutes. "Ladies, if you will please follow us to the field hospital for inspection, I am sure these gentlemen will see that your things are unloaded carefully and brought to your quarters," said Grauwin.

The prostitutes followed Grauwin and the orderlies up the hill to the field hospital, where they were examined for venereal disease and tuberculosis. The Legionnaires and colonials unloaded their belongings, including several reinforced cots, bedding, and heavy drapes to cut down on the noise during business hours.

It was late afternoon, and the sky was filled with dark clouds. Wallace Buford piloted his C-119 over the mountains. He was unflappable, a veteran pilot, like the other Americans flying for the French. His cargo, 6 tons of petrol, pushed the aircraft's load limit, and even at full power, the engines strained to keep altitude. He heard the pitch of the right engine change and watched the engine's head temperature gauge rise. The plane shuddered. "Oh shit," he said to himself. "Hang in there, baby. We're almost there."

The aircraft began to slowly lose altitude. Buford watched as the last mountain before the airfield rose in the windshield. His co-pilot's eyes widened with concern. "Ah, boss?" said the co-pilot.

"I see it. I'm not blind," said Buford. "Dump the load."

"All of it?"

"Yeah, all of it. Do it now and do it quick."

The co-pilot radioed back to loadmaster and relayed the order. The loadmaster opened the rear doors and, with the help of his assistant loadmaster, pushed out ninety 50-gallon drums of fuel sitting on pallets.

The drums tumbled in the air and crashed into the trees on the mountain slope. Fuel from the smashed drums spewed everywhere.

With its load lightened, the aircraft gained altitude and cleared the mountain.

The aircraft landed on the airfield at Dien Bien Phu and taxied off the runway. Buford and his co-pilot climbed out the door below the cockpit and headed toward the flight center. "Only thing I can think of is that she blew a head gasket on one of the cylinders," said Buford. "Get the mechanic to pull all the heads and take a look at each one of 'em, plus anything else he can think of that might have caused the rise in temperature."

"Will do, Boss," said the co-pilot.

"We ain't going back over those mountains until we know what went wrong," said Buford.

On the mountain slope, a Viet Minh corporal had watched the huge aircraft land on the airfield and park near the smaller planes. It was a tempting target, and his squad needed to sight in their howitzer. He did some calculations and aimed the howitzer. He ordered his gunner to fire. The private yanked the lanyard at the back of the gun, and the 105mm shell produced a loud crack as it left the barrel.

Buford and his co-pilot heard the familiar crack of artillery in the distance. "What the hell?" said Buford, turning back toward his aircraft.

The shell exploded forty feet from the giant air freighter. There was little mistaking the teeth-jarring detonation of a 105mm shell burst. Another crack and a second shell exploded ten feet off the left wing, pelting it with shrapnel. The final shell punched a hole clear through the cockpit and exploded next to the front landing gear. The front landing gear collapsed, and the plane tipped forward on its nose with its twin tail boom rising up in the air. The plane burst into flames.

"I think we are going to need more than one mechanic, Boss," said the co-pilot.

"Shut the fuck up," said Buford, unamused, as he watched his aircraft burn.

The Viet Minh lieutenant commanding the artillery battery ran through the tunnel toward the howitzer's encasement, just as the corporal and his crew prepared to fire a final shot aimed at the flight crew standing on the airfield and watching their aircraft burn.

"Cease fire now!" the lieutenant ordered.

The corporal and his squad snapped to attention.

"Who gave you permission to fire?" said the lieutenant.

"Sir, we were just sighting in our gun," said the corporal.

"And who told you to do that?"

"No one, sir."

"You have exposed your position to the enemy, corporal, and, more importantly, revealed that we have artillery that can reach their garrison and airfield. I should have you court-martialed. You've endangered our mission."

"I'm sorry, sir. I just thought –"

"Don't think, Corporal. I think for you. Do you understand?"

"Yes, sir."

"Check your camouflage, and for God's sake, don't fire your weapon until you receive a direct order from me."

"Yes, sir."

The lieutenant left knowing that shit rolls downhill, and he was going to hear an ear-full from his commanding officer.

Piroth and Langlais stood in the field command bunker in front of De Castries. "It was a 105mm, Colonel," said De Castries. "You told me that it was impossible for the Viet Minh to transport their artillery to this valley."

"Sir, with all due respect, the shells came from one gun," said Piroth. "And I agree, it was a 105, but that doesn't mean that the Viet Minh brought it here from their bases in China. They could have captured it from one of our garrisons, or it could have been left here from the Japanese. It's probably on its last leg of service and couldn't hit the broad side of a barn."

"It hit the airfield and destroyed a C-119."

"Yes, sir, it did. Fortunately, no one was hurt."

"Do you at least know its location?"

"We have a general direction of the gun's location. We will find the gun the next time it fires and destroy it with our counter-fire."

"I have no intention of waiting until it fires again, Colonel Piroth," said De Castries and turned to Langlais. "Colonel Langlais, find that damned gun and destroy it."

"Yes, sir," said Langlais.

"Gentlemen, you are dismissed," said De Castries, still steaming.

It was late afternoon, and the sky was dull over the valley. Bruno and a squad of scouts walked down a mountain trail and met Colonel Langlais at the head of a company of paratroopers. "Anything?" said Langlais.

"No, and we've checked out the entire sector," said Bruno. "Colonel, is it possible that the gun is on the backside of the mountain?"

"Anything is possible, but it would require that their gunners understand indirect fire, and our intelligence tells us they don't."

"I'm out of ideas, and the longer we sit still, the more chance the Viet Minh have to ambush us," said Bruno.

Langlais pulled out his map and studied it. "All right, let's check out the backside of the mountain," said Langlais.

Bruno walked up another mountain trail with Langlais. A scout sergeant came trotting down the trail. "We've got something," said the scout sergeant.

"You found the gun?" said Langlais hopefully.

"No, it's something else. A team of coolies and their commissar, digging into the mountainside."

"What are they digging?" said Bruno.

"We don't know. We couldn't get close enough without tipping them off."

"Bruno, bring up your flamethrowers," said Langlais.

A two-man fire team, one carrying a flamethrower tank on his back, crouched low as they approached the digging site. The flamethrower team leader, a corporal, moved closer to take a look. He could see the commissar supervising the digging team at the head of the tunnel. The French corporal waved the flamethrower gunner forward and opened the valves on the flamethrower's two tanks, one filled with compressed nitrogen and the other petrol mixed with a thickener. He used a handheld flint wheel to light the pilot flame, a trickle of gas inside the flamethrower's nozzle. The flamethrower gunner took a deep breath and stood up above the foliage. He took aim and pulled the trigger. A thirty-foot stream of fire spewed from the nozzle and engulfed the commissar and the Viet Minh guarding the entrance. "Cease fire," said the corporal. The shot only lasted two seconds. Two seconds was enough. The corporal wanted to conserve the petrol in the flamethrower's tanks for a second shot. The commissar and his men fell to the ground, dying.

"Move," said the corporal.

The gunner moved forward to get a better angle on the entrance and fired into the opening. The stream of flame bounced off the tunnel's walls and found its hidden targets. Four coolies ran from the tunnel with their clothes ablaze. The French corporal shot all of them with his submachine gun. It was the humane thing to do. The corporal signaled Bruno that they were done.

"Forward," said Bruno.

Bruno and a platoon of paratroopers ran up the mountainside and into the tunnel. Shovel and pick handles burned. Several coolies were burning inside the tunnel and were immediately shot by Bruno and his men. His men rushed past Bruno and rounded up any surviving coolies. Bruno saw a piece of paper burning on the ground. He stamped out the flames with his boot and picked up a scorched drawing. It was an engineer's crude drawing of a tunnel that reached from the back slope of the mountain to an artillery encasement on the front slope. Colonel Langlais approached. "Colonel, you should see this," said Bruno.

"Merde," said Langlais, recognizing the meaning of the drawing.

Langlais and Piroth once again stood in front of De Castries in his command bunker as he studied the singed engineer's drawing of the tunnel and encasement. "A tunnel? How is that possible? The manpower it would take..." said De Castries.

"Exactly, sir. Even if they have a few more guns, our intelligence reports show that they couldn't possibly have the manpower to build more than one or two tunnels and encasements in such a short amount of time. Sir, I think this is a ruse to draw our forces into the mountains so they can ambush us."

"Why a tunnel?" said Langlais.

"They can resupply their gun from the back slope without being concerned about our fighter-bombers or artillery," said Piroth.

"And the encasement?" said De Castries. "Can you destroy their guns with an encasement built into a mountain?"

Piroth hesitated and said, "It will be difficult if it is constructed according to this drawing."

"And what about our bombers? Can our bombers take out their guns?"

"Again, it will be difficult with that amount of earth above the encasement. It will act as a buffer and soften the impact of any of our bombs or artillery."

"They can fire on our garrison and airfield with impunity?"

"It seems so, sir," said Piroth.

"Colonel Langlais, you and your paratroopers must find those tunnels and destroy their guns. Our entire defense depends on it."

"Of course, sir," said Langlais.

It was just before sunrise when the paratroopers, under the command of Major Maurice Guiraud, moved out from strongpoint Claudine. The 1st Foreign Battalion of Paratroopers, known as 1st BEP, was an experimental battalion. Originally serving as Legionnaires, the battalion had been conscripted into the paratroopers and retrained. They were unique in that they could be used effectively for either offense or defense and were equally experienced in both tactics. They maintained their allegiance to the Legion, and with it the deep-seated esprit de corps that made them tough fighters.

Langlais had ordered Guiraud and his men to search the mountains at the far end of the valley for the enemy's artillery encasements. On the way, they were to reconnoiter a series of villages suspected of sheltering the enemy's anti-aircraft guns.

They reached Ban Phu at 9 a.m., Ban Co Hen at 10 a.m., and Ban Lung Con at 11 a.m. All three villages were abandoned and burned out by the Viet Minh. There were dried puddles of blood in the dirt. Pigs, chickens, and water buffalo had been slaughtered and left in the streets to bloat under the sun. The reek of putrid flesh was nauseating. Masses of blue flies swarmed around the carcasses with an angry hum as the soldiers passed.

The battalion moved on and reached Ban Huoi at around 1:30 p.m. In charge of 3rd Company, Lieutenant "Lulu" Martin stopped to take a compass reading. A shot rang out, and a bullet hit his hand, almost blowing it off. Heavy small arms fire erupted from the surrounding paddy fields and drove the company in the village to the ground.

Upon a nearby hillock, just past the far end of the village, Corporal Ty and his mortar squad opened fire, shelling the Legionnaires in the village with 24 rounds per minute of 80mm mortars.

It was a murderous rate of fire that took its toll on the French and drove them to find cover or hit the ground. Martin wrapped what remained of his hand in a field dressing and ordered his men to advance on the enemy mortar position. A fire team with a 57mm recoilless rifle firing low-velocity artillery rounds moved into position at the center of the village and fired at Ty's mortar squad on the hillock.

With anti-personnel shells exploding around him and his team, Ty was stubborn in the defense of his position and didn't want to give it up. After losing one of his men to a burst of shrapnel, it became apparent that his position would be destroyed by the recoilless rifle if he remained. He fired one last salvo and ordered his men to retreat, carrying their mortar and their dead comrade with them.

The last 80mm mortar shell exploded six feet from Major Verguet, Guiraud's second in command, killing two French sub-lieutenants almost thirty feet away. Miraculously, Verguet was not hit by the shell's fragments. Verguet and his men fought back and forth with the Viet Minh fighting from the hidden positions in the elephant grass and rice paddies that surrounded the village. The para Legionnaires rushed the Viet Minh's position, only to be driven back by the enemy's machine guns and 20mm mortars.

The Viet Minh finally retreated when their scouts spotted another French company coming up to reinforce the company in the village. Huts burned like bonfires. Dead villagers, pigs, and chickens were scattered across the ground. A thick layer of smoke hung over the village, teeming with the reek of cordite and gunpowder.

Guiraud arrived with another company and quickly appraised the situation. 3rd Company had been badly mauled by the ambush and was in no condition to continue the mission. He ordered a retreat of both companies.

As they left the village, they again came under attack from a separate Viet Minh battalion waiting in ambush on the backside of the village. The Legionnaires took heavy losses in both dead and wounded. The French fought a rear-action as they continued to retreat, chewing up the Viet Minh when they attacked, then retreating toward the garrison. The Viet Minh purposely stayed close to the French, engaging in close-quarter actions again and again. Guiraud considered ordering an airstrike on the Viet Minh force nipping at his heels but knew the situation was too fluid. The chance of hitting his own men was too risky. It took three hours to fight their way back to the umbrella of entrenched machine guns and recoilless rifles on strongpoint Claudine. Under fire from the French positions on the hillside, the Viet Minh battalion took heavy casualties and broke off their attack.

Guiraud was met by Langlais as he and his men entered the strongpoint's perimeter. Langlais was furious that Guiraud had not completed his mission and ordered him back out the next day.

The sky was clear, and the sun burned brightly. The Daisy Mae flew over the hills and mountains of the highlands. Coyle and McGoon sat in the cockpit. "Can you take the stick for a few minutes?" said McGoon.

"Sure," said Coyle. "Where ya going?"

"To get the man's autograph."

McGoon picked up a brown paper bag filled with books, walked out the cockpit door, and entered the cargo hold.

Graham Greene, the famous British author, and Lieutenant General 'Iron Mike' O'Daniel, the U.S. chief military advisor for Indochina, sat together talking. When offered the post, O'Daniel requested a drop in rank so he would not outrank General Navarre. It was O'Daniel that most influenced the Pentagon's decision on the amount of military aid and assistance to be given to France. It was aid that France desperately needed. "Indochina may be a sideshow compared to our military commitments in Europe, but it plays a key role in dispersing the Communists' resources," said O'Daniel. "Especially the Chinese. We're still cleaning up from the mess they made in Korea."

"General, let's be honest. Your country is fighting a proxy war against the Communists and using the French as your pawns. But the French are struggling. They are still rebuilding their army from its losses during WWII. Even with all your supplies and leftover weapons, they don't have enough troops to protect all of Indochina from the Communists," said Greene. "If the Communists take control of Indochina, there is no telling where they will spread to next. Malaysia? Thailand? The Philippines? Why not commit some of your soldiers to the French effort?"

"Committing ground troops to Indochina is a whole different ball of wax than just giving military aid. I don't think the American people have the stomach to support another war in a place that few could even find on a map. No, the role for the U.S. right now is to keep our focus on NATO and the Soviet threat in Eastern Europe. The French have economic interests in Indochina; the U.S. doesn't. Let them fight the Communists. We'll supply the weapons."

"Ah, gentlemen," said McGoon, "sorry to interrupt. I was wondering if I could get Mr. Greene's autograph. I'm a big fan."

"Of course," said Greene. "Which of my novels is your favorite?"

"Oh, ah… that one that they made into a movie," said McGoon.

"Third Man?" said O'Daniel. "I like that one, too, although the movie was a little hinky. All those Dutch angles, and who in the hell shoots a movie in black and white anymore?"

McGoon pulled out a stack of books and handed them one by one to Greene to sign. "Only one is for me. The rest are for my family. They're big fans, too."

McGoon walked back into the cockpit with his stack of autographed books. "I didn't know you were such a fan," said Coyle.

"I'm not, but when that guy dies, these babies could really be worth something," said McGoon.

"Dies? He's younger than you, McGoon."

"Yeah, but look at all the dangerous places he visits. That's pretty risky behavior. Odds are good that one of these days, some sniper or mortar shell will take him out, and when it happens, I'm gonna cry for Mr. Greene. All the way to the bank."

The Daisy Mae landed at the airfield in Dien Bien Phu, taxied to the apron, and parked in a bay made of sandbags stacked to the height of a man. The sandbag holding pen protected the aircraft from the enemy mortar fire that hit the airfield daily. O'Daniel and his staff exited the aircraft along with Greene. They were met by De Castries and Paule. "General O'Daniel, if you and Mr. Greene would ride with Paule and me in the jeep, I will be happy to give you a tour of the garrison," said De Castries.

"Thank you, General," said O'Daniel. "We know you are busy. We don't want to take up too much of your time."

"Nonsense, General. America's assistance is essential to our efforts and greatly appreciated."

De Castries hated to grovel to the American general but knew it was for the good of France and his men. They climbed into the jeep and drove off the airfield.

It was early evening, and the sky was clear over the remains of the Mayor's mansion. Coyle, Brigitte, and Bruno sat around a table on empty ammunition cases that Brigitte had scrounged from one of the battalion's supply sergeants. She had found a tablecloth and three unbroken plates in a sideboard that had been hidden under debris. The crystal glasses had all been broken in an artillery barrage. They shared several tins of rations Brigitte had heated over her little stove, and a bottle of wine Coyle had brought from Hanoi. It was a hodgepodge of elegance. Bruno was finishing a story, "… there I was, standing in the middle of the living room, looking like a chimney-sweep covered in suet, unarmed, secret documents stuffed in my pants, face to face with an SS Colonel with a glass eye standing in his living room and wearing silk pajamas while holding a Lugar."

"So, what did you do?" said Coyle.

"The only thing I could do. I told him I was finished cleaning his fireplace, and he owed me five francs."

Coyle and Brigitte laughed. Brigitte had heard the story several times before but still found it funny. Bruno kept adding little details to the story to make it more interesting. This time it was the silk pajamas.

"My daddy had a glass eye," said Coyle. "Lost the real one from a big splinter that got thrown from a falling tree. I remember this one time, my buddies and I were out tree top walking…"

"Treetop walking?" said Brigitte.

"Yeah, that's when ya climb to the top of a pine tree, and ya get it swaying, then ya jump to the top of the next tree. We'd have contests to see who could go the farthest. I held the town record for a couple of months until Timmy O'Connor took it away. Anyway, that night when I got home, my hands were bloody and covered in pitch. Of course, my daddy knew exactly what I had been doing and whupped my ass like you wouldn't believe. I was really mad at him, so that night, I snuck into his room and stole his glass eye. I only meant to keep it a couple of days, but he was so angry, I was too scared to give it back to him. I still got the thing."

"Are you going to give it back?" said Brigitte.

"Can't. He passed. I thought about tossing it in the coffin at his funeral."

"Ah. Of little use, but a nice gesture," said Bruno.

They passed the bottle around. Brigitte wanted Bruno and Coyle to like each other. It was the French way, the old lover and the new lover drinking and breaking bread together. Coyle, on the other hand, was jealous of Bruno's past with Brigitte. He knew it was petty, but he couldn't help himself. Coyle was no slouch when it came to his own war stories, but he found it hard to compete with the bold paratrooper. Why does he have to be so damn French? thought Coyle.

"Where are you from, Coyle?" said Bruno.

"Tennessee, in the eastern part of the United States," said Coyle.

"Ah, Nashville and the Grand Ole Opera," said Bruno.

"Yeah, but I wasn't from that neck of the woods. My family lived in the Appalachian Mountains in a little town called Fork Mountain. It's about 45 miles west of Knoxville. My daddy was a logger. He cut wood for the coal mines. They used his timber to support the shafts they dug."

"It was a good life?" said Brigitte.

"Yeah. Most of the time. Unless my daddy got hurt. Then things would get a little lean at the dinner table when he couldn't work. Logging was dangerous up in the mountains. When I was fifteen, I started working with him. Saw a logger cutting a tree once, and the damn thing split at the base. As it fell, the broken end hit 'im in the crotch and cut 'im in half, like a roasted chicken. Hell of a thing to see at fifteen. My daddy was the one that told his family what had happened. I kinda had a fancy for the man's daughter, but they had to move away shortly after he died. It was a shame. She was a nice girl. Always wore pigtails in her hair. She was a hell of a shot with a rifle, too. She could hit a squirrel on the run up a tree at fifty feet. Her family ate a lot of squirrel stew."

Brigitte listened to Coyle tell his story and wondered what she would look like with her hair up in pigtails. In the distance, they could hear artillery exploding and guns firing. Parachute flares dropped from a circling C-47 illuminated the surrounding countryside with an eerie green light. Orange tracer shells fired from machine guns streaked back and forth across the valley floor, the Viet Minh shooting at the French and the French shooting at the Viet Minh. Brigitte's little dinner party was strangely incongruent in the middle of the madness that surrounded them. But still, she loved it and didn't want the evening to end.

Bruno still loved Brigitte and refused to give up. He wondered how he could win her back against this Davey Crockett wannabe. He could see that Brigitte was fascinated by Coyle's backwoods mystique. Why did he have to be so damned American? thought Bruno.

BEATRICE

It had been raining all day, and the ground at strongpoint Beatrice was saturated. All vegetation on the hill had been cleared away to give the blockhouses and trenches a clear line of sight of the rice fields that surrounded the strongpoint's perimeter. Rivulets of water carved their way through the mud and made their way downhill until they found a trench.

Sergeant Rouzic and the German Legionnaire continued work on the blockhouse that would become their fighting position. The blockhouse had a firing portal facing downhill and was built along a trench line that was flooded, looking more like a farmer's irrigation ditch than a defensive position. The muddy water was streaming through the blockhouse entrance, and there was already two feet of water on the floor. They both used empty food containers to bail the water out through the front portal, but it was clearly a losing battle as the water continued to rise.

"What's the use? Let it fill up, and we'll bail it out once it stops raining," said the German Legionnaire, throwing down his improvised bucket.

"And if it doesn't stop raining?" said Sergeant Rouzic.

"Then we each get a pair of swim fins and drown the yellow bastards when they come to get us."

"Brilliant plan."

"German ingenuity."

Sergeant Rouzic conceded the battle to the rain and threw down his bucket. He opened a ration tin and munched on the contents. The German Legionnaire unbuttoned the fly on his trousers and urinated into the rainwater inside the blockhouse.

"Hey, what the hell do you think you're doing? I'm eating here," said Sergeant Rouzic.

"What does it matter? It all goes to the same place," said the German Legionnaire.

"You are a pig."

"For your information, a pig happens to be a very clean animal."
"Not if you're sleeping next to it."

The gunfire and mortar explosions continued as the sun set over the garrison. Two Legionnaires shoveled dirt into a freshly dug grave. It was a never-ending task. There was still a stack of forty bodies wrapped in sheets in need of burial, and they were running out of space. The French tricolor flag, now tattered, rippled over hundreds of white crosses covering the hillside.

Two hospital ambulances and several trucks pulled up to the cargo doors in the rear end of the Daisy Mae. The drivers and crew began unloading dozens of stretchers, each bearing a wounded soldier to be evacuated to Hanoi.

McGoon paced, waiting. Coyle was in a foul mood when he walked onto the airfield and over to the Daisy Mae. He couldn't figure out why Brigitte had invited Bruno to dinner. Bruno was full of himself, Coyle was sure of that, but he couldn't help but like the guy. He was beginning to understand why Brigitte once loved him and might still. After all, they were both French, sharing a common culture that he knew very little about. This all made Coyle uncertain about where he stood with Brigitte, and he was beginning to wonder if it was all just a big waste of time. "Finally. I was about to promote Kim-ly to co-pilot," said McGoon.

"Quit your belly-aching. I'm here, ain't I?" said Coyle.

"Don't get snippy with me. What the hell's got into you?"

"McGoon, don't. I don't need an ass-chewing right now."

"Well, Coyle, you be sure and let me know when I can chew your ass, okay?"

Coyle climbed up through the side door without responding. McGoon followed.

The sky was dull and overcast. The air in the valley was cooler than usual. The sun was getting low, and it would be dark soon. Langlais, a towel wrapped around his waist, walked up a hillside to an outdoor shower. It was a simple and efficient system. The wooden walls of the shower had already been scavenged by the engineers, allowing its users little privacy. He took off his towel, leaving his naked body totally exposed to any onlookers, and used an empty coffee can to dip into a barrel of rainwater. He poured the rainwater into an overhead bucket and pulled on an attached lanyard, causing it to tip and pour water over his head. He refilled the bucket with more rainwater and used a bar of soap to lather his hair and body.

On strongpoint Beatrice, Sergeant Rouzic stood in the newly-built blockhouse, staring out at the surrounding mountains. He heard the thumps of several 60mm mortar explosions at the base of the hill. The Legionnaires on Beatrice had grown used to the daily mortar barrages. He was unconcerned until he noticed that several of the shell-bursts were not the usual anti-personnel rounds but smoke rounds.

A veil of smoke obscured the rice fields surrounding the strongpoint and the approach trenches that the Viet Minh had been digging for over a month. The smoke cloud was growing heavier as more mortar rounds exploded, but he could still see through some of the thin patches. His interest was further aroused when he saw a dozen machine guns, mortars, and recoilless rifles being manhandled by their Viet Minh gun crews to forward firing positions closer to the perimeter. Moments later, two full battalions of enemy soldiers left the protection of the forest and ran across open ground, only to disappear into the trenches. "Oh, my god," said Sergeant Rouzic.

"What's wrong, Sarge?" said the German Legionnaire manning the machine gun.

"Find Colonel Gaucher and tell him we are about to be attacked," said Sergeant Rouzic.

"Really?" said the German, looking out the blockhouse firing portal.

"Move, Corporal," said Sergeant Rouzic.

The corporal scrambled out of the blockhouse. Sergeant Rouzic stepped behind the machine gun, pulled back the receiver handle, and chambered the first round. He swung the gun's barrel to where he thought the first Viet Minh sappers would exit their trench. He waited for the smoke to clear. It was going to be a long night.

Generals Giap and Thai, each with binoculars, stood on a mountain slope overlooking the garrison and runway. They could see the Daisy Mae, its rear cargo doors closed, starting its engines in preparation for takeoff. Giap looked at his watch-- it was 5 p.m. on March 13th, 1954. He knew that if they won, this battle would be a historic moment, and he wanted to know the exact time it occurred. If they lost, it really didn't matter.

"General Thai… you may begin," said Giap calmly.

General Thai barked out an order to his radio operator, and the operator used the radio to repeat the order to the artillery commanders in their firing positions around the surrounding mountains.

The familiar and distant crack of heavy artillery being fired caught Langlais' attention midway through his shower. It was the number and frequency of cracks that alarmed him. 140 howitzers and 40 heavy mortars fired during the Viet Minh opening volley. On average, one shell every second struck the French garrison. Langlais watched the hillside erupt with explosions from a rolling barrage that was heading straight for him. He hit the muddy ground and lay as flat as possible as the shell-bursts moved closer, like a tidal wave engulfing all in its path. He covered his ears and opened his mouth to release pressure inside his body should a shell land too close. The wave of explosions rolled past him tearing up the ground around him and moving up the hill. He was unhurt. He jumped to his feet and ran naked, covered in mud and soap, to his command post.

Brigitte was just starting her story on the typewriter when she heard the crack of artillery fire in the distance. She looked up and saw the orange glows from the hidden guns on the mountainside, like the beginnings of hundreds of small forest fires. She saw the first explosions on far-off strongpoint Beatrice, the first to get hit. She, too, was surprised by the number of explosions. As a war correspondent, she had watched many battles unfold with an opening artillery barrage, but this was different. It was more intense and growing like an angry, living thing. "Jesus," she said. "Those poor men."

There were more explosions on closer hillsides as more strongpoints came under fire. It occurred to her that her hillside with the mayor's mansion would also be a target. She picked up her helmet, grabbed her typewriter, and ran for her foxhole beside the mansion. The wall behind where she had been sitting exploded, bombarding the remaining furniture with pieces of brick and debris. The wall collapsed and crushed the couch where she had been sitting only moments before.

More shells rained down as she ran. Shell-bursts tore up the hillside all around her, like the rampage of an unseen demon. Nothing was safe. She stumbled over the uneven ground and dropped her typewriter. She heard the growing whistle of an artillery shell descending above her. She dove into her foxhole just as the shell exploded a few yards away. She scrambled up and looked over the edge of the foxhole at her typewriter. She thought about running to get it until she heard another 105mm shell coming down on her position. She ducked down into the foxhole, covered her head with her arms, and prayed. The explosion blew her typewriter to smithereens and left behind a crater the size of a car. She had witnessed two wars, but nothing like this. Brigitte curled up in the bottom of her foxhole and pulled down on the chin straps of her helmet. Dirt and debris rained down, covering her and filling the foxhole. She shook uncontrollably and felt like a coward as she prayed for God to spare her.

The Daisy Mae had already taxied to the end of the runway and throttled up her engines when the barrage began. Even over the sound of its engines, Coyle and McGoon could hear the thundering explosions, and they looked out the windshield to see the garrison being torn to shreds.

"Holy mother of Moses," said McGoon.

"Brigitte," said Coyle, staring out the windshield at the mayor's mansion on the hillside, with artillery shells exploding around it. He wanted to go to her and protect her, but he couldn't leave McGoon and the wounded they carried.

"Time to go," said McGoon, as he pushed the throttles forward and the engines roared.

The Daisy Mae inched forward, slowly at first, then gaining speed.

An artillery round hit the airfield's fuel depot and ignited five thousand gallons of fuel. The explosion and the fireball that followed were massive. The ground shook below the entire garrison.

"There goes the fuel depot," said Coyle.

Several shells dropped on the airfield. Some hit the steel plates that lined the runway and clanged like a hammer hitting a gong. The shell-bursts launched some of the plates into the air and left jagged spikes of steel sticking up from deep craters.

McGoon steered the plane clear but kept the speed up as they approached the end of the runway. The Daisy Mae lifted off. "Spank my bottom and call me 'Wilma.' That was a close one," said McGoon.

Deep within the forested hillside, a Viet Minh anti-aircraft gun fired at the Daisy Mae, still struggling to gain altitude.

A shell exploded next to the Daisy Mae. Coyle and McGoon felt the plane shudder. "We're hit!" said Coyle.

"No shit?" said McGoon. "Can't be that bad. We still have control."

"For now," said Coyle.

"Don't go getting negative on me, Coyle. We're gonna make it. I hate to crash. All that walking," said McGoon.

A second nearby explosion hit the aircraft, and the shards from the shell tore small holes in the sheet metal below the cockpit. They could hear the air whistling through the new holes like an out of tune flute. McGoon struggled to keep control. Coyle rose from his chair.

"Not the best time to take a leak, Coyle," said McGoon

"I'm going to find where they hit us."

"Yeah, good idea. Do that," said McGoon. "And Coyle… when we get outta this, we're demanding a raise the second we land, okay?"

"Yeah, when we land," said Coyle, unsure as he exited the cockpit.

"I don't mind risking my life, but damn it, I wanna get paid for it," said McGoon to himself.

Coyle entered the aircraft's hold. Several of the patients were dead from the shell's shrapnel and flying debris. A large rupture was torn out of the sheet metal on the port side of the aircraft. Coyle moved forward and saw a bloody hand hanging on to the sharp edge of the torn sheet metal. Coyle dove to the deck and belly-crawled to the breach. It was a medic hanging on from outside the aircraft. His body was dancing around in the two-hundred-mile-an-hour wind. Coyle reached out and grabbed the man's hand. The blood made it slippery, but Coyle hung on.

"Don't let me go," said the medic.

"I won't. I promise," said Coyle. "Hang on, and I'll pull you in."

Just as Coyle pulled the man partially back into the aircraft, several more anti-aircraft shells exploded outside the hole. Desperate to get the man back inside before more shell-bursts, Coyle pulled hard, and the medic landed inside.

"Thank you. Thank you," said the medic.

Coyle looked down to see both of the medic's legs gone and blood flowing into a great pool on the deck.

"You're gonna be okay," said Coyle taking his belt off to make a tourniquet.

"I don't think so," said the medic, and died.

Piroth stood in the main battery at the top of Strongpoint Isabel and watched thousands of enemy shells rain down on the French garrison. It was clear that General Giap and his ant army had accomplished the impossible by bringing his entire division of heavy artillery to the valley.

"Incredible," said Piroth to himself, as if admiring the enemy general's feat.

His radioman, a corporal, handed Piroth a hardwire handset. "It's General De Castries, sir."

Piroth stared at the phone like it was a deadly snake. He took the handset and raised it to his ear, "Yes, sir. I know, but… No, sir. Of course, right away," said Piroth. He gave the handset back to the radioman. "Order our batteries to counterfire."

"But where, sir?"

Piroth, almost despondent, looked out at over a hundred orange flashes from enemy artillery positions on the mountain slopes. "Everywhere, Corporal. Everywhere."

Langlais, still naked and out of breath, ran into his command bunker. Bruno was already there and waiting for orders. A young corporal stood nearby. "Corporal, give the colonel your trousers," said Bruno.

"Sir?"

"Your trousers, Corporal. Take them off and give them to the colonel. You can find another pair at the hospital. I am sure there will be plenty of dead shortly."

"Yes, Major," said the corporal as he unbuttoned his pants and handed them to Langlais.

"Bruno, take whatever men you can find and silence the anti-aircraft guns firing from the eastern mountain slope just beyond the airfield," said Langlais.

"Got it, Boss," said Bruno and exited the bunker.

In preparation for the enemy ground assault, Strongpoint Beatrice was hit especially hard by the Viet Minh artillery. Sergeant Rouzic watched the hillside in front of the blockhouse explode like a mounting tidal wave, churning up the tortured earth. The blockhouse shook violently with each explosion as the barrage advanced up the hillside like a hungry beast. Rouzic was surprised to see the German Legionnaire reenter the blockhouse. "You fool. What are you doing here?" he said.

"I told the colonel as ordered," said the Legionnaire.

"Why did you come back?"

"I am German. It's what we do," said the Legionnaire.

He took up his place behind the machine gun and checked the gun's chamber for a round. "Besides, you never were any good with a machine gun."

On the edge of the airfield, Bruno and a company of paratroopers leapfrogged their way forward toward the eastern mountain slope. They kept quiet by using hand signals and utilized whatever they could find for cover. A parachute flare was launched from the mountainside and illuminated their position. "Merde," said Bruno.

Tracer bullets from hidden machine guns streamed across the airfield and hit two of Bruno's men. Mortar shells exploded, taking out another man. Bruno and his paratrooper instinctively dove for the ground, hoping the mortar barrage would pass. It didn't. "We stay, we die!" yelled Bruno to his men.

He jumped up and waved his men forward, leading the way. His men, inspired by the courage of their leader, rose from the ground and charged, some firing their weapons, and others yelling "Vive La France!" They died by the dozens before they reached the machine guns. Enraged from seeing his men slaughtered, Bruno reached the tree line and jumped into a machine gun's nest. He plunged his knife into the gunner's chest, killing him. He turned on the gunner's assistant reaching for his rifle, and pummeled the man with his fists. The paratroopers overran the enemy firing positions, forcing the Viet Minh to abandon their weapons and driving them deeper into the woods. Once again, the French paratroopers had accomplished their objective, but at a heavy cost.

In the field command post, Piroth stood in front of De Castries and Langlais. "I don't understand how, but he brought up his entire division of heavy artillery. Our spotters have located over one hundred gun positions on the surrounding mountain slope. We believe each of the enemy's artillery guns is entrenched within an encasement like the one you and your men saw, Colonel Langlais. Our own batteries are having little effect. Even our bombers cannot silence them. I am so sorry, General," said Piroth.

"I don't think your condolences are much help at this point, Colonel," said De Castries.

"The enemy is expending ammunition at an incredible rate," said Piroth. "They cannot possibly keep it up."

"And yet you continue to underestimate them, and they continue doing the impossible," said De Castries. "Colonel Piroth, you are dismissed."

Piroth saluted weakly and walked past Bruno on his way out of the bunker. "I'm so sorry, Major."

"Major, are you wounded?" said Langlais upon seeing Bruno's uniform covered in blood.

"Me? No. It's not my blood, sir," said Bruno. "As ordered, the anti-aircraft guns around the airfield have been destroyed."

"Good work, Major," said Langlais. "Your losses?"

"I am still waiting for a final count, but heavy, sir," said Bruno. "And the Americans?"

"They are safe."

"Ah, well… good, the big one still owes me fifty francs from poker."

"Get some sleep, Major. It looks like we have our work cut out for us."

"Yes, sir."

Bruno saluted and exited. De Castries turned to Langlais. "Intelligence reports enemy strength at five full divisions," said De Castries. "How is that possible? The logistics required must have been incredible."

"No matter," said Langlais. "Soon, they will attack, and we will crush them."

"Soon? I doubt it, Colonel. They'll wear us down and strangle us a bit, yes?"

"Giap can't wait forever. He faces the same problem of resupply as we do, only worse. His supply lines must still cross three hundred kilometers of mountains, and without air support."

"Perhaps," said De Castries, looking very drawn and tired.

"Get some sleep, General," said Langlais. "Everything will look better in the morning."

Langlais saluted and exited, leaving De Castries with his nightmares.

Enemy artillery continued to explode all over the garrison, destroying defensive positions and killing the French. In tears, Piroth stumbled along a trench line, apologizing to the men hunched down inside. "I am sorry. I am so sorry," he said, oblivious to the danger.

He came to his command bunker and went inside. He knelt down and opened the footlocker at the end of his cot. He pulled out a photo of his wife, kissed it, and set it on the cot. He pulled out a grenade, hugged it to his chest, pulled the pin, and released the spoon.

"I am so sorry."

The grenade exploded, blowing his hands and forearms off and ripping open his chest. Piroth was dead.

As night fell, the bombardment continued. Two C-47s, dispatched from Hanoi, circled the garrison from overhead and dropped parachute flares.

Sergeant Rouzic and the German Legionnaire kept watch in the blockhouse. "Two hours of this. If they haven't attacked by now, what are they thinking?" said the Legionnaire.

"Quit your griping, or you'll jinx us," said Rouzic. "As long as they are shelling us, their men cannot attack."

"Still, I wish they would get on with it."

The shelling on strongpoint Beatrice suddenly stopped.

"Damn German," said Rouzic. Both men readied themselves.

The green glow of the flares revealed several teams of sappers carrying Bangalore torpedoes as they ran from the trenches just outside the perimeter of strongpoint Beatrice.

"There," said Sergeant Rouzic, pointing to the sappers through the dust and smoke. "Two o'clock. Sappers with Bangalores. They're going for the wire."

The German Legionnaire opened fire with the machine gun as Rouzic fed the ammunition belt into the gun's receiver.

Orange tracers streamed down the hillside from the blockhouse, giving away the machine gun's position. Four sappers were hit and dropped their long explosive tubes. Four more sappers sprung from their trenches, jumped over their fallen comrades, picked up the long tubes, and ran forward toward the perimeter. The Bangalores were made from hollowed-out bamboo tubes filled with explosives and were a Chinese version of the British Bangalore torpedoes. Each sapper slid his tube section under the triple concertina wire and moved out of the way for the next sapper, who attached another tube section and pushed the connected tubes further forward under the wire. The final sapper stuck a blasting cap in explosive clay at the end of the last tube section and lit the fuse with a brass trench lighter he had taken from a dead Legionnaire. He scrambled for cover.

The Bangalore torpedoes exploded, cutting the layers of concertina wire in several places, pitching the barbed wire high into the air. Several French mines also exploded between the wire and the first French trench. There was a path about twenty feet wide across the perimeter. The Viet Minh climbed from the trenches and ran through the opening. A single loop of barbed wire remained intact and blocked their route. The first soldier to reach it threw himself on the razor-sharp barbs and used his body as a bridge for the soldiers following him. Hundreds of boots trampled over him. He was crushed to death.

Once through the wire, the Viet Minh immediately spread out across the hillside. Dozens were killed by anti-personnel mines placed by the French engineers and hidden just below the surface. The surviving Viet Minh hit the ground, some diving into the craters formed from the exploded mines, and opened fire with their rifles and submachine guns. The French laid down murderous fire from their machine guns, mortars, and recoilless rifles, killing hundreds of Viet Minh.

The tracer bullets from the French machine guns revealed their firing positions in the blockhouses. Just outside the perimeter, the Viet Minh opened up with their recoilless rifles, taking out the blockhouses and killing the French gunners.

Viet Minh used airburst rounds launched from their mortars against the Legionnaires in the trenches, forcing them to keep their heads down or risk decapitation. The two sides fought for hours as the Viet Minh on the hillside crept upward under heavy fire from the French.

Feeding an ammunition belt into the machine gun, Sergeant Rouzic saw a platoon of Viet Minh approaching the final obstacle, a triple line of concertina wire laid across the ground just fifteen feet from the blockhouse. They cut through the wire and belly-crawled toward the blockhouse. The German Legionnaire was preoccupied with driving back the enemy from the main breach in their perimeter and did not notice the approaching danger. Sergeant Rouzic used one hand to keep feeding the machine gun belt and the other hand to pick up a small metal box with six switches on the top plate and wires leading out from the side. "Fire-in-the-hole!" he said and flipped the three switches on the left. Sergeant Rouzic and the German Legionnaire pressed themselves against the blockhouse wall away from the firing portal.

Three napalm canisters on the hillside exploded and engulfed the entire Viet Minh platoon with the burning gelatin. Flames licked the blockhouse portal and receded. "Clear," said Rouzic. The German Legionnaire resumed his position behind the machine gun with Rouzic at his side.

In Beatrice's command bunker, the battalion staff struggled to get a handle on the situation, as most of the phone lines had been cut by mortar and artillery rounds. Colonel Gaucher stood next to his radioman, barking out orders into the handset, "We need air support now, or we will be overrun!"

An artillery shell pierced the flimsy roof and landed in the center of the command bunker. The explosion that followed was thunderous and knocked everyone inside the bunker off their feet. There were bodies everywhere. Stunned but unhurt, the radioman stumbled to his knees. The bunker was filled with smoke and dust. There were small fires from burning maps and intelligence reports. As the dust began to clear, he saw the gauzy outline of Colonel Gaucher standing a few feet away. "Colonel, are you okay?" said the radioman.

Hearing no reply, the radioman rose, took a step forward, and saw that the colonel was missing both his arms and that the bone in his right leg was exposed above the knee. The commander of strongpoint Beatrice would be dead within the hour.

Sergeant Rouzic and the German Legionnaire continued to hang on, each time fighting back the Viet Minh assault. Rouzic could see the machine gun's barrel smoking from the heat of continuous firing. He knew the barrel would warp from the heat if it continued, but there was no lull in the fighting. "Barrel change!" he said. He put on a heavy pair of canvas gloves and waited until the last bullets on the belt fed into the machine gun's receiver.

"Go," said the German. Rouzic unscrewed the barrel using the gloves and swapped it with a cool barrel. The German opened the receiver and placed a new belt inside, slapping the top of the receiver down until it latched. He looked through the portal and watched as a wave of Viet Minh, believing the French machine gun was out of ammunition, rose from the hillside below, and charged toward the blockhouse. "Hurry up, or we're gonna die," he said.

"Don't be dramatic," said Rouzic. He gave the fresh barrel a final twist into place. "Ready," he said. The German Legionnaire chambered a round and took aim.

The Viet Minh were within ten feet of the blockhouse portal, and several were preparing grenades to throw through the opening when the German's machine gun opened fire and ripped them to shreds. More than a dozen died and rolled back down the hillside.

From across a rice field, hidden by a clump of elephant grass on the paddy's low dike wall, a Viet Minh recoilless rifle fired. It was a tracer round meant to help the gunner find his line of fire in the dark. There was no need.

The shell flew through the blockhouse portal and exploded on the back wall. The roof caved in and buried both men. Sergeant Rouzic was the first to recover and pull himself free from the rubble. He looked down and saw the lower part of a leg floating in the water at the bottom of the collapsed blockhouse. He checked to make sure both his legs were still attached. They were. He used his hands to dig through the debris until he found the German Legionnaire, still alive but screaming in pain, "Oh my god! My leg! Where is my leg?"

"Quit your bellyaching," said Rouzic. "You still have a knee." He pulled off the German's web belt and used it as a tourniquet on what remained of the leg.

With the bleeding stopped, Rouzic found a weapon and picked it up. He looked out and saw the Viet Minh again rising and running toward the collapsed blockhouse. With the machine gun gone, there was nothing to stop them and no time to retreat. This is it, he thought. This is where I die.

Two Bearcat fighters dove down from the sky and dropped their bombs on the Viet Minh assault in front of the blockhouse. The explosions killed dozens of Viet Minh and sucked up the air, making it impossible to breathe. The Viet Minh that survived the bombs were dazed from the concussions and became easy targets for the Legionnaires still in the trenches above. The Viet Minh under fire dove for cover, and the assault was stalled for a moment.

Sergeant Rouzic saw their chance. "Can you run?" he said.

"You're kidding me, right?" said the German, holding his bloody stump.

"All right. This may hurt a little. Just keep it down," said Rouzic. He picked up the German and lifted him over his shoulder in a fireman's carry.

The German moaned. With his submachine gun in one hand and the other hanging on to the German Legionnaire, Sergeant Rouzic ran out of the blockhouse and along the trench line. He stepped over the bodies of his fallen comrades and dodged behind the few Legionnaires still alive and fighting for their lives.

Sergeant Rouzic carried the German Legionnaire to the aid station on the backside of the hill. He saw the last ambulance preparing to leave and loaded the German inside. He turned to go back to his firing position and saw dozens of Viet Minh cresting the top of the hill. It was too late. "Go, go, go!" he said to the driver, emptying the clip in his submachine gun at the Viet Minh racing directly toward him.

Out of ammunition, Sergeant Rouzic climbed on the back bumper of the ambulance as it sped away. Beatrice had fallen.

In the garrison's command bunker, De Castries' radioman spoke into his handset, "Sun Two, say again."

Langlais entered the bunker and saw De Castries sitting in a chair and staring at a dirt wall. The radioman on Beatrice responded over the radio speaker, "Colonel Gaucher is dead, so is Major Pegot. Viets are over the wire and have overrun all our firing positions. Request fire mission on our position. Say again, on our position."

The command bunker radioman turned to De Castries, "General, your orders?"

De Castries was dazed and unresponsive. The radioman turned to Langlais. Langlais nodded.

"Sun Two, this is Sun Six. Fire mission incoming on your position. Andre, keep your head down and good luck," said the radioman. He switched channels to the artillery net and called in the fire mission.

Langlais walked over and put his hand gently on the general's shoulder, "Charles, can you hear me?"

De Castries looked up for a moment as if struggling to focus, "Yes, Colonel?"

"Colonel Gaucher is dead, and Beatrice has fallen. We must retake the strongpoint before the enemy can entrench. In the morning, yes?"

"In the morning… of course… everything will be better in the morning," said De Castries.

"I will see to it, sir," said Langlais.

"Yes," said De Castries. "You see to it, Colonel."

On strongpoint Beatrice, the last of the Legionnaires ran out of ammunition as the enemy overran their trench. Legionnaires and Viet Minh fought hand-to-hand using their bayonets, rifle butts, and entrenching tools to kill each other. A barrage of French artillery and mortar shells rained down on the hillside. Anyone not in a trench, regardless of uniform, was torn to shreds. The French made the Viet Minh pay for their prize.

It was silent, except for the occasional crack of a rifle. A thin veil of morning fog mixed with the smoke hanging over the valley. There was an acrid odor in the air from spent gunpowder and artillery propellant.

On strongpoint Beatrice, the Viet Minh tended to their wounded, searched for survivors, and carried off their dead. A company of Viet Minh took up positions in the trenches on the backside of the hill, facing the rest of the French garrison. Many leaned against their rifles and slept, exhausted from the uphill battle of last night. Hearing the heavy thrum of aircraft engines, a sleepy-eyed lieutenant looked up and saw a squadron of Bearcat fighter-bombers appear from over a nearby mountain. The planes dove down toward the hillside and dropped their bombs on the enemy positions. Dozens of Viet Minh were torn to pieces by the powerful explosions across the hill. Just when the Viet Minh thought it was over, the Bearcats swooped down again and unloaded the wing guns on the soldiers in the trenches. A dozen more died from the strafing. Their guns and bomb racks empty, the Bearcat pilots headed for home back in Hanoi.

Next came a rolling barrage of French shells. Every artillery gun and heavy mortar in the entire French garrison fired on the backside of strongpoint Beatrice. The incoming shells sounded like a freight train speeding through a tunnel. The murderous explosions tore up the trenches and killed most of the Viet Minh company. Any soldiers still alive were in shock from the concussions that had pounded their bodies. Blood poured from their ears, and their eyes blurred from swelling.

Below the hillside, Bruno and his battalion of paratroopers rose from the ground. Adrenaline pumped through their veins and their muscles tensed. They knew what was about to happen all too well. "Forward," said Bruno, taking the lead. His men formed three lines across the strongpoint's perimeter and walked forward at a brisk pace, matching their speed to his. Bruno did not want to wear out his men before they started up the hill's slope. Submachine gunshots from one of the Viet Minh defenders hit two paratroopers, wounding one and killing the other. "Charge!" said Bruno. The paratroopers shouted out a guttural scream as they ran up the hillside toward the trenches.

Several of the Viet Minh riflemen in the trenches had recovered and were firing down on the approaching paratroopers. Bruno's long-time radioman was hit in the eye and dropped to the ground. Bruno did not stop or even flinch on seeing the man that had been by his side for three years shot dead. His mind was focused on the trenches near the top of the hill. He and his men had to reach those trenches or die trying.

The hillside was wet from recent rain, and several paratroopers fell in the mud, then struggled to get back on their feet and rejoin their comrades. Mortars shells exploded across the hillside, killing several paratroopers, and still, Bruno and his men charged forward. As they approached the top of the hill, paratroopers in the first line opened fire with their submachine guns and raked the top of the trenches, killing several Viet Minh and driving others to cover below the trenches' forward rim. Paratroopers jumped in the trenches, and hand-to-hand battles broke out all along the line. The paratroopers were excellent fighters with or without weapons and quickly overpowered the Viet Minh.

Bruno, with several of his men firing their weapons at his side, jumped over the trenches and continued up the hillside. When they came to the top of the hill, they stopped. Between the fighter-bombers, the artillery barrage, and the French paratroopers, the Viet Minh on strongpoint Beatrice had had enough and were in full retreat down the hillside, back to the safety of the mountains. Bruno ordered his men to cease fire. Bruno and his paratroopers fell silent as they looked out over the hillside. Five hundred Legionnaires, many stripped of their uniforms and boots, lay dead in the mud. Tears welled up in Bruno's eyes. He wasn't a machine, after all.

With their men now off the hill and out of the way, the Viet Minh opened fire with their artillery. A fierce barrage of explosions rained down on Beatrice as the Viet Minh concentrated their artillery and mortars. Most of the strongpoint's entrenchments had been destroyed in the previous attack, and there was nowhere for the French to take cover. Bruno radioed Langlais, "We are taking heavy losses."

Langlais knew Bruno was not one to exaggerate, even when faced with overwhelming odds. "Can you hold if I send reinforcements?" said Langlais over the radio.

"Negative. They will just be more cannon fodder for the enemy. Your orders, Colonel?"

Langlais did not want to give up the ground the men under his command had bled to retake, but he could not afford to lose more paratroopers. "Pull back, Major," said Langlais.

Bruno gave the order to retreat. The French gave up the ground, and Beatrice was once again lost.

It was dark when Lieutenant Turpin woke in the bunker of Beatrice's aid station. He had been wounded in the leg and shoulder during the initial assault to take the strongpoint and had lost a good deal of blood before the French medic reached him and carried him to the bunker. He slept through most of the fighting and Bruno's counterattack. He looked at the bandages on his wounds. Both were stained with his blood and felt very sore when he eventually sat up.

He looked around the bunker. It had been abandoned, with only the dead remaining. The smell of death was intense. He wondered why he had not been evacuated with the other wounded. Maybe the medics thought him dead or simply forgot him. He was still weak but managed to climb the shallow stairs out of the bunker.

It was morning, and the light hurt his eyes. The valley below was covered in mist, and the sky was grey. He looked at the surrounding hillside. The destruction of the entrenchments was immense. Nothing remained undamaged. In the distance, he could hear artillery explosions and gunfire. The garrison was still fighting. That was a good sign, he thought. He was spotted by a Viet Minh scavenger squad looking for anything usable left behind by the French. The corporal in charge of the squad ran over, leveled his rifle at the French officer, and took him prisoner.

Turpin was taken before a Viet Minh major that spoke in broken English. He was given some rice and water, which he ate and drank. He was told that the Viet Minh were going to blow up the strongpoint but would agree to a brief ceasefire to allow the French to retrieve the bodies of their dead. Turpin was given two passes written in Vietnamese and told that he was free to return to his lines and deliver the message to the French commander.

The corporal that had captured him escorted Turpin to the base of the hill and pointed him in the direction of the French lines. As he walked in the mist, the lieutenant wondered if it was all a trick, and he was about to be shot in the back. He looked back, and the corporal was gone. Turpin turned back around and kept walking. The bandage on his leg began to unravel, and was dragged through the mud. He was too weak to do anything about it and only wanted to put distance between him and the Viet Minh. He walked on.

It took him the better part of an hour to find the French lines in the mist. He was sure the French would mistake him for a Viet Minh and shoot him, but the mist began to burn off as the sun rose higher, and things became more visible. He saw a hill up ahead. It was Dominique. He yelled out in French, and a Legionnaire yelled back. He moved forward slowly with his hands raised until the Legionnaire could get a good look at him and was convinced he was not a threat.

The Lieutenant was taken to the field hospital, where his wounds were examined. Before going into surgery to have the shrapnel removed, he relayed the message he'd been given by the Viet Minh major. A messenger was sent to General De Castries in the command bunker.

Langlais had been right. After three hours of sleep, De Castries had recovered from his malaise and was back in charge, barking out orders to his staff. He still had dark rings under his eyes, and his temper was short. Langlais entered the bunker. "A ceasefire?" said Langlais. "They are stalling. We must counterattack and retake Beatrice."
    "You and your men tried this morning," said De Castries, "and failed."
    "We must try again. We cannot leave that hilltop in the enemy's hands. They will move up their artillery and shell our positions, not to mention the airfield."
    "And how many men will you lose this time, Colonel?"
    "As many as it takes."
    "No. I have already sent a messenger to the Viet Minh. We are accepting their terms for a ceasefire at 4 p.m. If your men wish to do something useful,

have them bring back our dead."

"You waste our blood."

"No, Colonel. It is you that will waste your men's blood with another insane charge up a hill that you cannot possibly hold."

"We can hold if given the proper support."

"No, Colonel. You can't."

"Then tell me, General De Castries, if not Beatrice, where do we stop them?"

De Castries had no answer but was too tired to continue the argument. "You have your orders, Colonel," said De Castries. "Ceasefire at 4 p.m."

Langlais left the bunker without saluting. He was frustrated and desperately wanted to shoot something or someone. He just didn't know what or who.

It was just after noon, and the morning fog had burned off, leaving the sun to bake the tarmac at Cat Bi airfield. McGoon and Coyle surveyed the damage on the Daisy Mae. The maintenance crew was already working on cutting away the damaged aluminum support ribs and sheet metal panels around the hole in the side of the aircraft's hold. McGoon poked his finger through a small shrapnel hole in the left breast of the painted character of Daisy Mae.

"Damn it," said McGoon. "Ain't no way to treat a lady."

"Relax. It ain't nothing a bit of sheet metal, and a little paint won't fix," said Coyle.

"That may be, but it's disrespectful to hit her in the tit."

"Can't argue with that. Look, I'm sure she'll be fine. Good as new," said Coyle. "And now you can give her those bigger breasts you've been wanting."

"Coyle, that ack-ack must've knocked a screw loose in your brain or something. Ya can't give a woman bigger breasts just cuz ya want 'em," said McGoon. "It ain't natural."

"Yeah, I suppose you're right," said Coyle. "While she's getting fixed up, I could use a good co-pilot if you ain't too proud to fly with me."

"Can I bring my chair?" said McGoon.

"No."

"All right. I guess I'd be honored to be your co-pilot until the Daisy Mae is repaired. Better than sitting around watching the grass grow."

"Great," said Coyle, and continued to inspect the rest of the damage to the aircraft.

McGoon took a last look at the character's buxom figure. "Give a woman bigger titties… that'll be the day," he said and moved off to join Coyle.

It was early morning, and a light fog covered the valley floor. During the previous night, the Viet Minh and the French had fought for over twelve hours, with both sides sustaining heavy losses. Just two days after the fall of Beatrice, the trophy they fought for was strongpoint Gabrielle, and in the end, it was the Viet Minh that remained in control of the hill. It was a terrible loss for the French and allowed the Viet Minh to reposition their anti-aircraft guns on a hill directly under the French's northern flight path. Even with the hillside almost two kilometers away from the airfield, they had an unobstructed shot at any plane taking off or landing. The noose was tightening.

A jeep drove General Giap and General Thai to the base of the hillside. The two generals stepped out and looked up through the thinning mist. The hillside was littered with an equal number of Viet Minh and French bodies. They numbered in the thousands. Two platoons of Viet Minh soldiers continued the search for wounded and carried away the bodies of their comrades. Some of the bodies were intertwined from fighting hand-to-hand with their enemy. Other bodies were hung up in the loops of concertina wire around the perimeter and in front of the French trenches and blockhouses. Many of those killed were just teenagers, the age of the students Giap once taught at the university.

"Madness," said Giap.

"A necessary tragedy," said Thai.

"Was it, General?"

"What do you mean?"

"Why were our assault trenches so far from the French perimeter? Our men were forced to attack over open ground and were cut down by the enemy's machine guns."

"Our sappers entrenched as far as they could, given the time and resources they were granted."

"Then we must expand their resources and the time they are allowed. I will not see our men slaughtered because of impatience."

"Sir, the council agreed upon the fast strike, fast win strategy."

"They did. But that was before this carnage. Our men's morale will sink to new depths if they believe their generals are wasting their lives and the lives of their comrades. I am the commander in the field, and I have the authority to fight the battle as I see fit, with or without the council's approval."

"Yes, sir."

"You will instruct our engineering commanders to dig our trenches up to the first French trench line before we launch an assault."

"That will take weeks, General."

"Then let it. We will use the extra time to bring up more artillery and ammunition."

"But the rains, sir," said General Thai. "The monsoon season will soon be here, and with it the mudslides and floods. We will not be able to maintain our supply lines at the current rate."

"Better our men get wet and hungry than die at the hands of the French," said General Giap.

General Thai knew Giap's temperament and mindset. Giap was slow to anger and measured his words before speaking. They had fought together for many years. He considered Giap his friend. Losing his temper was unusual for Giap. Thai decided not to press the issue any further. "Do you wish to arrange a ceasefire with the French so they can retrieve the bodies of their fallen?" said Thai.

"No," said Giap. "Let them rot."

ISABEL

It was night, and a thin fog had settled in over the valley. Firefly flares slowly fell from above and gave the countryside a greenish glow. The distant sound of artillery explosions and gunfire were a constant reminder of the unceasing battle that raged between the Viet Minh and the French.

Major Sudat and his company of engineers waited on the muddy banks of the shallow river that flowed between the airfield and strongpoint Huguette. Sudat peeked over the embankment and gave a hand signal to his platoon leaders. The engineers and riflemen climbed out of the riverbed. They carried their equipment and supplies across the open ground toward the airfield, trying to keep noise to a minimum.

Reaching the runway, a platoon of riflemen took up defensive positions to protect the engineers. Sudat quickly surveyed the damage. Enemy artillery shells had torn up the PSP and blown craters in the runway. The garrison's lifeline to the outside world was a tangle of steel and dirt. It was engineering company's responsibility to fix the runway faster than the enemy artillery could destroy it and not get killed in the process. The French army engineers were a tough breed and accustomed to working under the most hazardous conditions.

Like a field hospital surgeon, Sudat performed triage and identified the most critical repairs. He needed at least a thousand yards of runway to land a C-47 and twelve hundred yards to land a C-119, which could carry nearly four times the amount of badly needed supplies, ammunition, and replacement troops. He signaled for his men to get to work on repairs.

The heavy steel plates did not just attach to each other like a child's puzzle; they were bolted together to keep them from shifting during the landing of the heavy aircraft they were designed to support. Once breached, each plate needed to be cut from its surrounding plates and replaced with a new one. It was a labor-intensive job that required several men with crowbars and welding torches. There were dozens of craters and hundreds of broken plates.

The lieutenant in charge of the rifle platoon went rigid when he heard the voices of a Viet Minh patrol obscured by the fog. He signaled to Sudat and the engineers, then slowly pulled his pistol from its holster, knelt on one knee, and watched the edge of the fog. The engineers stopped working and picked up their weapons. They stooped low and kept quiet. The engineers were fierce warriors in addition to being skilled workers, but if a firefight broke out, they would be fighting on open ground and could be easily flanked by the larger Viet Minh forces. The enemy patrol passed, and the voices faded. The lieutenant gave the all-clear signal, and the engineers returned to work. It was going to be a long and dangerous night.

Major Sudat reported to General De Castries in the garrison's main command bunker. "General, the airfield is once again open for aircraft, but I cannot guarantee how long it will stay open. The perforated steel plates we used to build the runway are a real son of a bitch to repair when they are damaged."

"Thank you, Major," said De Castries. "How many feet are useable?"

"Twelve hundred feet, sir. We can land the C-119s."

"Excellent. Good work, Major. See that your men get some rest. I am more than certain we will need them again shortly."

"As am I, General," said Sudat, saluting and exiting the bunker.

It was night, and a steady drizzle set in over the valley. Its cooling effect was a welcome relief from the heat and humidity. The new C-119, piloted by Coyle and co-piloted by McGoon, cleared the last mountain before descending into the cloud cover over the valley. It was a dangerous move, not being able to see more than a few feet ahead of the aircraft's nose, and knowing that the valley was surrounded by mountains and scattered with hills. McGoon and Coyle kept a close watch on the altimeter and studied the map carefully, tracking their progress.

The Viet Minh anti-aircraft gunners heard the aircraft's engines but could not spot the plane against the low cloud cover. Their mortar crews shot parachute flares into the night sky and still saw nothing.

Just before reaching the airfield, McGoon and Coyle brought the C-119 down out of the clouds. The Viet Minh opened fire with everything they had in range, but it was too late. The aircraft hit the runway hard, and Coyle reversed the blades on her two engines, using them to reduce her speed while riding the wheel brakes.

The C-119 taxied off the runway and over to the apron. Enemy artillery shells rained down in hopes of hitting the aircraft and destroying its cargo. It was a long shot without being able to visually correct their fire through the drizzle and only pitted the airfield with more craters. The C-119 stopped in front of three trucks and several jeeps, used to ferry supplies from the airfield to the supply depots around the garrison. The assistant loadmaster opened the rear doors on the aircraft, and the ground crew went to work, unloading the badly needed cargo.

Coyle climbed out of the doorway below the cockpit. McGoon followed. "I'll be back before morning," said Coyle.

"Make damn sure ya are, Coyle. We don't wanna be dodging ack-ack in the daylight," said McGoon.

Coyle ran across the tarmac toward strongpoint Elaine. The drizzle had stopped, but the ground was still wet and slippery. Coyle kept low as he ran across the base of the hill called Elaine. A gust of wind hit his wet pants, and he felt a chill up his back. He came to a four-foot-high barbed wire fence that stretched along the perimeter of the hill. He looked through the darkness for a way through the fence. An enemy sniper shot slapped the mud next to his left foot. Coyle hit the ground and lay as flat as possible on the wet grass. "Hey, asshole," said a faceless voice in the darkness. "Get your butt in here. You're giving away our position."

"Sorry," said Coyle to the voice. "Which way do I go?"

"There's an opening in the fence five meters to your left."

"Got it."

Coyle crawled to the opening and entered the perimeter. He crawled to the closest trench and slithered over the side. There was a dead Legionnaire on the floor of the trench.

"This way," said the voice.

Coyle hunched over below the edge of the trench and walked in the direction of the voice. He stepped carefully over the Legionnaire's body but accidentally stepped on his hand. "Hey, you bastard. Watch where you are stepping," said the Legionnaire.

"Sorry," said Coyle. "I thought you were dead."

"Not yet," said the Legionnaire.

The Legionnaire lying on the bottom of the trench was using a homemade geophone--built from his mess kit and a stethoscope borrowed from the field hospital--to listen to the ground. "Little yellow bastards dig an assault trench, and we build a countertrench to cut them off. You'd think we were gophers."

The Legionnaire heard something through the geophone and motioned for Coyle to be quiet. The Legionnaire listened to the sound of digging and determined the direction. He motioned the direction to his men, and they went to work digging their countertrench. Sergeant Rouzic, one of the few survivors of Beatrice, stepped forward from the shadows of the trench. "Cat and mouse with shovels, yes?" he said. "You are an American pilot?"

"Yeah. I fly a boxcar," said Coyle.

"A boxcar?"

"A plane. A big one."

"Ah, yes. You are lost?"

"Yeah, I guess. Can't get my bearings too well in the dark."

"The airfield is that way," said Sergeant Rouzic, pointing in the direction Coyle had just come.

"No. Not the airfield. I am looking for Brigitte Friang."

"Ah, yes. The journalist. She is over at the field hospital near the command bunker," said the sergeant, pointing in the opposite direction.

"Oh my god, is she hurt?"

"No, no. The hospital is overcrowded with wounded. She volunteered to help."

Coyle was surprised when the dirt wall next to him started to crumble and fall away. Sergeant Rouzic pulled a grenade from his pocket and motioned for Coyle to keep quiet and get out of the way. Several Legionnaires moved up beside the sergeant and readied their weapons. More dirt fell away, and the head of a Viet Minh sapper poked out of the hole. The Legionnaires opened fire and shot the enemy soldier in the face, killing him. Sergeant Rouzic pulled the pin on his grenade and pitched it down the enemy tunnel. It exploded, and several Viet Minh screamed in pain. The Legionnaires pushed past the dead soldier and entered the enemy trench, firing their rifles and submachine guns and throwing grenades. "Good luck, Yankee," said Rouzic as he followed his men, disappearing into the darkness. Coyle was alone. He walked down the French trench in the direction the sergeant had pointed.

Coyle moved past a line of wounded soldiers waiting for treatment as he entered the garrison's field hospital. The smell of rotting flesh, loose bowels, and vomit hit him like a hammer, nauseating him. Wounded leaned against the tunnel wall and lay on a floor made muddy from blood. A doctor, assisted by Nurse Guinevere, worked to save the life of a seriously wounded soldier who'd lost an arm and a portion of his chest from an enemy mortar shell. He died. The doctor went on to the next patient without any remorse. Not having slept in two days, the doctor was like a zombie, without feeling.

"Monsieur Coyle, are you hurt?" said Guinevere.

"No. I'm looking for Brigitte Friang, the journalist. They said she was here," said Coyle.

"Ah, yes. She is down that tunnel, then the second room on the left," said Guinevere, pointing.

"Nurse, are you okay?"

"Yes, just a little tired."

"Can I help?"

"No, no. You'd just be in the way. I've got it. You go find Brigitte. She needs a rest."

Coyle looked around at the chaos. "I guess it can't get much worse," said Coyle.

"Oh no, Monsieur Coyle," said Guinevere, "it can get much worse."

Coyle found Brigitte in a small room dug off the main tunnel. She was kneeling next to a Legionnaire who was burning up with fever from a gangrenous leg wound. "Mother," said the Legionnaire.

"Shhh. I am right here," said Brigitte, cleaning the sweat off his face and chest with a cool washcloth.

"I'm so cold. I heard men crying."

"It's just the crows outside the window. You're safe at home with me."

"And papa?"

"He's outside cutting wood for the fire. You need to sleep now. Everything will be better in the morning."

The Legionnaire closed his eyes and fell back to sleep. She turned to see Coyle in the doorway. She rose and walked into his arms. "Take me away from here," she whispered.

The night was waning. Coyle held Brigitte close as they sat against the living room wall of the mayor's mansion. "I've got to get back to the airfield. We could use a nurse for the flight back," said Coyle.

"I can't leave, Coyle," said Brigitte.

"Can't or won't?"

"Does it matter?"

"I suppose not. I could stay."

"It's not your war. Besides, the garrison needs you to keep flying supplies and reinforcements. We're short on pilots."

"I suppose I'd better get going, then."

Coyle and Brigitte rose. Coyle hugged her tight and kissed the top of the head. "Take care," said Coyle.

Brigitte pulled his face closer and kissed him passionately. He wasn't sure if she loved him, or she just needed the feel of another human. He didn't care and kissed her back. They broke their embrace, and Coyle left.

A jeep pulled onto the runway and stopped in front of Coyle's C-119. General De Castries stepped out along with Paule Bourgeade, his 28-year-old secretary. "I don't understand why I need to go," said Paule.

"You are twenty-eight and invincible. Of course, you do not understand," said De Castries, taking her by the arm and escorting her to the aircraft.

"My life is no more valuable than any of the men fighting here."

"To you, maybe not. But to me…"

De Castries turned to McGoon, who was finishing the preflight check.

"Monsieur, do you have room for one more?" said De Castries.

"Well, it don't look like she weighs more than a feather pillow, but it ain't up to me to say. You'll have to ask the pilot," said McGoon, pointing up to the cockpit where Coyle was already sitting.

"This is ridiculous. If they can take me, they can take another wounded soldier instead," said Paule.

"You're going. That's all there is to it," said De Castries.

"Monsieur," said De Castries, waving his arm to get Coyle's attention.

Coyle opened the side windshield and said, "What can I do for you, General?"

"If you would be so kind as to take my secretary back to Hanoi with you?"

"Sure. She can sit in the navigator's seat. It's empty."

"General, please…" said Paule.

"Get on the damn plane, Paule," said De Castries.

Paule knew that tone in his voice, and what would follow was not something she wished to experience. She had lost the argument. She boarded the plane.

It was sunny and hot at Cat Bi airfield. There was no sign of the afternoon rain that normally cooled down the heat of the day. A messenger ran across the tarmac to a waiting French fighter with its engine already running. He climbed up the side of the aircraft, stood on the wing, and handed the pilot a canvas bag marked "Top Secret." He climbed down and moved off as the pilot shut his cockpit windshield and taxied to the runway. The fighter took off and banked hard toward the valley of Dien Bien Phu. The pilot hated the intelligence missions to deliver reconnaissance photos, even if they were important. It was a waste of his talent and just as risky as a combat mission. He was a well-trained warrior, not a delivery boy.

The French fighter climbed over the mountaintop and swooped down into the valley. The pilot opened his cockpit windshield and prepared to drop the canvas bag as he approached the garrison. A flak shell exploded off his left wing. It surprised the pilot, and he acted instinctively, grabbing the stick with both hands and pitching the aircraft hard to one side to avoid the flak shell he knew would follow the first. The momentum of the aircraft's spin carried the canvas bag out of the open cockpit. The pilot grabbed for it, but it was too late. It dropped to the earth below.

A Viet Minh rifleman sat in his trench, finishing his daily bowl of rice and fish sauce. He heard a dull thump behind him. He turned around and saw the canvas bag sticking in the mud at the bottom of the trench. He could tell that it was French by the writing printed on the outside. He didn't know what it meant because he couldn't read, but he thought it might be important. After all, it came from the heavens. He would take it to his commanding officer once he had finished his meal.

Standing in his command tent, General Giap examined the French reconnaissance photos. They showed the entire valley in fine detail, including the French trenches and, most importantly, the French artillery pits. He turned to the Colonel that had brought the photos and said, "You say they were dropped from a passing plane?"

"Yes, general. One of our men found them," said the Colonel. "We believe it is a trick. The French are hoping to fool us with fake photos to convince our leaders into attacking the wrong areas. I was going to destroy them but thought I should show you first."

"A wise decision, Colonel. Are these the current positions of our trenches?"

"Yes, sir. As of yesterday."

"Incredible."

"Sir?"

"Colonel, when fate offers you a gift, it is best not to refuse it," said Giap. "Have copies made for our artillery commanders."

On strongpoint Huguette, a French gun crew worked in an open artillery pit half-filled with mud and water. One of their four 155mm cannons had already been damaged beyond repair by a Viet Minh artillery shell. A second gun was of little use, leaking oil from a burst gasket on its recoil piston. A third gun had been fired so many times, its barrel had been bored smooth and was no longer capable of spinning the shells it fired, reducing its accuracy to nil.

The gun crew heard the familiar whistling rush of multiple artillery shells descending on their position. A very accurate barrage rained down. The explosions inside the open pit killed the entire gun crew and destroyed all the remaining artillery guns. Fate had tipped the scales toward the Viet Minh.

With few French artillery guns remaining in the valley and the supply of unused shells dangerously low, the Air Force was called in to retaliate against the Viet Minh artillery assault. French spotters had identified several enemy gun positions on one of the surrounding mountains. The French no longer used bombs to take out the Viet Minh artillery positions. The encasements were too well built and capable of withstanding even the largest French munitions. The Air Force settled on a new tactic that seemed to have varying degrees of success. The Bearcat fighters flew low across the valley floor and used their under-the-wing rockets to pierce the enemy encasements. The rockets entered the gun encasement on the front of the mountainside and destroyed the enemy artillery, along with its gun crew. It was a difficult shot, but the Bearcat pilots became more and more effective in the tactic as the battle continued.

The Viet Minh artillery commander suspected the French would use their aircraft to retaliate against his barrage. He purposely used his artillery guns on one mountainside and no others. He had his gun crews coat the inside of each barrel with a thin layer of gunpowder so they would give off an extra bright flash when fired and could be easily spotted by the French. He wasn't surprised when he heard the approaching drone of the French fighter engines. He was prepared for them.

The squadron of Bearcats flew over the mountaintop and swooped down into the valley. The pilots banked hard and turned their fighters towards the mountain. They flew low and lined up their sights. The Viet Minh had moved six anti-aircraft guns into the valley and formed a hidden defensive line in front of the mountain. The tactic worked as planned. The French Bearcats flew right above the anti-aircraft guns, and the gun crews opened fire. Three Bearcats were blown out of the sky before the French squadron commander realized what was happening and broke off the attack.

It was day, and the sky was cloudless. The Legionnaires on strongpoint Isabel had been surrounded by the Viet Minh soon after the attack on Beatrice and were cut off from the French supply lines. Their hillside was 5 kilometers to the south of the main garrison, and they were slowly starving to death. Isabel had a small auxiliary airstrip that was now outside their perimeter and therefore useless for resupply. Ammunition was becoming a problem as several of the strongpoint's mortars had run out of shells.

Even with strict rationing, it had been over a week since the soldiers within Isabel's perimeter had eaten their last meal. Water was also in short supply, and the men suffered from the hot sun and the humidity that seemed to wring their bodies of moisture. Their lips were cracked, their faces burned, and their tongues swollen. Disease accompanied their starvation as their bodies lost the energy to fight off bacteria. Many of the soldiers developed fevers and infections from the smallest of wounds. The battalion field hospital was well beyond its limit with wounded and sick. But even in their worsened condition, the Legionnaires would not yield and continued to fight off the nightly harassing attacks by the Viet Minh.

Langlais entered De Castries' Command bunker. The garrison staff was busy, moving quickly from one task to another, but strangely quiet and whispering. Langlais found De Castries sitting with his head resting on the table with a map of the valley. He was asleep.

"General?" said Langlais.

De Castries woke and realized he had fallen asleep. The strain of command and exhaustion were evident. He straightened his uniform. "Yes, Colonel," said De Castries.

"Sir, Colonel Lalande and the Legionnaires on Isabel haven't received any supplies in over a week. They are starving and almost out of ammunition."

"What about the airdrops I requested?"

Langlais spoke slower than normal and felt the need to repeat facts that he knew De Castries had already heard but may not be remembering.

"As you know, our Air Force has lost a large number of aircraft and crews to the enemy's anti-aircraft guns. General Dechaux has placed a twelve thousand-foot floor for flight operations over the valley. At that altitude, the enemy receives more of our supplies than our troops. The enemy has captured several of our artillery guns and heavy mortars from the three strongpoints that have fallen. They are using our own artillery and mortar shells against us. Airdrops are no longer an option."

"What do you suggest, Colonel?" said De Castries.

"We need to resupply by land. A truck convoy. My men can protect—"

"Not your men, Colonel," said De Castries, cutting Langlais off. "The paratroopers must be reserved for capturing positions and offensive operations."

"Offensive operations? Sir, with all due respect, if we lose Isabel, we lose the garrison's southern anchor. The Viet Minh will have us surrounded. And once they do, they will consolidate their forces and attack us in full force. That cannot be allowed. We must save Isabel."

"And we will, but not with paratroopers. Send a company from Group Mobile 9 to protect the convoy."

"Sir, Colonel Gaucher, and his men were wiped out on Beatrice. Group Mobile 9 no longer exists," said Langlais.

"Yes, of course. I just..." said De Castries, struggling to remember. "Look, Colonel, I don't care who you send, just not your paratroopers."

"Sir, my men stand the best chance of breaking through to Isabel."

"I don't have time to argue with you, Colonel," said De Castries losing his temper. "You have your orders."

"Yes, sir," said Langlais. He snapped to attention, saluted, and left.

Exiting the bunker, Langlais stopped and pulled out his last pack of cigarettes. His face revealed the deep concerns he had about the mental fitness of this commanding officer and his ability to direct the defense of the garrison.

It was first light in a grey morning sky. Major Sudat and his engineers were just finishing their nightly repairs on the garrison's main runway. They were exhausted but felt like they were making real progress. They had widened the runway, making it safer to land, and most of the damage to the perforated steel plates had been cut away and repaired. A hanging mist still protected them from being spotted by the Viet Minh patrols. The major thought it strange that he hadn't heard any enemy patrol since 4 a.m. He heard a cacophony of cracks in the distance. It was a sound he knew only too well. "Down!" he shouted and hit the ground with his men.

The entire arsenal of Viet Minh artillery and mortars had fired in unison. The shells rained down on the airfield with incredible thunder. The runway exploded in a torrent of steel and dirt. Several engineers were shredded and hurled through the air when a 120mm mortar shell landed next to them. Most of the enemy shells exploded on impact. A few were French shells captured during the airdrops and had time-delayed fuses that allowed them to bury themselves deep in the earth and then explode a few seconds later. The results were craters as deep as a man.

The shelling stopped almost as soon as it began. It was only one volley, but that was enough. Sudat and his men stood up and looked out at the airfield. All their work had been destroyed in less than a minute. Dozens of craters. Steel plates were torn and bent skyward. The airfield was again closed. No more supplies or reinforcements could be flown into the garrison.

It was late afternoon, and the sky was cloudless. No rain in sight to relieve the men in the garrison from the heat and humidity. Three C-47s flew over the mountains and into the valley. They dove downward to 600 feet. Their cargo was a company of paratroopers led by Captain Botella. Three drop zones on strongpoint Elaine were to be used to split the enemy's fire. The paratroopers would jump low and only have 30 seconds in the air. The hope was a reduction in casualties from enemy fire. The enemy anti-aircraft guns thundered. Hundreds of black puffs of smoke surrounded the three aircraft. The aircraft took numerous hits before reaching the drop zones. In one of the planes, three paratroopers and a jumpmaster were killed when an anti-aircraft shell exploded just as the jumpmaster opened the cargo door.

The veteran paratroopers knew a low jump was risky but preferred it to hanging like a Christmas ornament as the Viet Minh ground troopers took potshots at them in the air. The recent recruits were more nervous and prone to mistakes. Their sergeants watched them carefully and reminded them several times what to do once they left the aircraft. A slap in the face was not uncommon if a newbie wasn't paying enough attention. All the paratroopers jumped clean except for a young private. When it came to his turn to jump, he panicked and yanked on his parachute's main handle instead of waiting for the static line to open the parachute. His parachute opened too soon and caught on the plane's tail stabilizer. The plane dragged him like a puppet until his parachute finally ripped, and he fell to his death.

With their passengers gone, the pilots of the three C-47s throttled up their engines to gain altitude. It was all about altitude over the valley. Once the French aircraft hit nine thousand four hundred feet, the Viet Minh anti-aircraft guns could no longer hit them with any measure of accuracy, and at fourteen thousand feet, the enemy shells self-detonated. The higher they rose, the safer they'd be. That was the thinking. They thought wrong. As they rose, anti-aircraft guns spread throughout the valley were able to spot them. They opened fire, and the puffs of black smoke increased as they flew higher. At fifteen hundred feet, one of the C-47s was hit twice in the space of a few seconds. The first shell hit the aircraft's tail and tore into the rudder. The second shell exploded in front of the starboard engine and pelted it with molten fragments of metal. The engine burst into flames. The pilot had no choice but to feather the prop on the burning engine and cut off the fuel in hopes the fire would burn out and allow him to restart it later. The aircraft slowed and lost altitude. As it descended back toward the valley, the anti-aircraft gun crews were merciless, like a pack of hyenas that had culled an injured gazelle. The aircraft's crew was killed by shrapnel, and the plane crashed into a rice paddy.

The paratroopers landed on the three drop zones and scrambled to reunite with their comrades. The enemy fire was fierce. Several paratroopers were killed and wounded as a Viet Minh mortar found a sweet spot in the middle of a rifle squad that had just regrouped. The paratroopers moved up the hillside to the position they had been assigned. They had traded the weight of their entrenching tools for more ammunition, which they were assured they would need. They used helmets and rifle butts to dig temporary foxholes. The company had lost twelve paratroopers, equaling 10% of their fighting strength in the first ten minutes of battle in the valley. It was an eye-opening experience for the new recruits, and not one they would soon forget.

Lieutenant Alain Gambiez commanded the company of Algerian Legionnaires charged with breaking the siege around strongpoint Isabel. He was twenty-three-years-old and the son of a general, Navarre's Chief of Staff. This was his first command of a company, but his inexperience didn't make him timid. He was aggressive and wasn't afraid to "kick some ass" when his men required it. He knew what was expected of him and was determined to complete his mission. He was his father's son.

It was early morning, and the Legionnaires had already been traveling for several hours. A light fog masked their movement and the movements of their enemy. French scouts patrolled ahead. The convoy of trucks was escorted on either side by two columns of riflemen and made use of a dry riverbed for additional cover. Reaching the closest point to the hill on which the strongpoint was located, the convoy emerged from the riverbed and drove back onto the road. Lieutenant Gambiez knew that if they were to be attacked, this place, with its open ground, would be perfect for an enemy ambush. The fog was beginning to lift as the temperature rose with the sun. Soon, the convoy would be exposed.

Colonel Lalande was strongpoint Isabel's commander, and he watched the approaching convoy through a pair of binoculars. His radioman, a corporal, was by his side and looked out at the convoy. "Will they have food, Colonel?" asked the corporal.

"Yes," said Lalande. "And ammunition."

The Legionnaires escorting the convoy tensed and kept a sharp eye out for the enemy as the trucks crossed the last 300 yards of open ground to the French perimeter on Isabel. The convoy was forced to stop when the company's scouts encountered multiple enemy ditches carved into the road. Seeing no way around, Lieutenant Gambiez ordered one of his platoons to fill in the trenches enough for the trucks to pass.

A recoilless rifle shell fired from a hidden position and hit the lead truck, blowing it apart and destroying the badly needed supplies and ammunition. The lieutenant ordered one of his platoons forward to attack the Viet Minh firing position and pin down the gun crew before they could destroy more trucks.

Just as the lieutenant and his men overran the first recoilless gun position, two more trucks exploded from shells fired from the opposite side of the convoy. Heavy machine guns from Viet Minh trenches at the base of the hillside opened fire on the Algerian Legionnaires and the convoy. The Viet Minh had formed a reverse wedge to trap the convoy they knew would eventually come to relieve the strongpoint. The French had driven into the center of the wedge and were now paying the price for their recklessness.

Lieutenant Gambiez and his men were cut off from the convoy by the enemy machine guns. The Legionnaires kept firing as they backed up the hillside toward the safety of the French trenches on Isabel. Lieutenant Gambiez was hit in the knee and crumpled to the ground. The bullet had struck an artery, and he was bleeding badly. His kneecap was shattered, making it impossible to walk. It hurt like hell, but he hushed his scream to a moan. Two Algerian Legionnaires picked up their commander and carried him to a French trench on the hillside. A quick-thinking Legionnaire pulled off his web belt and used his bayonet to make a tourniquet above the lieutenant's knee. The bleeding slowed, and the Legionnaires carried their lieutenant up the hillside to the strongpoint's field hospital.

Below the hill, the rest of the Algerian Legionnaires escorting the convoy were badly mauled by the Viet Minh. The convoy had no choice but to retreat or be destroyed, and the Algerians reluctantly gave up the field to the Viet Minh.

The Legionnaires on Isabel were ordered to cease fire by Colonel Lalande when he saw the convoy retreating. He and his men needed to conserve the little ammunition they had left. Lalande and his radioman looked down at the burning trucks with sadness. The suffering of the Legionnaires on Isabel would continue.

In great pain, Lieutenant Gambiez was carried into the field hospital. Dr. Rezillot, the battalion surgeon, went to work on the lieutenant's wound. It was too dangerous to give the lieutenant morphine with such a high amount of blood loss. Mercifully, the lieutenant fainted. The doctor cut open the flesh around the knee and clamped the bleeding artery. Without repairing the damaged artery, the lieutenant would most likely lose his leg, but the doctor didn't dare operate further for fear of more blood loss. The doctor checked the lieutenant's vital signs. His blood pressure was very weak. He looked at the blood type on the lieutenant's dog tags. It was the same as his own. The doctor attached a needle to a rubber tube and another needle on the opposite end. He plunged a needle into the lieutenant's arm, and then the other needle into his own. He squeezed his fist in a rhythmic pumping and gave the lieutenant a direct transfusion of blood. He gave the lieutenant as much blood as he dared without becoming faint himself. There were others that needed him, and he was already anemic from lack of nourishment.

Navarre's Chief of Staff, Lieutenant General Fernand Gambiez, was at his desk, managing the daily mountain of paperwork required to run an army. A messenger delivered a cable to the general. He opened it like he had opened the dozen other cables he had received that day, but this one stopped him cold in his tracks. The cable read that his son had been seriously wounded and was in the field hospital on strongpoint Isabel, still under siege. The general was numb and found it hard to breathe as if someone was standing on his chest. A passing captain saw the look on his face, "General, are you okay?"

General Gambiez thought for a moment before answering the captain, "Yes, Captain. I'm fine."

Unsure, the captain moved off, leaving the general to his thoughts, which would later become his nightmares.

General Gambiez stood by General Navarre as his commander finished signing a stack of orders. "Thank you, Fernand," said Navarre, with his usual cold politeness.

General Gambiez took the stack of signed orders, placed them in a folder, and walked to the door. "Fernand, any word on your son?" said Navarre.

"I am assured he is still alive," said General Gambiez.

"I have been informed that they will be mounting another attempt to break the siege. I am sure he will be one of the first to be evacuated."

"Any idea when?"

"I'm not sure. There seems to be some uncertainty on the matter, but soon, I would imagine."

"Soon may cost him his leg."

"Yes, I heard. Bad luck nicking an artery."

"Sir?"

"Yes, Fernand?"

"There is still an option to land a small plane on the auxiliary airstrip. He could be evacuated."

"I'm afraid the airstrip is outside the perimeter, and the Legionnaires are low on ammunition. It would cost too many lives and resources to secure it without a resupply first."

"I understand, sir. It was just a thought. Let's hope they break the siege."

General Gambiez exited. Navarre thought for a moment and picked up the phone to his secretary sitting right outside the door, "Sergeant, the request for resupply by De Castries… there were two field radios. Where were they to be sent within the garrison?"

"Yes, general. An additional set for garrison command, and one to replace a damaged set on Isabel."

"Get me General Dechaux, Sergeant."

"Right away, sir."

Navarre pulled a piece of stationery from his desk and started to write by hand. He stopped and thought for a moment and tore up the letter. He opened another drawer, pulled out a blank piece of paper, and started writing again. His phone rang, and he picked it up, "General, I just received a request for two field radio sets for the garrison. It is critical that they receive these radios."

"We'll make sure they make it out in the next airdrop," said Dechaux.

"No, General. We cannot risk them being damaged or lost to the enemy. What about flying them in?"

"Landing at the garrison's airfield until it is repaired would be suicide."

"I see. What about landing it on Isabel's airfield? The pilot could take the back route and fly over the southern mountains, where the enemy's anti-aircraft guns are fewer."

"That might work, but the auxiliary airfield on Isabel is still in no man's land."

"Use a helicopter. It can land inside the perimeter, can it not?"

"Yes, sir. It can."

"See to it, General."

"Yes, sir."

Navarre hung up the phone and finished his handwritten letter.

Two field radio sets, along with twenty ammunition cases and sixteen cases of food rations, were loaded into a Sikorsky H-19 Chickasaw helicopter, another American hand-me-down, its rotors already spinning. A messenger from a C-47 that had just landed exited the aircraft and ran over to the helicopter. He handed a sealed envelope addressed to Dr. Rezillot to the helicopter's co-pilot. "It's from the C and C. Make sure the doctor reads it, or it's your ass," said the messenger.

"Will do," said the co-pilot.

The messenger stepped back. The pilot twisted the collective next to his seat and throttled up the engine. Once the blades were at speed, he pulled up on the collective, changing the blades' angle of attack, and the helicopter took off.

The H-19 helicopter swooped over the mountains, hugging the treetops at full speed, just under 90 knots. For a helicopter, it was fast but still slower than an aircraft, which made it an easy target for nearby anti-aircraft guns. It didn't encounter any resistance until it was a mile from Isabel, then all hell broke loose. The Viet Minh shot everything they had at the helicopter and hit it several times. It was a big beast and could take a beating. The pilot didn't reduce his speed until he was over the French perimeter. As the helicopter flew over the hilltop, the pilot pulled back on the cyclic and flared out the aircraft, tilting it at a sharp upward angle to let the rotor slow it down. The helicopter stopped its forward momentum and hovered. He pushed down on the collective, and the helicopter descended until it landed, then he twisted the collective to throttle down the engine to a slow spin. The Legionnaires cheered and ran to unload the helicopter. The co-pilot jumped out and asked the closest Legionnaire the location of the field hospital.

Inside the field hospital bunker, Dr. Rezillot and his medical team were preparing four seriously wounded patients for transport. The co-pilot entered, asked for the doctor, and handed him the envelope. The doctor opened the envelope and read the letter. His face showed his disdain for the contents. He walked over to one of the patients and took his vital signs. "Remove this man from the evac. His vital signs are too weak to survive the changes in altitude," said the doctor.

"Yes, doctor," said a medic. "Who will go in his place?"

"The lieutenant with the knee injury… Gambiez," said the doctor. "We still may be able to save his leg if he gets treatment soon."

The medics loaded the helicopter with the stretchers, one of which held

Lieutenant Gambiez. The medics stepped back. The pilot twisted the collective to rev up the helicopter's engine. The first mortar round hit fifteen feet in front of the helicopter's cockpit and shattered the windshield. The medics on the ground dove for cover. The second round was a direct hit. The helicopter exploded and burst into flames, killing all those onboard, including the wounded lieutenant.

It was early evening, and the sun had set. It was dark in General Gambiez's office. He sat at his desk, holding the cable that informed him of his son's death. General Navarre entered and flipped the light switch. Gambiez was surprised by his commander's visit and stood to attention. Navarre signaled for him to sit. It was the first time in all his years of service that Gambiez had seen Navarre in his office. "I'm sorry for your loss, Fernand," said Navarre.

"Thank you, sir."

"I have been told by his commanders that he was a brave and faithful soldier that knew his duty."

"He was, sir. And a good son."

"If there is anything I can do?"

"The families, sir."

"The families?

"Yes, sir. The families of the helicopter pilots. I'd like to write them and thank them for their sacrifice. They tried to save my son, and I think their families would be comforted by that thought."

"Of course, General."

"Thank you, sir."

Navarre left the office, flipping the light switch. Gambiez was again alone and cried in the dark.

The Viet Minh artillery batteries were slowly chipping away at the French artillery batteries. The French still could not identify the locations of the Viet Minh batteries unless they were spotted by scout planes during repositioning. This only happened once. Three Viet Minh trucks, each pulling a 105mm howitzer, were crossing a series of rice paddies on their way to strongpoint Beatrice, which was now in the possession of the Viet Minh. A scout plane was doing a routine patrol over the mountains when the sun burned through the morning mist, and the pilot spotted the small caravan. The excited pilot immediately radioed in the coordinates.

The artillery gun team on strongpoint Dominique received their fire mission over the radio from the nearby Fire Direction Center. The orders specified the type of ammunition, fuse setting and propelling charge, bearing, elevation, and the method of adjustment to be relayed to the team by the Forward Observer. Each gun team member knew exactly what to do and when to do it. They were a well-oiled machine that could fire up to ten rounds per minute. The howitzer's split-frame was picked up by the team members and traversed into an approximate position. A gunner leveled the sight on the side of the gun and used it to call out adjustments to the two crew members that dialed in the final elevation and bearing by turning hand cranks. The breach on their cannon was opened and given a quick swab with a ram to clean out any excess gunpowder or dirt that might affect a clean shot or jam the shell once fired. A 105mm shell was inserted into the steel tube, and the breach was closed. An assistant gunner held the lanyard taut and yanked it hard when given the order to fire. The howitzer gave out a loud crack and echo when the shell left the barrel.

One of the trucks was stuck in the middle of a rice paddy with mud covering its rear axle. When the French shells began to drop, the other two truck drivers abandoned the stuck vehicle and headed for the trees. The truck stuck in the rice paddy was the first to get hit. The French artillery shell landed in the truck's bed, and the explosion ignited several cases of ammunition. The truck flipped up in the air, carrying the howitzer with it, and both landed upside down in the mud.

The French gun crews on Dominique saw the explosion and cheered. They fired three more rounds at the Viet Minh howitzer to ensure its complete destruction, then changed their focus to the other two trucks rushing to the safety of the forest.

As the trucks neared the tree line, the French created a wall of explosions directly in the trucks' path, forcing them to change direction and travel back across the rice paddies. From there, it was just a matter of continually cutting off the Viet Minh drivers' escape routes until they were riding around in circles. The French gun crews took potshots until the Viet Minh drivers abandoned their trucks and fled across the rice paddies on foot. A few minutes later, the trucks and their howitzers slowly sank in the mud and were destroyed by the French guns.

The Viet Minh artillery commander was incensed at the loss of three of his precious 105s, and his vengeance was swift. He immediately ordered a barrage on the French artillery pits on Dominique.

Shells dropped on the French artillery at a rate of one per second. Dominique's open pit gun crews were ripped to shreds. Eighty-seven highly-trained gunners and loaders died. The French artillery on the other strongpoints acted as counter-batteries and returned fire, hoping to silence the Viet Minh guns. They were unsuccessful. The bombardment of Dominique's artillery pits went on for 30 minutes. It was a bitter rampage. Five of the remaining French 105s were destroyed, their barrels pierced by molten shards of metal from the enemy shell-bursts. The main ammunition depot on Dominique suffered a direct hit, blowing a hole the size of a building into the side of the strongpoint's hillside. A great yellow-orange ball rose into the sky for the entire garrison to see. The ammunition lost was sorely needed and would be impossible to replace.

The Viet Minh had expended more than half of their available artillery shells and would need to wait until more ammunition could be captured from the French airdrops or brought up through the mountains before launching another heavy barrage. The Viet Minh artillery commander knew he would be scolded by his superiors for such an extravagance, but he felt it was worth it.

When De Castries was informed of the loss, he could not believe it and went into a deep depression. He kept to himself in his bunker and did not eat, drink, or sleep for two days. When asked for orders by his staff or his field commanders, he simply replied, "Do what you think best." The garrison was leaderless. Although the constant shelling and gunfire didn't help, it wasn't the noise of violence that unhinged De Castries. It was the expectations of the men under his command and his superiors. He couldn't stand the thought of letting them down.

Warned of the situation by one of De Castries' staff officers, Dr. Grauwin entered the command bunker unannounced and gave De Castries a quick medical exam, which was his prerogative as the chief medical officer in the garrison. It was clear De Castries was dehydrated and anemic. He immediately gave the general an IV of saline to rehydrate his body. The fluid seemed to help lift the haze from De Castries' mind, and he became lucid and more aware of the situation he was facing. Even a commander could be relieved by a doctor that felt the officer was seriously ill or emotionally unstable. De Castries realized that as a general officer, such an event would be the end of his military career. He assured the doctor he would immediately eat and drink. He ordered the IV removed and ordered the doctor back to the hospital so he could attend to the more seriously wounded. The doctor obeyed and exited the bunker.

Langlais was aware that De Castries was not sleeping and knew that the doctor had paid him a visit. Langlais went to the hospital to check on his wounded paratroopers. While in the bunker, he made his presence known to Grauwin. His hunch paid off. Grauwin asked to speak with him in private. Langlais was not surprised when informed of De Castries' condition and asked if the doctor would relieve De Castries on medical grounds. The doctor refused, saying that if De Castries was drinking and eating, there was nothing he could do. It was not a medical emergency, and his hands were full with the wounded. Langlais understood, thanked the doctor, and left the bunker.

The command bunker was busy as the general's staff carried on operations as best they could without clear direction. The air was stale and filled with dust falling from the timber-reinforced ceiling every time an enemy artillery shell landed nearby. The electric bulbs overhead faded in and out with the cycles of a generator strained to its capacity.

De Castries sat on the edge of his cot, contemplating the revolver in his hand. Colonel Langlais, Bruno, and several other paratroopers entered the bunker. On seeing the colonel, De Castries let the hand holding the revolver fall to his side and rose to his feet. Bruno nodded to the radio operator and the other staff officers. They each grabbed a pack of cigarettes and left the bunker, leaving the paratroopers alone with their commander. "What is this, Colonel?" said De Castries.

"General De Castries, the Legionnaires on Strongpoint Isabel have been abandoned. Without food, water, and ammunition, Colonel Lalande's battalion will perish, and with it, the garrison's only serviceable artillery. Sir, you are failing to grasp the seriousness of the situation. You are no longer capable of commanding," said Langlais.

"What?" said De Castries.

"My officers and I feel it would be best if you allow us to take over all operations of the garrison."

"Colonel, this is treason. I could have you shot."

"Yes, sir. And I you."

De Castries raised the revolver in his hand and aimed it at Langlais. Langlais didn't flinch, but his officers raised their weapons and aimed them at De Castries. "God damn your soul, Pierre!" said De Castries.

"Better that one man dies than ten thousand," said Langlais.

It was a standoff that De Castries would clearly lose. While he wasn't afraid to die, the thought of ending his military career in a mutiny gave him pause. He wanted a way out, but he was still suffering from lack of sleep, and his mind was clouded.

"Christian, nobody blames you," said Langlais. "And nobody needs to know."

"What do you propose, Colonel?" said De Castries.

"As far as the world knows, you will remain in command and continue to communicate with General Cogny and the general staff in Hanoi, but decisions concerning military operations and the defense of the garrison will be made by myself and my officers," said Langlais. "Christian, let us save the garrison."

De Castries considered the proposal and what was best for the men under his command. He recognized that he was beyond exhaustion and was not thinking clearly. He lowered his gun and nodded his acceptance. He sat back down on his cot. The mantle of command had been lifted, and he was relieved. His eyes felt heavy. He just wanted to sleep. Bruno walked to the bunker doorway and called the general's staff back inside, most of which would not make eye contact with De Castries, and secretly relieved that Langlais was now in charge. Langlais walked over to the radio operator. "Get me Captain Hervouet."

There was a light fog over the valley, and the ground was soggy. The smell of wet earth filled the countryside. It was just before sunrise when Bruno and his paratroopers took up positions against the bank of the dry riverbed below strongpoint Isabel. On the road and behind the paratroopers, three Chaffee tanks with their long cannons appeared through the fog and moved into their firing positions. The French waited patiently as the sun rose until they could spot the Viet Minh hidden in the nearby trenches and in the surrounding fields of rice.

The Viet Minh fired with their recoilless rifles first in a bid to take out the tanks. The first volley missed and gave away the Viet Minh positions.

The French paratroopers and the tanks returned fire and knocked out three of the four recoilless rifle positions, killing the gunners and loaders.

The Viet Minh heavy machine guns were the next to open fire and reveal their positions.

The paratroopers let the tanks take the fight to the enemy and kept low, out of the machine guns' deadly line of fire. The tanks shelled the machine gun positions, destroying the guns and killing the gunners.

Ty and his mortar squad had been ordered to reinforce the Viet Minh assault against the French strongpoint. He and his men set their mortar behind the dike around a nearby rice field. They were out of the enemy's direct line of fire but still close enough to watch where their rounds dropped and effectively adjust their fire.

It was Bruno that recognized the reflection of Ty's binoculars, spotting the French positions for his mortarmen. Bruno knew instinctively what was happening and ordered the lieutenant of one of his platoons to send a squad and take out the mortar position.

The remaining recoilless rifle fired on Hervouet's Chaffee and hit the river embankment beside it. The three tanks fired on the enemy position and destroyed the Viet Minh gun and its crew. Standing in the turret's hatchway, Hervouet felt his tank slip sideways and saw the river embankment beside him crumble. He ducked back inside, grabbing for anything he could find to support himself. The river embankment collapsed, and Hervouet's tank with it. The tank did a complete rollover into the dry riverbed and landed on its side. Inside, Hervouet lost his grip during the rollover and had both his arms severely broken, with a bone sticking out of one of his wrists.

A squad of riflemen moved along the edge of the rice field, careful to keep out of sight of the enemy spotter. They moved up as far as possible without being detected. They jumped over the dike and opened fire on Ty's mortar squad.

Only Ty survived the first volley unscathed. His men manning the mortar were dead or badly wounded. He could see clearly the French would overrun his position in a matter of seconds. There was no time to save the mortar, but he refused to abandon it to the enemy. He picked up a nearby rock and ran to the mortar as the rifle squad charged his position. He grabbed a shell from the ammunition case and slid the shell into the tube, followed by the rock on top of it. He ran like hell. The mortar round hit the pin at the bottom and ignited, launching the shell upward in the tube. The shell's tip hit the rock and exploded, destroying the mortar and showering the approaching rifle squad with hot shrapnel. Ty was hit in the flesh of his left calf by a small piece of the mortar tube, but otherwise unhurt. He ran with a limp back to the safety of the forest. The French riflemen were too busy tending to their wounded to chase after him.

With the threat of the machine guns and mortars gone, the paratroopers climbed the river embankment and charged the Viet Minh trenches at the base of the hillside. The Viet Minh opened fire with their rifles and submachine guns, killing a dozen paratroopers as they approached.

From above on the hillside, the Legionnaires of Isabel joined the fight, charging downward behind the Viet Minh and leaping into their trenches. Neither side had time to reload their weapons while facing their enemy just a few feet away. The knives came out. Both sides fought hand-to-hand for over an hour.

The Viet Minh tried to reinforce their positions but were cut off by the surviving tanks' guns and a squadron of Bearcats armed with rockets that had flown in from the airfield at Luang Prabang, Laos. Both sides took a brutal beating, but it was the Viet Minh that finally retreated. The French won the day, and the siege of Isabel was lifted.

The Legionnaires on Isabel cheered the convoy and paratroopers as they unloaded the supplies they so desperately needed. It was a good day for the French. They had so few.

BATTLE OF THE FIVE HILLS

Ty sat in the Viet Minh aid station. A medic dug the piece of shrapnel from his calf. It was a painful procedure. The Viet Minh medics only used morphine on the worst of injuries and for officers of high rank. Ty's commanding officer entered the aid station. Ty tried to stand at attention. The commanding officer ordered him to sit back down and let the medic finish his work. "You lost your squad and your weapon," said the officer.

"Yes, sir," said Ty, embarrassed.

"You spiked your mortar tube?"

"Yes, sir, with a shell and rock as I was instructed.

"Good work, Corporal. Can you still walk?"

"Yes, sir. It is not a serious wound."

"We do not have another mortar or crew available. You are being reassigned to an engineering company. You will report as soon as you are finished here," said the officer, handing Ty a written order.

"Thank you, sir," said Ty, pleased. He had finally made it. He was going to be a sapper.

In the night sky above the valley, anti-aircraft shells exploded around a squadron of C-47s and C-119s, dropping supplies and ammunition from their cargo holds. A shell burst directly below the port engine of a C-47 near the front of the squadron. Everything seemed normal until the engine exploded, tearing off the wing and sending the aircraft into a death spiral.

In the cockpit of their C-119, McGoon and Coyle watched through their windshield. "Shit. There goes Henri and his crew," said McGoon. "You see any chutes?"

"No," said Coyle.

"Damn. I liked Henri. Did you know he was a Dodger's fan?"

"No."

McGoon opened the small side window, pulled out his field revolver, and fired at the forest below. "Chew on that, ya little yellow bastards!" he said.

"You ain't gonna hit anything," said Coyle.

"I could get lucky… for Henri," said McGoon.

The cargo crews finished the drop and closed their cargo doors. The surviving aircraft of the squadron headed for home.

In the valley below, Bruno and Langlais watched the parachutes carrying the crates of supplies and ammunition drop downward and land outside the perimeter. "Merde," said Bruno.

"At this rate, the Viet Minh are getting more of our supply drops than we are," said Bruno.

"And eating better," said Langlais.

"I hope they choke on the pâté," said Bruno.

The artillery barrage intensified on Huguette. Bruno and Langlais hit the ground. A large explosion on the side of Huguette's hillside shook the ground, and a yellow and orange ball of flame rose into the air. Bruno and Langlais belly-crawled over to see what was hit. "The supply depot," said Langlais.

The supply depot billowed out smoke and fire as the garrison's precious supplies were engulfed in flames and lit up the night sky. The air was filled with the smell of burning tobacco. "Damn, they hit the tobacco stuffs," said Bruno.

Bruno and Langlais, both smokers, took in a deep breath and inhaled the tobacco smoke. "Giap is gnawing away at us piece by piece. Soon there will be no garrison to overrun. This has to stop," said Langlais.

American and French pilots sat in the briefing room, arguing with their commanders. "Gentlemen, the forces on the ground are doing everything in their power to eliminate the anti-aircraft positions around the airfield, but you must realize the difficulty of the situation," said the Air Force Colonel. "We have requested flak jackets from the Americans. They should be arriving shortly."

"Flak jackets will not keep our aircraft from being blown out of the sky," said an American pilot.

"Five aircraft in one week and for what? Half of the supplies we drop fall into enemy territory. The enemy is using the ammunition we drop to kill

Frenchmen. It is ridiculous to risk our aircraft and our lives for so little," said a French pilot.

"You are correct. That is why Air Command is asking that we drop back down to twelve hundred feet for the next series of drops," said the Colonel.

The crowd erupted into chaos at the news.

"That is suicide," said an American pilot.

"Now, you've gone completely insane," said the French pilot.

"It ain't in our contract to get our asses shot off. No combat missions. That's what it says," said McGoon. "I say we go on strike unless we are properly compensated for the additional risk."

"You would hold the men in the garrison hostage?" said the Colonel.

"We ain't holding nobody hostage," said McGoon. "It's just a matter of risk versus reward. That's all."

"Twelve thousand or twelve hundred feet, it ain't gonna make much difference. We need to put aircraft on the ground, so we can drop off essential supplies and pick up the seriously wounded," said Coyle.

"Wait a minute, Coyle," said McGoon. "Now you're talking crazy."

"Just pipe down and listen," said Coyle. "I've been doing some thinking, and I've got a plan that just might work."

"It's that 'might' part that's got me concerned, Coyle," said McGoon.

Coyle moved to the chalkboard and drew a diagram. "We fly a decoy plane, something with a big engine that'll make a lot of noise and be able to skedaddle when the Viet Minh open fire with their anti-aircraft guns. We follow it with a second plane, throttle back the engines, and glide in so the Viet Minh gunners can't hear it over the first plane's engine. We land without lights on the airfield.

"I'm sorry. Did you say, 'land without lights?'" said McGoon.

"Okay. Maybe we keep it dark, then have the ground crew light it up just before landing," said Coyle.

"That's better," said McGoon, feeling like he had contributed to Coyle's plan.

"It can't be any worse than landing on a carrier in the middle of the night. You've done that, ain't ya?" said Coyle.

"I suppose," said McGoon.

"We all know they got seriously wounded stacked up in the hospital, and they are almost out of medical supplies. We get a plane on the ground, we're gonna save some lives," said Coyle.

"Only catch is, we need a couple of pilots that are crazy enough to fly both planes," said McGoon.

"And they'd have to be good," said Coyle, looking McGoon straight in the eye. "Real good."

The sun set at Haiphong's Cat Bi airfield. It was hot and humid. The sky was clear. The waning moon had already risen, giving little light to the surrounding countryside.

Coyle performed his pre-flight check on a Lockheed P-38 Lightning. It was a relic from World War II and was decommissioned near the end of the war. It had been abandoned on an airfield in Laos when it ran out of fuel after an aerial battle with the Japanese. The French Air Force was not anxious to sacrifice any more of their aircraft on Coyle's crazy plan. The P-38 would not be missed if it went down over Dien Bien Phu.

He had taken one of the French mechanics with him when he went to retrieve it. The engine and the hydraulics were still in fairly good shape, but the tires had rotted and needed to be replaced.

Coyle knew the aircraft well. He had trained on it in San Francisco and thought it was perfect for this mission. With two 1,600 horsepower Allison V-12 piston engines, the P-38 was a fast beast and loud. Its rocket hard points were empty to make it lighter and give it extra speed. After refueling, he had flown it back to Cat Bi Airfield. "You sure you remember how to fly that thing?" said McGoon approaching.

"Like ridin' a bike," said Coyle.

"I suppose."

"I appreciate this, buddy," said Coyle.

"I ain't doing it for you, Coyle. We pull this off, people are going to write about it in the newspapers, maybe even the history books. We're gonna be famous. I figure that could be worth something."

"If we pull it off," said Coyle, unsure.

"Ah Coyle, there ya go getting' negative again," said McGoon. "I swear, when we get back to the states, you should audition for the role of Grumpy at that new Disneyland they're building out in Californ-I-A. You'd be a shoe-in."

Coyle shook McGoon's hands and climbed into their aircraft, Coyle in the P-38 and McGoon in Coyle's C-119. They each climbed into the cockpits. Buford sat in the co-pilot's chair beside McGoon. Each aircraft's engines spun to life with a deafening roar, and they rolled to the runway.

It was a moonless night. The airfield at Dien Bien Phu was quiet. Distant shelling illuminated the sky and mixed with the thunder from approaching rain clouds. The two aircraft hugged the top of the last mountain before the valley. Coyle, piloting the P-38, took the lead, throttling up his engine and climbing higher. The P-38 was a twin tail and had a similar contour to the C-119. Coyle hoped to confuse the Viet Minh anti-aircraft gunners with the plane's silhouette in the night's sky. If the gunners, who had never seen a P-38 before, thought it was the larger C-119, they might aim higher and overshoot, thinking it was farther away.

McGoon, in the C-119, throttled back his engines to just above stall-speed, but enough to keep him out of the forest canopy as he descended into the valley.

In the forest below, the Viet Minh gunners heard the P-38's engines, swung their anti-aircraft guns around, and waited for a target.

The P-38 was painted dark blue and was hard to see against the night sky. It was moving fast. The anti-aircraft guns opened fire. Coyle reached the edge of the forest in front of the airfield and swung around back over the forest. He could see the C-119 approaching in the distance. Coyle opened fire on the anti-aircraft guns hidden in the forest with his aircraft's nose-mounted .50 caliber machine guns. The noise was thunderous, and further masked the C-119's engines.

Below, the anti-aircraft gunners were taken by surprise, confused by the fast-moving cargo plane shooting at them.

The C-119 approached the airfield, and McGoon lined up the aircraft to where he thought the runway might be.

A Viet Minh mortar crew shot several parachute flares into the sky and illuminated the airfield and the C-119 on final approach. The anti-aircraft guns swung around and opened fire on the slower target.

"Coyle, gig's up. Get the hell out of here," said McGoon over the radio.

Coyle continued to fire at the anti-aircraft guns to divert them back to his aircraft and away from the C-119.

"Light 'em up, boys," said McGoon over the radio.

The airfield ground crew ran along two outer edges of the runway and dropped flares.

Only a hundred feet from the front of the runway, McGoon could see his alignment was off, and he was going to miss. He pitched the C-119 hard, and the wings almost scraped the ground. Back on course, he steered her back level and landed. The ground crew stomped out the flares as the C-119 passed, obscuring the runway once again.

With the C-119 safe, Coyle dove the P-38 down to the treetops, making it harder for the anti-aircraft crews to spot him. "That was some kinda flying, McGoon," said Coyle over the radio.
    "Not too bad yourself, Coyle," said McGoon over his radio.
    "Check on Brigitte for me, will ya, McGoon?"
    "You got it, buddy."

McGoon parked the C-119 in a specially prepared bunker made with extra high sandbags and large enough to fit the massive aircraft. They pulled a camouflage net over the C-119. The net was painted the same color as the soil around the runway to further mask the aircraft from the Viet Minh artillery spotters. Ground crews unloaded the badly needed medical supplies and ammunition.

Envious that McGoon would see Brigitte before he did, Coyle swung his P-38 around and headed back to Hanoi.

The morning fog covered the runway. Medics and ambulance drivers loaded up the wounded into the hold of the C-119.
    Buford and McGoon completed the final check of the aircraft. "All right, Buford, let's mount up and head for home," said McGoon. "I'm in desperate need of a visit to Mama Sing's."
    "What's Mama Sing's?" said Brigitte as she walked up behind McGoon.
    "Oh, it's a bar in Hanoi," said McGoon, embarrassed.
    "Really? And here I thought it was that whore house near the river."
    "Oh, well… I wouldn't know about that. Must be two of 'em."

"Oh, of course," said Brigitte.

"I'm glad I got to see ya before we leave. How are you doing?"

"I'm fine, but who is asking?"

"Well, me… and Coyle."

"He was flying the other plane?"

"Yeah. Crazy bastard."

"What you did was very brave."

"Ah, well, someone had to give it a shot. Probably won't work again, now that the Viets know what we're doing."

"Still, thank you. You saved many lives," said Brigitte, standing on her tippy-toes and giving McGoon a kiss on each cheek.

"You take care of yourself, young lady," said McGoon.

"I will. And give Coyle my love."

"Your love?"

"Yes. Life is too short not to love, yes?"

"Yes. He ain't gonna be much use for the next couple of days once he hears it, but all right. I'll tell 'im."

"Take care, McGoon."

"Always do."

McGoon climbed into the C-119, waved goodbye one last time to Brigitte, and closed the cockpit door. The back doors on the cargo hold shut, and the C-119's engines cranked to life. Still covered in fog, the C-119 lifted off the runway, climbed to twelve thousand feet, and returned to Hanoi without incident.

General Navarre was sitting on the patio of his command headquarters finishing his morning coffee and going over reports. Captain Pouget walked out onto the patio, picked up the phone extension, and brought it over to the table. "Excuse me, sir. The phone is for you. It's General Cogny calling."

"Very well," said Navarre.

Captain Pouget went back inside. Navarre took a final sip of coffee before picking up the receiver. "Good morning, Rene. How are things?"

"Good morning, sir. I am afraid we have lost another strongpoint at the garrison. Anne-Marie has fallen. The Thai colonials abandoned their positions late last night, leaving the hilltop defenseless except for a few French officers. The officers had no choice but to retire the position or be taken prisoner."

"You assured me that the Thai were reliable," said Navarre, incensed.

"They were, sir… until we abandoned Lao Chau."

"It was Viet Minh that killed their families, not the French."

"Yes, but it was the French that had promised to protect their families. Viet Minh spies from the villages in the valley have been handing out leaflets to the Thai patrols. The leaflets question the French loyalty to the Thai and say we would not defend their villages when attacked again. The Viet Minh promised leniency to their families if the Thai put down their arms. It was a compelling argument."

"And the French officers, did they try to stop them?"

"Of course, sir. But it was a mutiny of the entire battalion. Summary execution would only have angered the Thai and encouraged them to join the Viet Minh rather than just going home to protect their families."

"Pragmatic in the face of defeat, I suppose," said Navarre.

"There's more bad news to report, sir."

Navarre sighed and said, "Continue."

"In addition to Anne-Marie and Gabrielle, the Viet Minh have retaken possession of Beatrice. Once the Viet Minh move up their artillery and heavy mortars, they will be able to hit our farthest positions on the garrison."

"And the counterattacks?"

"There won't be any, sir."

"Why, in God's name?"

"Without a steady supply of reinforcements and supplies, General De Castries feels it would be too risky."

"Leaving the strong points in the enemy's hands is risky."

"Of course, sir," said Cogny.

"And what is the current disposition of the enemy forces?"

"The Viet Minh are busy digging assault trenches in front of strongpoints Dominique and Elaine, sir. I believe it is only a matter of a few days before their assault begins," said Cogny. "General, perhaps it is time to reconsider Operation Condor?"

"We've been through this, Rene. Colonel Godard's battalion is needed to pin down the enemy's flank and prevent any backdoor invasion of Laos."

"I understand, sir. It's just with the three strongpoints now gone, the Viet Minh are sure to move up their anti-aircraft guns so they can fire directly on the airfield at close range. If the airfield is cut off…"

"Then we will resupply the garrison by airdrop."

"Yes, General, but it's the reinforcements that concern me. Almost all of our paratroopers are already in the valley. We only have one brigade of paratroopers in reserve. Giap's artillery is putting tremendous pressure on the garrison, and we've already lost over four thousand men. The garrison cannot continue to fight without reinforcements, and for that, we need the airfield."

"I agree that the airfield is key, Rene. But we must plan for all possible scenarios. Dien Bien Phu is not our only battlefield."

"Exactly, sir. So, I was thinking, we could send Colonel Godard's battalion by way of Nam Ou and then through the limestone pass. That would continue to cut off any possible enemy route to Laos while his forces were on the move. Even if Godard's battalion never made it all the way into the valley, Giap would be forced to respond, and that could relieve the pressure enough to allow us to reinforce the garrison at Dien Bien Phu and mount an effective counterattack. It would be a feint before a lunge if you will."

"Can the engineers repair the airfield?"

"It's pretty badly torn up, but the chief of engineers assures me it can be repaired if there is a letup from the enemy artillery, and his men can work freely."

"Very well, Rene. You can have your battalion, but if they are in danger of being overrun, Godard and his men must return to their garrison near the Laos border. We cannot afford to lose them."

"I agree. General, one last thing before you go. Perhaps we should draw up a break-out plan should the garrison be in danger of falling to the enemy? A worst-case scenario, for sure."

"But prudent," said Navarre. "Draw up your plan. But remember, Rene… as long as our forces continue to fight in Dien Bien Phu, they are tying down five divisions of Ho Chi Minh's best soldiers. Divisions that cannot be used to attack our forces in the Red River Delta, Laos, and other key points vital to our survival. Yes, we have sustained heavy losses, but so has the enemy, and they will continue to lose men until the end."

"And so will we, sir," said Cogny.

"Victory rarely comes without sacrifice," said Navarre.

"So, the men at Dien Bien Phu are to be sacrificed for the greater good?"

"I did not say that," said Navarre with a sharp tone. "Honestly, sometimes I question where your loyalties lie."

"With France, sir. Always with France," said Cogny.

This was not what Navarre was hoping to hear from his key commanding general. Navarre knew that when it was over, win, lose or draw, the story of Operation Castor would be told. He wanted to ensure it was his version of events that prevailed.

It was raining over the valley, and visibility was at a minimum. Coyle and McGoon flew in Coyle's new C-119 just below the clouds and studied the terrain below, comparing it to their maps and recon photos.

"Have you given any more thought to what you're gonna call her?" said McGoon.

"Call her?" said Coyle.

"Your plane, Coyle."

"Haven't really given it much thought."

"It's bad luck not to name her."

"Well, I guess I better get on it, then. I suppose I could name her after my mom."

"Oh, that's inspiring."

"I like my mom."

"I think you're missing the point."

"How about 'Brigitte?'"

"Nope."

"Why not?"

"It's about inspiration, Coyle. Her boobs aren't big enough."

"They're bigger than a champagne glass."

"Really?"

"I'm not having this conversation with you," said Coyle.

"There it is… I think," said McGoon, pointing to a hillside.

"You're the bird dog," said Coyle.

McGoon picked up the radio and told Kim-ly to prepare for the drop.

The cargo doors on the back of the aircraft opened, and Kim-ly released the parachute pallets from their restraining cables. Kim-ly and his assistant loadmaster pushed the pallets along the deck rollers to the end of the hold. The buzzer sounded, and the cargo light turned green. Kim-ly and his assistant loadmaster pushed the pallets out as fast as possible. The pallets dropped one-by-one over the edge, and their static lines snapped tight, releasing their parachutes. Just as the crew pushed the last pallet toward the back, a shell from an anti-aircraft gun in the valley below exploded near the open doorway. The red-hot shrapnel from the shell-burst hit Kim-ly in the chest, killing him instantly.

In the cockpit, Coyle and McGoon saw the flak exploding around the aircraft. The right pane of the front windshield cracked from the impact of a small piece of shrapnel, surprising McGoon. He checked his face and chest for possible injuries. There were none.

"Shit. They've got our altitude," said Coyle.

Knowing instinctively Coyle's next move, McGoon grabbed the radio and warned the cargo crew, "Hang on, boys. It's gonna be a rough one."

Coyle banked the aircraft to one side to break away from their flight path and shake loose the anti-aircraft gunner's line of fire. With the rear cargo doors open, the aircraft was sluggish.

The last pallet rolled out of the doorway at an angle, along with Kim-ly's lifeless body. His safety line dangled the body out the back of the plane like a tailless kite dancing in the wind.

"Get those doors closed. We need altitude," said McGoon over the radio.

The assistant loadmaster removed a folding knife from his flight suit and cut the safety line, freeing Kim-ly's body to fall to the earth. He was saddened by the loss of his boss and closed the doors.

The C-119 rose into the safety of the clouds and disappeared.

Most of the pallets of supplies and ammunition floated down and landed safely on the strongpoint's landing zone. It was a good drop. The last pallet was off course and landed outside the strongpoint's perimeter in no-man's land. The two crates on the pallet were marked, "VINOGEL – WINE CONCENTRATE."

As was the tradition in the French Foreign Legion, April 30th was Camarón Day- the annual celebration commemorating the siege of 65 Legionnaires in a hacienda in Camarón de Tejeda, Veracruz, Mexico. The conduct of the Legionnaires, who refused to surrender to a Mexican force of over 3,000, led to the Legion's mystique and became synonymous with bravery and a fight-to-the-death attitude.

It was well after sunset, and the light was fading fast. Bruno and a squad of paratroopers accompanied Brigitte to the command center on strongpoint Elaine, where she had been invited to join the festivities. Hiking up the hillside, Bruno and Brigitte passed the trench where Sergeant Rouzic and the other survivors of Beatrice had been stationed. The Legionnaires looked anything but festive.

"Sergeant Rouzic, what's wrong?" said Brigitte.

"Those damned American pilots dropped our supply of wine outside the perimeter, and we have nothing to celebrate with," said Sergeant Rouzic.

"So, let's go get it," said Bruno.

"That's crazy, Bruno. It's just wine," said Brigitte.

"No. Camarón Day is a matter of honor for the Legion," said Bruno.

"You're a paratrooper," said Brigitte.

"Yes, but that's French wine, and the enemy will recover it if we do not. This I cannot tolerate," said Bruno. "Sergeant, will you accompany me for a little stroll into no man's land?"

"It would be my honor," said Sergeant Rouzic, emptying several rucksacks.

The two men crouched down low as they moved toward the perimeter. "Idiots," said Brigitte, and followed them.

Brigitte and the squad of paratroopers climbed down into the closest trench to the perimeter and watched as Bruno and Sergeant Rouzic belly-crawled beneath the barbed wire. They crept over to the lost pallet, thirty feet into the no man's land between the French and the Viet Minh trenches, and broke open the wooden side of one of the crates. They pulled out the cans of wine concentrate and stuffed as much as they could carry into the rucksacks.

A mortar-launched flare ignited overhead, illuminating the battlefield. A Viet Minh machine gun opened fire at Bruno and Sergeant Rouzic as they scrambled back to the French perimeter. The Legionnaires and paratroopers in the trenches returned fire. Bruno was the first to make it through the wire. Sergeant Rouzic's rucksack was snagged in the wire, but he refused to abandon it. Bruno crawled back to help him and was hit in the hand by a Viet Minh bullet, which blew off his index finger. Bruno searched the mud for his severed finger. Sergeant Rouzic freed the rucksack and crawled over to Bruno.

"What are you waiting for?" said Sergeant Rouzic.

"I'm not leaving without my finger," said Bruno.

Sergeant Rouzic searched the mud and held up the finger, "I've got it."

The two men crawled back and tumbled into the safety of the trench. Brigitte pulled a can of Vinogel from one of the rucksacks and opened it. She poured the concentrate over the bloody stump on Bruno's hand, cleaning off the mud. "Merde. It stings worse than it tastes," said Bruno.

Next to the legion's flag and battalion's battle ribbons, Bruno's finger wrapped in a shoelace hung on the flagpole inside the command bunker. Several empty cans of Vinogel lay next to a half-empty bucket of wine. Bruno and Brigitte stood at attention, wavering from intoxication. The battalion commander pinned home-made strips on their shoulders. "For meritorious service to your country above and beyond the call of duty, you, Mademoiselle Brigitte Friang," said the commander, "and you, Major Marcel Bigeard, are hereby awarded the honorary rank of Private in the French Foreign Legion."

Bruno saluted with his bandaged hand. Brigitte followed his example. The Legionnaires toasted their new comrades and shouted, "Vive la France!" Bruno and Brigitte took another drink of Vinogel. Bruno fell backward, unconscious.

"Wimp," said Brigitte and joined him on the ground, using his chest as a pillow.

Monsoon rains poured down on Colonel Godard's mile-long relief column hiking up a steep mountainside. The Legionnaires struggled to keep their footing in the slippery mud and grass. Godard ordered his executive officer to rest the men and the pack mules carrying the ammunition and supplies. Seeing the signal to stop, many of the men collapsed in place and fell quickly to sleep. The quartermaster approached Colonel Godard as he reviewed their position on a map.

"Colonel, we've lost another two mules. We either need to slow down or lighten their loads," said the quartermaster.

"Slowing down is not an option. We're already four days behind schedule," said Colonel Godard.

"I understand, sir, but Hanoi cannot expect us to cross these mountains during the monsoon season."

"You underestimate a general's capacity to watch his men suffer," said Godard. "We keep the same tempo. Give the mules an extra ration of grain, and shift some of their load to the men if you must. But if I were you, I would do it with my pistol in hand."

"Yes, sir."

The quartermaster saluted and walked away in the pouring rain.

"God help us if the Viet Minh attack the column," said the battalion executive officer. "I doubt the men could give them much of a fight."

"Oh, I don't know about that, XO. Bullets flying over your head are an excellent motivator," said Colonel Godard.

"So is sleep," said the XO.

"Humph. Sleep is overrated. The men will do fine when the time comes," said Colonel Godard.

It was night. The air was heavy with smoke and the smell of spent artillery shells. Parachute flares launched from French mortars and dropped from the aircraft circling high above the garrison lit up the darkness with their familiar green glow.

Three of the howitzers in Brunbrouck's battery had already been destroyed by Viet Minh counter batteries and the gun crews killed. The remaining seven howitzers were hot from firing most of the night. He needed to let them cool or risk weakening the barrels until a shell cooked off inside and killed another one of his gun crews. He had heard about crews urinating on the barrels to cool them down, but he wasn't really sure that would work. Besides, his men hadn't stopped in several hours, and judging by the sweat stains on their uniforms, probably didn't have much to offer.

Brunbrouck heard the gunfire and grenades exploding above on Dominique's hilltop. There was one hell of a fight going on up there, he thought. His West Africans grew anxious on seeing the Algerian troops running down Dominique's hillside. It was full-on rout, the likes of which Brunbrouck had never seen before. The Algerians ran through Brunbrouck's position up the opposite hill until they reached the French trenches on the hilltop of strongpoint Elaine. Brunbrouck was concerned that his own men might join them. Fear was like a grass fire in high wind. It spread quickly, and there was little anyone could do to stop it.

Dominique was falling and with it his right flank. Brunbrouck radioed Colonel Langlais' command bunker and informed the radio operator that Dominique had fallen. A captain came on the line and argued that it was impossible that the strongpoint had fallen.

"I don't know what is possible and what is not. But I am reporting that two hundred Algerians are running through my position as we speak. If you do not believe me, then, by all means, come and see for yourself," said

Brunbrouck.

Langlais came on the line and said, "Versailles Six, this is Gauss-Pierre. Is your position in danger of falling?"

"Gauss-Pierre, there is a large buildup of Viet Minh in the assault trenches in front of my position. Half my men have been killed or wounded by enemy counter batteries. I am requesting reinforcements immediately."

"I'm sorry, Versailles Six. All our reserves are already committed. We have nothing to give you. Can you retreat?"

"Gauss-Pierre, all the vehicles in my unit have been destroyed. I have no transportation to haul my artillery."

"Versailles Six, you are authorized to spike your guns and retreat."

"Gauss-Pierre, I will not give up my guns. I would rather die."

"All right, son. We'll send what we can. Good luck, Versailles Six."

"Thank you, Gauss-Pierre. Versailles Six, out."

It didn't take long before he and his men came under fire and became occupied in defending their own firing positions. The Viet Minh attacked in waves, as was their doctrine. As a tactic, a human wave was surprisingly effective in demoralizing the defenders, but any victory usually came at a heavy cost, especially against modern weaponry.

The French quad-50s on both hillsides opened up with a thunderous rattle. Tracer bullets streaked orange across the night sky. Their high-velocity bullets didn't take down just one man but cut through multiple layers of men, leaving large empty swatches in the enemy's line. The enemy hesitated and hit the ground.

The quad-50s continued for another minute, raking the enemy on the ground, and then went silent one after the other. They were out of ammunition. Brunbrouck knew he was in trouble.

Another blast from their bugler and the Viet Minh rose and resumed their charge. They hit the mines first, and dozens were killed. Any that made it past the layer of mines were caught in the concertina wire and immediately picked off by Brunbrouck and his men. Again, they hesitated and hit the ground. The Viet Minh sappers ran up with their Bangalore torpedoes. They created a ten-meter-long charge, which was long even for a Bangalore, and ran it underneath the three layers of concertina wire and across the top of the mines. The initial explosion from the Bangalore and the mine explosions that followed rocked the earth below them. The barbed wire was torn and flew up into the air, coming back down in a tangle like a twisted-Slinky. It did its job and blew open a breach in the French defensive perimeter. Another bugle call and the Viet Minh were on their feet again, rushing forward and firing their weapons.

It was clear to Brunbrouck that his position was about to be overrun. There were just too many of them and too few on his side. It was time. "Zero point!" he yelled to his men.

Brunbrouck had spent an entire day training them, practicing the same actions over and over again. They were prepared, and that gave his men confidence. The gunners spun the small wheel on the side of each gun that adjusted the altitude of the barrel until they hit their bottom point, which was level with the ground. They used their sights to aim their guns at the metal shell cases filled with dirt that they had prepositioned ten meters out. The loaders opened the breech, emptied the spent shell casing, reloaded the breech with a high-explosive shell with its fuse set to "immediate," and slammed the breech closed. The loader called "Up" and gunner called "Ready."

The Viet Minh poured through the breach and spread out across an assault line with several layers, as they were trained to do. Several Viet Minh stepped on mines, which exploded, hurling the soldier into the air and killing several men around him. They did not stop until they reached their assigned position, then hit the ground, laying as flat as possible to avoid shrapnel, and continued to fire their weapons at the French. When a substantial number was reached, their commanding officer shouted, and the Viet Minh rose and charged forward. Brunbrouck waited until the first line of Viet Minh had passed the shell cases and yelled, "Fire!"

The artillery shells left the seven gun barrels and struck the metal cases in an instant. The rolling boom of explosions so close to their guns shocked the French gun crews. The blast walls that they built saved them from the hail of shrapnel. The air concussed, and Brunbrouck and his men struggled for breath. One of his men screamed. His hand had been a little too high above the blast wall, and a shard of Viet Minh jaw bone with several teeth still in it was sticking out of his wrist.

Brunbrouck looked over the blast wall. To his surprise, there was no sign of the Viet Minh, not even body parts. The explosions had vaporized the entire assault line. There was nothing left except a large dark stain on the ground. In the distance, he could see another line of Viet Minh forming up to assault his position. Brunbrouck wasted no time and gave the order to reload.

The remaining shell cases filled with dirt had been knocked over by the blast but still made good targets for the gunners.

It took two more volleys from the French guns before the enemy had had enough and retreated. The Viet Minh losses had been massive. Brunbrouck had guessed correctly. Three shell cases filled with dirt for each gun was all that was needed.

He heard the vehicles crossing a bridge over the river behind him. A small convoy of trucks sent by Langlais pulled up behind his position. "Load 'em up," he yelled to his men.

It took twelve minutes to hitch up the howitzers and retreat from the position. It was overrun by the Viet Minh a few minutes later.

A GOOD MAN

Navarre sat at his desk, talking to Cogny on the phone. "The garrison is down to a fighting force of fewer than four thousand men, and many of those are wounded," said Cogny. "General, if the garrison is to maintain a viable defense, we must commit our final para reserves."

"And send another battalion to their death?" said Navarre. "How long can they hold out without reinforcements?"

"Without reinforcements, the Viet Minh will overrun the last strongpoints in the garrison within the week."

"If I commit our reserves, can you guarantee me that the garrison will survive?"

"No, sir. But I can guarantee you that it will fall if you don't."

"The airfield? Is there any chance we can repair it?"

"No, sir. It's too far gone, and even if we could repair it, we don't have the necessary supplies."

"And Colonel Godard's relief column?

"They are still bogged down in the mountains fifty miles away. They will never reach the garrison in time."

"Then, our men have no escape."

"No, sir."

Navarre took a long moment to consider his options before continuing his conversation with Cogny, "Our negotiations in Geneva are on the verge of a breakthrough. General Giap has committed over half of his available forces to the highlands. We, on the other hand, have only committed a tenth of our own. His supply lines are stretched to the limit, and the monsoons are coming. The roads he built will wash away, and he will be unable to resupply his men. He cannot let the siege continue for much longer. Every minute our garrison holds out increases our position at the bargaining table."

"Then you agree to send reinforcements?"

"No. The garrison must stand with the men they already have on the ground. You may continue the supply drops, but no regular units are to be committed. Inform General De Castries that he must not surrender the garrison at any cost."

"But these men… they are the best France has to offer. Their loss would decimate our fighting ability for years to come."

"Yes. It is an incredible sacrifice, Rene. Let us hope it is not wasted."

Navarre hung up the phone. Captain Pouget entered. "The supply reports you requested, sir."

"Thank you, Jon."

The Captain turned to leave but hesitated and turned back to Navarre.

"Sir?"

"Yes, Jon?"

"Sir, in this position, one hears things."

"You have my confidence, Jon. You may speak freely."

"Thank you, General. Is it true that the Americans have offered us a squadron of heavy bombers to break the siege at Dien Bien Phu?"

"Yes, Jon."

"…and two atom bombs?"

Navarre hesitated, "The offer was considered and rejected."

"But why, sir? Our men are dying."

"American involvement would give the Chinese and the Russians the excuse they need to enter this war. It is bad enough that we may lose to Ho Chi Minh, but to the Chinese and the Russians… never," said Navarre. "I know it's difficult, but politics are a harsh reality in the game we play."

"Game, sir?"

"Yes, Jon. To think of it otherwise would drive me insane. Is there anything else?"

"General, there is a group of volunteers that will be parachuting into Dien Bien Phu tomorrow night. With your permission, I wish to join them."

"Jon, your post here is invaluable."

"Thank you, sir. That is very kind, but still, I ask."

Navarre hesitated. He did not want to lose the captain to a hopeless cause, but he understood his sentiment and admired him for it. There was a part of him that wished he himself could volunteer but knew that was just bravado-foolishness.

"Of course, Jon," said Navarre. "You may go."

"Thank you, General," said Captain Pouget, saluting. "It has been an honor serving you."

Navarre stood and shook the Captain's hand, "Good luck, Captain."

Captain Pouget nodded and exited the office.

It was late afternoon at Cat Bi airfield. Coyle and McGoon inspected the repairs on the Daisy Mae. New sheet metal covered the rupture in the aircraft's side, and the bullet holes in the fuselage had been patched. The Vietnamese artist stood on a ladder and finished the repair on the painting of Daisy Mae, her breasts having been enlarged.

"Lookin' good, girl. Lookin' good," said McGoon.

"They're bigger, aren't they?" said Coyle.

"Her breasts? Yeah, I figured why not? She's just a cartoon character, Coyle. You can do anything you want to a cartoon. That's what makes 'em so fun."

"You wanna grab some supper? There's something I wanna talk to you about," said Coyle.

"Sure. What's the big secret?"

"No secret. I'm buying."

"Well, in that case,… lead on, my captain."

The sun was setting, and it was still hot and humid. Coyle and McGoon sat on the patio of a café, finishing their meal.

"It's gonna be a busy night," said McGoon. "Buford and I got a supply drop down to Hue, then back to Hanoi to pick up a bunch of volunteers that wanna parachute into the garrison. Fool's courage, if you ask me. Ain't much left that they can even land on."

"Yeah, about that…"

"Hey, did I tell you my business idea? Ya know, with all the money the Frenchies are paying us, we oughta be looking to invest some of it, like a nest egg for when we get back to the States. And this idea is gonna make a million bucks. I'm willing to cut you in on it once all of this is over."

"That's nice of ya, McGoon, but I don't know if I'm gonna be available."

"Now there you go shooting down an idea before you've even heard it. And this was a real winner, too. But now you'll never know because you're just too ignorant to even listen."

"I'm sorry, McGoon. It's just that…"

"Look, Coyle, you don't want to be my partner, just say so."

"It's not that."

"Unlike you, I got plenty of offers from people with vision. Yep. You just missed a golden opportunity, buddy. Chance of a lifetime. And cuz you're too pigheaded to even give it a listen, you're gonna end up a dumb, broke hillbilly the rest of your life."

"Okay, McGoon. What's your idea?"

"Too late. I've moved on."

"No, really, I wanna hear it. I'm listening."

"Yeah? Well, I can't tell it to ya."

"Why?"

"Cuz in all the hubbub, I forgot it."

"You forgot it?"

"You know I don't respond well to negative thinking."

"Million bucks, huh?" said Coyle.

"We'll never know," said McGoon, looking at his watch. "Oh, shit. I'm late. I gotta go. You got this, right?"

"Yeah, I got it," said Coyle. "I didn't get a chance to tell ya…"

"We'll talk later," said McGoon, jumping up and flagging the nearest trishaw.

"Yeah, later," said Coyle.

McGoon jumped in the front of the trishaw and pointed in the direction of the airfield. The driver pedaled, and the trishaw disappeared around the corner.

Dark clouds moved in over the Cat Bi airfield. The Daisy Mae pulled to a stop in the cargo loading area. The tail doors opened, and the hold was empty. The ground crew entered the hold and folded down the two rows of passenger seats on the inner wall of the hold. A group of volunteer soldiers, each holding a weapon and wearing a parachute, lined up outside the aircraft. Few had jumped before. The uneasiness showed on their faces. Captain Pouget was at the front of the line and seemed calmer than the rest. "All right, boys. Let's load 'em up. We got a schedule to keep," said McGoon, walking out the rear doorway.

The line moved forward as the soldiers filed into the aircraft and took their seats. McGoon just stood on the cargo ramp and smiled until he saw the second to the last soldier… it was Coyle. "Hey, Coyle. What're ya doing?" said McGoon.

"I tried to tell you, McGoon," said Coyle. "But you never let me get a word in edgewise."

"Tell me what, Coyle?"

"I volunteered."

"It ain't your war."

"It is now."

"Boy, somebody whupped you with the stupid-stick. You ain't even French."

"They don't care. They'll take anyone that can fire a rifle."

"Coyle, don't do this."

"I love her, McGoon."

"Okay. I get that. But there's got to be a better way than jumping to your death. We can try your two plane change up again. I'll take the P-38 this time, and you land in the Daisy Mae with Buford, so you can find her and…"

"It ain't gonna work, McGoon. You and I both know that airfield is too torn up to land. 'Sides, she won't leave."

"That's her decision, Coyle, not yours."

"Yeah. I realize that. But I can't leave her there. Not alone."

Heavy drops of rain splattered on the tarmac.

"You haven't thought this through, Coyle. The Viet Minh are gonna keep pounding away until that garrison falls, and when it does, there ain't gonna be nothing left."

"I know."

"Then, why do it? You ain't saving anyone."

"You're probably right. But at least we'll be together."

"And that's worth dying for?"

"Yeah, McGoon. It is."

"God damn it, Coyle. You can be so pigheaded sometimes."

"You just don't get it, McGoon. And I doubt you ever will."

"Get what?! You sacrificing your life ain't gonna add up to a hill of beans. We paid our dues in the Pacific fighting the Japs. That was our war. That was worth dying for. This is just a sideshow. And it don't matter how it turns out. It ain't gonna change anything. The Commies are gonna keep pushing us, and we're gonna keep pushing back. Let the Frenchies fight 'em as long as they can. It's all gonna end up in our lap anyhow."

"Like I said, you just don't get it," said Coyle.

Coyle entered the Daisy Mae and took the last seat. The big raindrops turned into a downpour. The pattering on the sheet metal was amplified by the cavernous hold and sounded like Buddy Rich's snare drum. McGoon stood outside, soaking wet, staring at Coyle and the other volunteers. "World's gone insane, I tell ya," said McGoon. "Fucking insane!"

It was dark and raining. The Daisy Mae cleared the last mountain as it entered the valley. McGoon pushed the wheel forward and lowered the elevators on the tail booms, forcing the aircraft downward.

"McGoon, what are you doing? Orders say we drop 'em at twelve thousand feet," said Buford.

"Yeah, well, orders ain't the pilot of this aircraft," said McGoon. "We drop 'em at twelve thousand, half of 'em will miss the drop zone. We're going down to six hundred."

"McGoon, that's crazy. Even if we make it through the flak, they'll only have thirty seconds in the air. Most of these guys have never jumped."

"Well, they ain't gonna learn any younger. Six hundred feet, and that's all there is to it," said McGoon and turned to Buford, "You with me, Buford?"

Buford thought long and hard before answering. "Yeah. I'm with ya, McGoon. I'll give the jumpmaster a heads up."

"You're a good man, Buford. A good man."

The Daisy Mae flew fast and close to the treetops as the mountain slope descended to the floor of the valley. Hidden anti-aircraft guns swung around and opened fire. Dark clouds of flak burst around the aircraft.

Inside the hold, the volunteer sitting next to Coyle slumped over, revealing a hole the size of a half dollar in the side of the aircraft. His parachute was torn badly, and his shirt was stained with blood. Coyle bent down to help him. He was already dead.

A buzzer sounded, and the rear doors swung open. Coyle and the other volunteers could see the flak bursts outside the rear of the aircraft. There were more than enough little black clouds to kill all of them. The jumpmaster ordered the volunteers to stand up and hook up. Coyle stood and hooked his parachute's static line to the wire running down the middle of the hold. Coyle helped hook up the volunteer behind him, who was too scared to remember the jumpmaster's instructions on the ground. "Just follow me when the time comes," said Coyle. The soldier nodded.

A shell burst just outside the doorway. A small piece of shrapnel hit the volunteer behind Coyle in the upper arm, and blood flowed. The man vomited at the sight of his own blood. The vomit hit the deck and splattered on Coyle's boots. "Nice," said Coyle.

Coyle reached into the man's front pocket and pulled out a wound packet. He ripped the packet open with his teeth and tied the gauze around the man's arm to stop the bleeding. He unhooked his and the man's static lines and helped him sit back down. "You've done your duty," said Coyle.

"Vive La France," said the grateful man.

"Yeah, whatever," said Coyle as he went back to his place at the head of the line and rehooked his static line.

In the cockpit, McGoon and Buford's eyes were focused on the drop zone in the distance beyond the edge of the forest. "I'm gonna need your help pulling her up in time. We're gonna stay low and avoid the flak until we reach the edge of the forest, then we're gonna pop up to six hundred feet and drop the troops," said McGoon.

"Their chutes are barely going to have enough time to open," said Buford.

"Better than getting shot or dropping behind enemy lines."

"Yeah, I guess you're right."

"Coming up on the edge. Now!"

McGoon gunned the engines as he and Buford pulled back on their wheels and pulled the elevators to their limit. The Daisy Mae rose sharply, and gravity pushed them back into their seats.

In the rear, the volunteers struggled against the weight of their parachutes and rucksacks. Some stumbled and fell and were helped back to their feet by their comrades. "Ready," said the jumpmaster.

The Daisy Mae leveled out above the drop zone. "Go," said McGoon. Buford flipped the switch for the drop light.

Inside the hold, the red light turned green. "Go!" said the jumpmaster.

"Away!" said Coyle, and jumped.

Coyle's static line snapped tight and pulled open the cover on his parachute. He held his breath until his chute popped open, and his harness jerked him upward. He floated downward and saw the battle raging below. Tracer bullets from machine guns flew in both directions across the battlefield. Explosions lit up the French trenches and blockhouses. He saw something falling out of the corner of his eyes and heard a scream from above. He turned just in time to see a volunteer with a failed parachute rushing past him and falling to his death. Coyle didn't want to see the impact. He looked away and saw the other volunteers with their parachutes open floating downward. They had been given brief instructions on how to steer their parachutes toward the drop zone. Some had clearly not listened or had forgotten in all the excitement and were heading away from the French lines. Mercifully, it was all over before they noticed.

Coyle hit the ground hard and rolled down the hillside. The ground was wet and muddy. He slid toward a line of barbed wire on the edge of the perimeter. He dropped his rifle and reached out with his hands and grabbed at the mud. His boot caught the edge of a rock and stopped his sliding just above the line of barbed wire. Bullet hits slapped the mud around him. He released his parachute straps and scrambled back up the hillside to retrieve his weapon. He crawled into the nearest trench. Strangely, it was empty. No matter, he thought. His war would start here. He looked up and saw the Daisy Mae banking hard to the right as it passed over the edge of the forest and headed back to Hanoi.

Several of the volunteers still in the air veered off course and landed in no man's land between the French and Viet Minh lines. A Viet Minh machine gun killed three. The others hit the ground and laid flat. They were trapped and had no idea where they were or what to do.

Captain Pouget was one of the last to land. He came down hard in rolls of barbed wire. The wire wrapped around his legs and tore his trousers. Machine gun tracer rounds zipped over his head. He stopped struggling and lay as motionless as possible, hoping the gunner would think he was dead and move on to another target. It worked. After a moment, he attempted to untangle himself from the barbed wire. It was no use. The more he tried to unwind his legs from the wire, the more he became entangled. He needed a pair of wire cutters. An idea came to him. He unbuttoned his pants and carefully slipped out of each pant leg. The wire's barbs scratched up his legs, but it was better than remaining in the enemy's field of fire. He left his pants tangled in wire, crawled over to the nearest trench, and dropped down inside. He landed on Sergeant Rouzic.

"Hey, asshole, watch where you're stepping," said Rouzic, who had been reassigned to this position. A flare above the trench ignited, and the sergeant saw that he was talking to a captain. "Oh, sorry, Captain. Couldn't see your insignia.”

“Carry on, Sergeant,” said Captain Pouget.

Sergeant Rouzic looked down at the Captain’s scratched up legs, “Sir, where are your pants?”

“Tangled in the wire. Where is your quartermaster?”

“Dead, sir. Mortar got ‘im last night.”

“I need to find a pair of pants before I report in.”

“Pants? Pants we’ve plenty of. Live bodies to wear ‘em is a different story.” Sergeant Rouzic reached down into the water at the bottom of the trench and pulled up a dead soldier beset with rigor mortis and bloated. “What size do you wear?”

Captain Pouget, having sat in an office most of his career and not accustomed to the realities of war, vomited.

In a nearby gully, Bruno and his men had been waiting for the parachute drop. They were in a dry river gully that was starting to fill with rainwater. Brigitte was with him. One of Bruno’s paratroopers with a bazooka opened fire on the Viet Minh machine gun and blew it to bits.

Bruno crawled out of the gully and over to the lost volunteers. Like a tour guide, he signaled with his hands which way to go. They followed him back to the gully.

The Daisy Mae’s flight path back to Hanoi led right over the top of a hidden anti-aircraft gun position. The Viet Minh corporal in charge of the gun squad was patient and waited until the enemy aircraft was right above his gun before ordering his men to open fire.

Coyle, standing in his trench, watched as a stream of orange tracers rose from the forest and hit the Daisy Mae’s left engine. “Oh God, no,” said Coyle as he watched the flames burst from the engine.

Inside the cockpit, McGoon and Buford struggled with the controls as the aircraft shuddered and bucked. “Damn it. Just when my chair was starting to get good and comfy,” said McGoon.

“One thing’s for sure,” said Buford. “We ain’t making it back over those mountains on one engine.”

“I think our only shot is to swing her around and try to land her on the airfield,” said McGoon.

“Not much of a shot. The airfield is in pretty bad shape.”

"Yeah, well, we're a little short on options here, Buford."

"Okay, McGoon. Land her on the airfield. At least we'll be near French lines."

Bruno and Brigitte watched the Daisy Mae from the gully. "They'll be okay," said Bruno. "They'll make it. The Americans are not too smart, but they are lucky."

From his trench on the hillside, Coyle watched the Daisy Mae turn around over the forest and fly toward the runway. Even in the dark and the rain, he could see the number of holes in the runway and the broken and twisted steel plates reaching up like the claws of a devil. He knew it would be a miracle if McGoon could land on it without tearing out the undercarriage of the Daisy Mae. Coyle ran back along the trench to get closer to the airfield. He reached the closest point to the airfield and jumped out of the safety of the trench and onto the bare hillside. Enemy bullets slapped the ground around him, kicking up dirt and mud. He ran down the hillside, slipping and sliding on the mud and what was left of the grass. He came to the perimeter and jumped over the barbed wire, and prayed he didn't land in a minefield. He didn't. He ran across the open ground toward the airfield. Tracer bullets streamed around him, and mortars shells exploded nearby. He knew he was a tempting target but figured he'd be harder to hit if he just kept running flat out and didn't stop.

Bruno watched the crazy soldier running across the open ground. "Fool," said Bruno, and then he took a closer look. "Is that Coyle?"

Brigitte turned and saw Coyle running. "Oh my god, Bruno, do something."

"1st Platoon, on me," said Bruno to his men. "The rest of you take our new guests back to headquarters and get them something to eat."

Bruno ran down the gully in the direction Coyle was running, followed by 1st Platoon and Brigitte.

Inside the Daisy Mae, McGoon lined up the aircraft for the final approach as best he could with just one engine. Buford reached for the landing gear lever. "Wait," said McGoon. "Maybe we should belly-land her. The wheels are just going hit those craters and shear off anyway. I figure we're better off without 'em."

"You ain't gonna be able to steer without wheels," said Buford.

"Ha. I think steering is gonna be the least of our concerns."

Buford took his hand off the landing gear lever and nodded his agreement to McGoon. "Okay. I think this is it," said McGoon.

The Daisy Mae flew over the leading edge of the runway just a few feet off the ground. McGoon and Buford wrestled the controls to bring her down on her belly. The aircraft hit the runway with a shower of sparks that lit up the night, and both engine props bent under. The Daisy Mae bounced back into the air. They forced her down again, and this time, she stayed on the runway. Sparks turned to flames as the wing fuel tanks ruptured, but she was going straight down the runway, and that was the best they could hope for until a shell from a Viet Minh recoilless hit one of her tail booms and exploded. The tail boom ripped off the back of the wing and hit a broken steel plate on the runway. The Daisy Mae spun around clockwise as she continued to slide and veered to the left of the runway. Her left wing dug into the wet ground and flipped the entire fuselage into the air. The Daisy Mae cartwheeled three times as she disintegrated into pieces, throwing off her engines, wings, and remaining tail boom. The cargo hold and cockpit stayed together and tumbled to a stop on the left edge of the airfield.

Coyle ran toward the burning hulk. He dodged the burning parts and pieces of sheet metal scattered across the ground. He reached the rear of the hold where one of the rear doors had broken off. He climbed inside and moved toward the cockpit. Both door hinges were broken, and the cockpit door was ajar.

On the airfield, a Viet Minh rifle company approached the wreckage of the Daisy Mae. Bruno and his men opened fire, cutting them off and pinning them down. The Viet Minh returned fire. Bruno's men took up defensive positions around the wreckage. Bruno and Brigitte moved toward the wreckage of the cockpit and cargo hold.

Inside the Daisy Mae, Coyle pulled open the broken cockpit door and tossed it to one side. He hesitated, afraid of what he would find inside. He entered the cockpit.

It was a tangle of twisted sheet metal with hanging control panels and wires. The entire front of the cockpit had collapsed. McGoon and Buford were still in their seats. Buford was dead, his neck broken. McGoon groaned. His head bled from pieces of the windshield that had shattered and cut him during the crash. Coyle moved to his side and looked down. A large gash in McGoon's chest was bleeding badly. McGoon looked up, "Coyle?"

"Hey, buddy. Nice landing," said Coyle.

"Yeah. One for the history books," said McGoon, weakly. "How's Buford?"

"He's seen better days, McGoon."

"Dead?"

"Yeah."

"Oh, that's a shame. He was a good man."

Coyle looked down at the front control panel sitting on top of the two pilots' legs. "McGoon, can you feel your legs?"

"Not really."

"It's okay. I'm gonna get you outta here."

"That'd be good. I'm kinda getting a little parched. I sure could use a beer," said McGoon.

"A couple of beers sound real good right about now," said Coyle.

"Hey, Coyle?"

"Yeah, McGoon?"

"I remembered my idea."

"Oh yeah? What was it?"

"Lobster farms."

"You don't even like lobster, McGoon."

"I don't wanna eat 'em. I want to grow 'em and sell 'em. You know, to tourists and stuff."

"Like by the sea?"

"No. Like in Nashville or Cincinnati, where they ain't got any."

"How are ya gonna grow lobsters?"

"We buy an old oil storage tank, clean it out really good, fill it with saltwater and grow 'em in there."

"McGoon, that ain't a half bad idea."

"Ain't it, though?"

"Worth a million," said Coyle, starting to choke up.

"I knew you'd like it once ya heard it," said McGoon.

"Coyle?" said Brigitte as she entered the cockpit, followed by Bruno.

"Help me get him free. I figure once we get him out from this control panel, we can cut his chair loose and carry him out."

Bruno and Brigitte moved to help Coyle lift the control panel. McGoon groaned in pain. Both his legs were crushed. Unable to free him, they let the control panel back down.

"We need something to cut the control panel. There should be a toolbox in the cargo hold," said Coyle.

"I'll get it," said Brigitte.

"I need to check on my men," said Bruno. They exited through the doorway into the hold.

"Hey, Coyle?" said McGoon.

"Yeah, McGoon?"

"I'm sorry 'bout what I said. You know, about Brigitte?"

"Don't worry about that now, McGoon."

"She's one hell of a woman, ya know?"

"Yeah, she is."

McGoon groaned as if something had changed inside him.

"You okay, McGoon?"

"Oh, yeah. Just a little stiff. Hey, Coyle?"

"Yeah, McGoon?"

"We're gonna be rich," said McGoon, smiling.

"Yeah, we are, buddy," said Coyle, smiling back with tears in his eyes.

McGoon slumped over in his chair and died. Tears rolled down Coyle's face. He tried to catch his breath but couldn't believe the incredible pain he felt. Brigitte and Bruno returned with the toolbox. They could see McGoon slumped over, and Coyle's face told the rest.

"Is he…?" said Brigitte, tears welling up in her eyes.

"Yeah," said Coyle.

Coyle took the toolbox from Brigitte and fished through it. He pulled out a hacksaw and tried to free McGoon's body from the wreckage.

"Coyle, I'm sorry for your friend," said Bruno. "The Viet Minh are flanking us. We have to go now."

"I'm not leaving without him," said Coyle.

"Coyle, we stay, we die," said Bruno.

"Coyle, please," said Brigitte.

"Go," said Coyle.

"I'm not leaving without you, Coyle," said Brigitte.

"Bruno, take her away," said Coyle.

"She's not going to go without you, Coyle. And I'm not going to force her."

"You're a chicken-shit. You know that, Bruno?"

Several bullets ricocheted off the sheet metal inside the hold as the Viet Minh closed in on the wreckage of the Daisy Mae. "My men need me, Coyle," said Bruno. "We must pull back with or without you."

Coyle looked at Brigitte. He couldn't stand the idea of her getting hurt or killed because of him. He released McGoon's body and left with them.

ELAINE

Corporal Ty was assigned to a squad of sappers digging an assault trench in front of strongpoint Elaine. He hunched down behind a four-foot thick and six-foot-wide roll of straw mats used to shield his squad of sappers from enemy snipers and mortar rounds. He and his men were fortunate. The French were running low on ammunition, and they only fired when they had a clear target. Even with his wound still being quite tender, Ty took his turn digging the trench along with the others in his squad. Digging while hunched over or kneeling was back-breaking work and tired the men quickly. They were making good progress when a lieutenant jumped into the trench and informed Ty that the battalion's colonel wanted to see him. Ty put down his shovel and followed the lieutenant out of the trench.

It was night, and the firefly flares continued to light up the garrison and the surrounding countryside. The ever-present explosions and gunfire were now just white noise and only caught attention when the tempo increased. On top of the hill called Elaine, Coyle, emotionally drained and irritable, sat against the last remaining wall in the mayor's mansion. He stared at the heap of debris with a half-buried painting of Napoleon on a white steed untouched by the battle raging around him as hundreds of men fought and died. "Generals never die," he said to himself.

Bridget was nearby, boiling coffee grinds she had already used twice before. Bruno stood by her, looking over at Coyle. "The Americans are brave. I will give them that," said Bruno.

"Bruno, what will happen to him?" said Brigitte.

"He is a volunteer. They will assign him to the forward trenches as cannon fodder for the Viet Minh assault."

"Bruno, you can't let that happen."

"It is not up to me, Brigitte."

"Bruno, I am asking you to keep him with you. To keep him safe."

"And how are you asking, my dear Brigitte?"

"As a friend. For old times' sake, yes?"

"As a friend?"

"Bruno, you know I love you."

"But you are not in love with me?"

"No. That time has passed. But if I ever meant anything to you, please help him."

Bruno had fought many battles in his lifetime, and he knew the face of defeat all too well. He had lost the battle for Brigitte's heart long ago, but he had still held out hope until that moment. He saw it in her eyes and heard it in her voice. She is in love with that stupid, brash, uncultured American, he thought. "I will see what I can do," said Bruno.

Brigitte kissed him on the cheek, "Thank you, my little Bruno."

Bruno just smiled in response.

The surviving field commanders gathered in the French command bunker. Most had bandages over their wounds, and they all looked like they hadn't slept in a week. Their uniforms were torn in spots, caked with mud, and stained with blood. Every few seconds, they heard the dull thud of an explosion somewhere in the garrison, and dirt was knocked loose from the timber-reinforced ceiling. Coyle stood by Brigitte while she took notes with a pencil and pad. She knew that her reports were more important than ever if the garrison was to survive. Even at this late hour, it was still her job to make it known what had happened here and how these men had been abandoned. She would not let the French generals and the politicians turn a blind eye without consequences.

Captain Hervouet, both his arms in plaster casts, gave his report to Langlais. "We still have one tank fully operational and two that are unable to move, but still have service of the cannons and machine guns," said Hervouet. "Ammunition, of course, is the main challenge. Including myself, I have sixteen men in my squadron still capable of fighting."

"Captain, your arms are in casts. How do you propose to fight?" said Langlais.

"I still have my teeth, yes?"

Everyone smiled. They were too tired to laugh.

"Thank you, Captain. Major, your artillery?" said Langlais.

The young major now in charge of the remaining artillery rose to his feet.

"As you know, the heavy mortars are out of ammunition, and all the cannons in the main garrison have been destroyed. We still have a 155 on Isabelle, but I am afraid it is of little use beyond a few hundred feet. The rifling in the barrel has worn smooth," said the major. "Colonel, for all practical purposes, our artillery is finished."

"I see," said Langlais. "No use flogging a dead horse, then. Have your remaining gun crews take up small arms and join the Legionnaires in the trenches."

"Yes, sir."

"Gentlemen and I use that term loosely," said Langlais to more smiles, "Intelligence reports enemy strength at fifty thousand plus. We, on the other hand, have fewer than three thousand still capable of fighting."

"Hardly seems fair. Should I send them a few of my paras to even things up?" said Bruno to more smiles and a few weak chuckles.

"To avoid giving the enemy any more supplies than they have already captured, Hanoi has elected to discontinue our supply drops. The garrison will stand or fall with what we have on hand," said Langlais.

"What about our reinforcements?" said Hervouet.

"Colonel Godard's relief column is still stuck in Laos. Resistance has been much heavier than expected, and, of course, the rain and the mountains don't help the situation. At this point, it is probably easier for us to get to him than he to us. Which brings me to my next item. Hanoi has made it clear that any surrender on our part would deal a heavy blow to the peace talks in Geneva. It is, therefore, my decision not to surrender the garrison under any circumstances. We will fight until we can fight no more," said Langlais. "Should the enemy overrun your position, I am authorizing individual commanders to take any remaining forces under their command and attempt a breakout. With a bit of luck, you may be able to link up with Colonel Godard's relief column."

"Colonel, that's fifty miles away through enemy-held territory," said Hervouet.

"Well, Captain, you still have your teeth," said Langlais. "The breakout plan is codenamed "Albatross." Before you make your attempt, you are to blow up any remaining ammunition and equipment. We leave nothing for the enemy."

Knowing the briefing was ending, the commanders rose to their feet.

"Gentlemen, it has been a privilege commanding with you. You have served your country with honor," said Langlais as he snapped to attention and saluted his men. "Viva La France."

"Vive La France!" said the men in unison, saluting back.

Langlais dismissed the officers, and they filed out of the bunker, some saying goodbye to their comrades for the last time. Langlais pulled Bruno aside and said, "You will take care of Brigitte and the American?"

"Yes, sir. I will do my best."

"Bruno, the Viet Minh have raised the bounty on your head."

"I am honored. I hope to match their expectations," said Bruno with a smile.

"No one would feel you any less of a man if you were to slip through the wire before the final assault."

"Colonel, I appreciate the concern, but fear only clouds one's judgment. A soldier in my position must be willing to greet death with honor," said Bruno. "It is my intention to make them earn their bounty."

Langlais shook his hand and said, "Good luck, Major."

"It has been my honor, sir," said Bruno, and left the bunker.

It was raining when Captain Hervouet reached the field hospital. Hundreds of wounded soldiers sat and lay on the muddy ground near the hospital entrance, waiting their turn for treatment. Many had died waiting. The steps carved into the hospital entrance had been compacted to a muddy ramp. Hervouet, with both his arms in casts, could not keep his balance on the slippery mud and, after several failed attempts, finally resorted to sliding into the hospital on his butt. "Merde," he said, feeling the wetness on the back of his pants.

Once inside, he made his way down the crowded main tunnel and entered what he thought was an empty examination room. He rifled through the instruments until he found a pair of shears used to cut through small bones and ligaments. Guinevere entered, "What are you doing, Captain?"

"Mademoiselle, if I could impose on you to remove my casts," said Hervouet.

"But your arms… they haven't healed," she said.

"Yes, but it is my head that worries me. I cannot close the hatch on my tank with these casts."

Guinevere sighed, took the shears from his hand, and cut away Hervouet's casts.

Ty crawled on his knees through a long, narrow tunnel dimly lit with oil lamps every twenty-five feet, just enough to give the sappers that dug the tunnel light to work. The tunnel was deep underground and had an upward angle to it. The floor was soft and muddy from the water that seeped in from the ceiling and surrounding walls. In his pocket, he carried an American Zippo lighter that the Colonel had given him. "It is dependable, like you, Corporal," the Colonel had said.

In Elaine's command bunker, Bruno stood over several maps and aerial photos, discussing the escape plan called "Albatross" with his platoon commanders. Coyle and Brigitte stood nearby and listened. "Once we join Godard and his column, we will make our way to Laos. Any questions?"

"Major, it seems cowardly to give up the garrison," said another Lieutenant.

"We will survive and fight another day, Lieutenant," said Bruno. "Anything else?"

"Major, we have reports that the Viet Minh have stopped digging," said a Captain.

"Good," said a lieutenant. "They were keeping me up at night."

"When did they stop?" asked Bruno.

"About three hours ago," said the Captain.

Bruno took a moment to consider the information. "Does anyone remember the time of the last artillery barrage?" said Bruno.

"About the same time," said a lieutenant.

"What's he thinking?" said Coyle quietly.

"I don't know," said Brigitte.

Ty reached the end of the tunnel and entered a cavern filled with over a hundred small drums of gunpowder mixed with packages of high explosives. He stood and found the three-foot-long fuse that the Colonel had told him would be there waiting for him. They could not risk a longer fuse that might burn out in the moist tunnel, the Colonel had explained. It would be useless to flee once the fuse had been lit, but that Ty would not suffer more than an instant, and his name would be remembered forever in the history of his country. It was a great honor he had been given. Ty lit the fuse. Tears welled up in his eyes as he looked back on his life in those brief moments before the explosion ended it. He loved playing piano in his music teacher's house, joking with his friends while drinking beer along the river, reading in the university library filled with knowledge just waiting to be uncovered, and the soft caress of his mother's hand when he was sick with a fever.

Inside the command bunker, Bruno realized what was about to happen. "Everyone out of the bunker," said Bruno.

"What? Why?" said a lieutenant.

"Now!" said Bruno.

Coyle and Brigitte joined the others and moved toward the bunker's doorway when they heard a dull thud and a deep rumble coming from beneath the bunker's floor.

The entire top of the hill disappeared in a geyser of dirt mixed with barbed wire, broken timbers, and bodies. Everything shot thirty-feet straight up into the air.

Inside the maelstrom that was once the command bunker, Coyle landed with a thud and was quickly buried with falling dirt and debris.

A thick cloud of dust enveloped the tortured remains of the hilltop. It was quiet.

Coyle gasped for air and coughed up the dirt in his mouth and throat. He couldn't see through the dust and dirt still falling like heavy black snow. He clawed his way up from a layer of dirt and debris. He searched for any sign of Brigitte. He saw a bandaged hand and dug around it until he uncovered Bruno's face. Bruno was choking to death. Coyle stuck his fingers into Bruno's mouth and cleared out the dirt. "Don't you die on me, you French bastard," said Coyle.

Bruno coughed and gasped for breath.

"Brigitte's under the dirt. Help me find her," said Coyle.

Coyle went back to searching for Brigitte. Bruno used his one free hand to clear more of the dirt from his mouth and nostrils. He dug himself out and joined Coyle in the search. Bruno uncovered a rifle and used the butt of the gun to dig through the dirt.

Below the hillside, a battalion of enemy soldiers climbed from their assault trenches. Additional explosions from Bangalore torpedoes took out the French barbed wire and cleared many of the mines that surrounded Elaine's perimeter. A wave of Viet Minh charged up the hillside. They quickly overran the trenches and blockhouses, the Legionnaires inside still stunned by the mine explosion.

Coyle heard the approaching machine gun fire and grenade explosions. He looked over the edge of the crater and saw the line of Viet Minh charging toward the edge of the crater that was once the top of the hill and killing anyone in their path. "Bruno, they're coming," said Coyle as he continued to dig.

Bruno didn't bother looking over the edge of the crater. He knew what was coming. He tossed down the rifle and searched the debris. He found a submachine buried in the dirt and pulled it out. He knew it would be a miracle if the gun didn't jam, but it was all he could find. He pulled out the clip and opened the gun's chamber by sliding back the bolt. He clanked the gun and the clip together, letting the dirt inside each fall free. He looked down the barrel and saw daylight. He blew as hard as he could into the top of the clip and again in the open chamber of the gun to clear any remaining dirt. He slapped the clip back into the gun and released the bolt. It chambered the first bullet and slammed closed. That was a good sign. He jumped to the rim of the crater and laid the gun on the edge, and opened fire. After five rounds, the gun jammed.

The Viet Minh continued to advance up the hillside.

Bruno pulled out the clip, blew on it, pulled open the bolt, cleared the jammed bullet with his fingers, slapped the clip back into the bottom of the gun, and chambered the next run. He fired again.

Several Viet Minh charging up the hill fell to Bruno's hail of bullets. The rest of the line hit the ground and returned fire. Bruno fired his last round. He looked for another clip. There was none in sight. "Coyle, I'm out of ammunition. We have to leave," said Bruno.

"I'm not leaving without her," said Coyle.

"She's gone, Coyle."

"No. She's here. We can find her. I know it."

"Damned American," said Bruno as he knelt and dug.

Bruno found a small boot. "I think I have her," said Bruno.

Coyle crawled over, and they dug around Brigitte until they could pull her body free. Coyle cleared her nose and mouth of dirt. She wasn't breathing. Bruno crawled to the edge of the crater and looked over the rim. The Viet Minh were twenty-feet from the top and coming fast.

"We have to go now, Coyle."

"She's not breathing."

Coyle breathed into Brigitte's mouth several times. She coughed and gasped for breath. "Okay, let's go," said Coyle. They each took one of her arms and ran with her toward the opposite side of the crater. She continued to cough, gasp, and spit out dirt. They disappeared down the backside of the hill just as the Viet Minh appeared over the top. The three were safe, but Elaine was gone.

More than half of the original garrison had been overrun and was now under the control of the Viet Minh. With the capture of each hillside, the Viet Minh repositioned their artillery and poured down direct fire on the remaining French positions. Surviving French troops were forced to crowd together on the remaining strongpoints, providing the Viet Minh snipers with plenty of exposed targets. Ammunition and food were almost nonexistent. Even drinking water became scarce when the water purification system had been damaged by a well-placed Viet Minh mortar shell. Only the French Air Force kept the Viet Minh at bay. French bombers and fighters pounded the Viet Minh trenches, killing hundreds. Undaunted, the Viet Minh advanced, digging their assault trenches and surrounding the French. There was no way out of the garrison.

The French suffered but did not give up hope. They knew their enemy was suffering, too. They had heard reports that captured Viet Minh soldiers had said that if the garrison held out for two more weeks, the Viet Minh would be forced to pull back because of lack of supplies and ammunition. They also knew the peace negotiations in Geneva could produce a ceasefire at any moment. And then there were the Americans, who were still considering military intervention on behalf of the French. The American long-range bombers were within range of the garrison. One strike from a squadron of new B-29 Superfortresses had the power to inflict incredible damage and break the will of the Viet Minh in the valley.

The French position was shrinking and getting more desperate by the hour, but they would not surrender. If the Viet Minh were to capture the garrison, they would have to take it from the French, and the French would make them pay a heavy price for every inch.

STALIN'S SYMPHONY

It was night and raining heavily. A Viet Minh lieutenant ran down a mountainside and found his commanding officer, a captain in charge of an artillery company. The young lieutenant was out of breath and stood at attention. "Lieutenant, you are an officer. Send a runner next time," said the captain.

"Yes, sir," said the Lieutenant. "I just thought you'd want to know as soon as…"

"Know what, Lieutenant?"

"They're here."

It took a moment for the captain to realize what the lieutenant was talking about. "Show me," said the captain.

The lieutenant led the captain to a clearing in a forest grove. A camouflaged net had been stretched over the treetops to prevent any passing planes from spotting the clearing. Twelve metal sleds covered with heavy canvas tarps to protect their cargo from damage sat in the clearing. The porters that had dragged the sleds into the valley stood at attention as the captain approached. The captain pulled a knife from his pocket and cut away the rope holding the tarp on one of the sleds. He pulled back the tarp to reveal the six tubes of a Russian-made Katyusha rocket launcher, nicknamed "Stalin's Organ," mounted with steel support beams attached to the base of the sled. Another 24 pushcarts carried the launchers' ammunition—over one thousand 82mm rockets originally designed to be fired from the wings of aircraft and now redesigned to be launched from the ground. The ground rockets were not nearly as accurate as artillery guns or mortars but packed a much more powerful punch on impact. They produced a devastating barrage when the entire battery of seventy-two rocket tubes was fired in unison. Although their destructive power was potent, their real benefit was the terror they struck in the hearts of the enemy. Only the very bravest and the dead could stand their ground under a Katyusha rocket attack.

Down to their last few rounds of ammunition, Bruno and a small group of paratroopers gathered on a hilltop and looked out over the valley. The garrison was a shamble, pitted with craters like a tortured moonscape. Viet Minh artillery and mortar shells continued to rain down on the remaining French positions. The French artillery guns were destroyed, and the mortars were out of ammunition and silent. The neatly laid out concertina wire was broken and twisted into steel bundles like giant balls of yarn. The French had long since given up repairing it. There was no more the French could do without supply drops and ammunition. Only strongpoint Isabel, four kilometers away from the fighting, remained defiant. The Viet Minh commanders planned to deal with Isabel once the main garrison had fallen.

By Bruno's side, Coyle and Brigitte watched and waited. It was time to attempt a breakout and hopefully live to fight another day. Coyle still had his Air Force revolver with four remaining shells hidden inside his jacket. He would save the final bullet for Brigitte to keep her from being raped by the Viet Minh, as he had been told to expect by several paratroopers and Legionnaires. He prayed it wouldn't come to that and wondered if he had the courage to pull the trigger.

Bruno pulled up his pant leg to reveal a square silk cloth tied around his calf. "What's that?" said Brigitte.

"It's a map. Just in case the Viet Minh forget to shoot me," said Bruno.

He untied the strings and opened the cloth. It was embroidered, so it would stay legible even when wet or stained with blood. It showed the escape route and the path to Godard's relief column. Brigitte pulled out a pencil and pad from her pocket and copied the map. Bruno handed her his compass. He knew it would be confiscated should he be lucky enough to be taken prisoner and that Brigitte and Coyle would need it to find the relief column.

"You must stay close to me. I will lead an assault with whatever men I have left. We'll drive a wedge into the enemy's front. On my signal, you will split off and make your way out of the garrison. You will head south into the forest along the far side of the airfield. It's lightly patrolled, and most of the enemy troops will be watching the final assault on the garrison. It's your best chance. Take as much food and water as you can carry. You'll need it," said Bruno, handing them each a rucksack filled with supplies. "Stay off the trails and watch out for mines and booby-traps. When I am finished here, I will try and join you. But don't wait. Keep moving until you find Colonel Godard's relief column."

Tearful, Brigitte hugged him and kissed him on each cheek. "Stay safe, little Bruno."

"Of course," said Bruno.

Bruno reattached the silk map to his calf and pulled down his pant leg. He turned to Coyle and said, "Take good care of her, Coyle. She is everything I fight for."

Coyle nodded and offered his hand. Bruno batted his hand out of the way and gave him a hug.

"Americans," said Bruno.

"French," said Coyle.

Bruno picked up a submachine gun. With no more orders to be given, he would fight in the last battle. They moved off down the hillside with Bruno's men by their side.

In the command bunker, Langlais and what remained of his staff burned aerial photographs, maps, and communiqués in several empty oil drums. "That's the last of it, Colonel," said a lieutenant.

"Very well, Lieutenant. You and the others may join your units," said Langlais.

His staff stood at attention and saluted their commander. He saluted back and dismissed them. Apart from the radio operator, his staff picked up their weapons and exited the bunker. Langlais sat down next to the radio operator, ready to issue his final commands to the garrison.

General De Castries, wearing a neatly pressed uniform, entered the bunker. His eyes were bright, and he seemed in perfect control. Langlais rose to greet him.

"Colonel, I assume everything is in order?" said De Castries.

"Yes, General. As well as can be expected under the circumstances," said Langlais.

"Very well. While I appreciate your past efforts on my behalf, your presence is no longer required in the command bunker. I will be tending the radios from here on out. Colonel, you may rejoin your men."

Langlais hesitated, unsure, and then stood at attention and saluted his commander, "Thank you, sir. I was happy to be of service."

De Castries saluted back. Langlais picked up his weapon and left the bunker.

In a hillside trench, a small fire hidden by a jacket heated the last coffee grinds at the bottom of a mess kit. Sergeant Rouzic was alone. All the men he had commanded were dead or in the hospital. Waiting for the water to boil, he looked out at the hillside below and could see the Viet Minh sappers busy digging the last few yards of their assault trenches. It would all end soon enough. He just wanted to finish the last of his coffee before they killed him. That's all he asked.

Someone approached from behind him in the trench. Sergeant Rouzic turned and raised his weapon. It was the German Legionnaire that he had saved. He was using a rifle as a crutch. A bloody bandage used to cover his stump had come loose and was dragging in the mud. "I thought you'd be dead by now," said Sergeant Rouzic.

"Mercy hates Legionnaires, especially Germans," said the Legionnaire.

Sergeant Rouzic used the top of his mess kit to pour in half the coffee he had made and gave it to the German. The German took a sip and grimaced. "Oh god, you French need to learn how to make coffee," said the German.

Sergeant Rouzic just smiled, grateful not to be alone. Their uniforms were in tatters and covered in mud. They hadn't shaved or even washed in several weeks and smelled like wet dogs. It didn't matter. Nothing really mattered at this point, just the horrible coffee they shared. Together, they looked out at the mountains surrounding the valley. The trees were still lush green and thick.

"It would be a beautiful country if it wasn't for this war," said Rouzic.

"Damn all wars," said the German Legionnaire.

"Damn all wars," said Sergeant Rouzic.

In the forest clearing, the Viet Minh artillery captain stood next to a battery of twelve Katyusha rocket launchers, each with six tubes aimed in the direction of the French garrison. In the trees above, sappers released the camouflaged net to open the sky up to the rockets. The captain covered his ears with his hands and gave the order to fire. Within twenty seconds, all seventy-two rockets were launched with thunderous whooshes from the ignited propellant. The ground shook, and the surrounding trees quivered from the power of their combined engines.

The unknowing Legionnaires and paratroopers on Huguette had grown accustomed to the enemy's artillery barrages. They simply took cover in a nearby trench or blockhouse until the barrage passed. Nothing had prepared them for what was about to happen. There was a high-pitched trill overhead. It was different from the sound of artillery shells, and all eyes turned upward to see the rockets arcing across the sky, leaving trails of smoke. The enemy rockets exploded all at once across the entire hillside, and the air shattered. There was no time to seek cover, and anyone caught above ground was torn to shreds from the long metal shards from the shattered rocket casings. A torrent of dirt, barbed wire, and body parts flew everywhere. The soil and rock that held the hill together shook so violently from the explosions it became loose and began to resettle.

Inside the hospital, the timber-reinforced ceilings rained down dirt and small rocks into the open wounds of the soldiers being operated on by the surgeons. Several of the tomb-like patient cells caved in and smothered the wounded soldiers lying inside. The hospital's tunnels filled with thick dust, making it impossible to breathe.

The trench walls crumbled and collapsed, burying hundreds of soldiers and making their dirt-filled weapons inoperable.

The ceilings in the blockhouses collapsed, crushing the occupants with wooden beams and burying them with three yards of compacted dirt from above.

Even the concrete used to construct the command bunker cracked and buckled in places, crushing radios with loose slabs of concrete, tearing wall maps, and burying their precious recon photos beneath the debris. The wires in the overhead lighting snapped and swung down, breaking the light bulbs and sending the command bunker into darkness.

When the rockets finally stopped, and the ground stopped shaking, the surviving soldiers dug themselves out from under the debris and looked up over their trenches and out of their blockhouses. The entire garrison was in ruins. The barbed-wire fences that protected their perimeter were broken in several places, and most of the mines had exploded and created craters that could be used by the enemy as protected firing positions. The strongpoint was open for attack, and the soldiers inside the perimeter knew it. They were in shock, and for the moment, whatever morale was left was crushed.

As each of the strong points in the French garrison had fallen, the Viet

Minh had consolidated their forces. Unlike previous attacks on the strongpoints, the Viet Minh had more than enough soldiers available for a final attack from all directions.

The enemy bugles sounded, and the ground forces rose from their trenches and charged forward in the thousands. Machine guns and recoilless rifles paved their way, keeping the heads of the French soldiers down in their trenches.

The sappers were first in the assault and cleared away the French mines and barbed wire with their Bangalore torpedoes.

Next, the rifle companies charged up the hill, firing their weapons and throwing grenades.

Small machine gun squads and bazooka teams were the last up the hill and were used to support the infantry whenever they got pinned down by the French defenders.

When the French soldiers heard the Viet Minh battle bugles, they knew what was coming. Those still able to fight scrambled to find their weapons buried under the mud and dirt. They were lucky if they got off the first shot before the gun jammed, and they were forced to clean out the dirt and mud from the gun's receiver and ammunition clip. Several gun barrels and breeches exploded from mud blockage and blinded or killed the rifleman using it, or in some cases, an unlucky soldier beside him. It didn't make much of a difference anyway. The French were almost out of ammunition and had only issued a few cartridges per man. The French machine guns blew through their final belts within the first minutes of the battle. The machine gunners were forced to spike their barrels and bury the guns' receiver bolts so the enemy could not use them. The few remaining recoilless rifles had been fired so many times over the past few weeks that the rifling in their barrels had worn smooth. Without spinning, the shells were terribly inaccurate beyond a few hundred feet and usually missed their intended targets.

The French commanders had one last surprise to offer the Viet Minh. The quad-50s anti-aircraft guns that had protected the airfield had been held in reserve and repositioned to cover the hillside. The meat grinders' barrel clips were still full of ammunition, and their gunners would use every shell for one last slap in the face before the enemy delivered its final coup de grâce on the garrison.

Just a few yards before the charging Viet Minh reached the French trenches, the quad-50 gun crews opened up and unleashed hell. The sound was deafening. The storm of bullets tore into the enemy horde, killing hundreds. The quad-50s' high-velocity bullets ripped bodies apart and left few wounded. The scene of their comrades being shredded into pieces stopped the Viet Minh soldiers in their tracks, and they hit the ground and prayed they weren't next. The surviving French soldiers cheered, but their adulation was short-lived. The deadly barrage from the meat grinders came to an end when the last shells fired, and the smoking gun barrels went silent.

The Viet Minh mustered their courage, rose, and resumed their assault up the hillside.

The French fought bravely, mostly hand-to-hand when the Viet Minh jumped into their trenches or entered their blockhouses. The French didn't last long, as they were soon overpowered by multiple enemy soldiers using the bayonets on the ends of their rifles.

In their trench, Sergeant Rouzic and the German Legionnaire fought side by side as they had always done. They fired the last of their ammunition at the human wave as it approached. They could both see that there were too many and that they would soon be overrun. The first Viet Minh that reached the trench jumped down next to Sergeant Rouzic. The sergeant raised his rifle and pulled the trigger. It clicked empty. The Viet Minh raised his own rifle straight at Sergeant Rouzic's face. The Viet Minh's throat exploded in blood from the bayonet of the German standing behind him. The German was riddled with bullets from another Viet Minh standing at the top of the trench, and crumbled into the mud at the bottom of the trench, and died. Still, another Viet Minh jumped into the trench and plunged his bayonet into Sergeant Rouzic's stomach, pinning him to the trench wall. The getaway driver of the famous bank robber, Pierrot-le-Fou, slumped over and died.

Below the hill, Hervouet, his arms now free of their casts, rode on top of his tank, firing the last few rounds of his machine gun. The tank gunner fired his last shell at an enemy machine-gun emplacement destroying it.

A Viet Minh bazooka team moved up a gully paralleling the tank. The gunner rose over the lip of the gully and fired the bazooka into the side of the tank just a few yards away. The explosion took the gunner's head off.

Inside the tank, the loader and driver were sprayed with hot molten metal and killed instantly. Standing on the commander's seat with half his body out of the tank, Hervouet's legs were hit with the red-hot metal, and his pants caught fire. Hervouet pulled himself up and out of the hatchway. He jumped off the tank and rolled to put out the fire on his pants. He pulled out his knife and used the tip of the blade to pry out the smoking pieces of molten metal lodged in the flesh of his leg. His pants still smoldering, Hervouet was hit in the back of the head by the rifle butt of a passing Viet Minh soldier. Unconscious and his final tank destroyed, Hervouet's fight was over.

It was the massacre everyone was expecting when strongpoint Huguette was finally overrun by the Viet Minh. As usual, the assaulting force showed little mercy to the French defenders, for they, too, had suffered great loss and had watched their friends and family die at the hands of the French over the years of occupation. Most French soldiers did not surrender but were shot or beaten into submission by their Viet Minh captors.

Bruno, Coyle, and Brigitte watched from a hillside trench and listened on a handheld field radio as the garrison was overrun. The French were in chaos. "It always happens faster than you would expect," said Bruno. "Remember, stay close until you see my signal."

Bruno dropped the radio in the mud and fired one round of his remaining ammunition into the casing. It was destroyed. He moved up beside his men, fighting from their position in the trench and using up the last of their ammunition.

The Viet Minh approached the edge of the trench. Bruno nodded to a lieutenant, holding a mechanical detonator with two wires attached. The lieutenant wound the handle and yelled, "Fire in the hole!" The paratroopers and Legionnaires ducked down below the edge of the trench. The lieutenant pushed down on the handle and released the magneto inside the detonator, sending an electrical charge through the wires and setting off seven napalm canisters buried beneath the mud. The entire front of the trench exploded in flames, incinerating the enemy.

Bruno signaled to Coyle and Brigitte. They ran along the trench toward the airfield as Bruno had instructed.

Bruno and his men scrambled up the front of the trench and jumped through the fire left by the napalm explosions. They charged into the enemy, firing the last rounds in their weapons and then using them as clubs. Bruno fought like a madman, killing several Viet Minh before he was finally surrounded by six Viet Minh. They had been ordered not to kill the officers.

Even with their bayonets just inches from his body, Bruno kept swinging until one of the soldiers hit him in the face with the butt of his rifle, breaking his nose and rendering him unconscious. Fortunately, none of the soldiers realized who he was and never tried to collect the bounty. Two of the soldiers dragged him off to join the other prisoners. Bruno never surrendered.

Inside the command bunker, De Castries and the radio operator listened to the final pleas from the garrison. "Our position is being overrun. We are out of ammunition. They have reached the bunker. I am destroying my radio. Andre, if I don't make it, tell my wife I love her. Falcon One, out."

"Wilco, Falcon One. Good luck, Lamar. Out."

The radio went silent. The operator turned to De Castries and said, "That's the last one, sir."

"Get me, General Cogny."

"Yes, sir."

The operator moved from the field radio to the command radio used to communicate with Hanoi. He raised the operator on the opposite end.

"General De Castries for General Cogny," he said.

After a few moments, Cogny spoke, "Charles, how are you holding up?"

"I am afraid it is over, sir," said De Castries. "The garrison has fallen."

"I see. And the men?"

"They fight to the end as ordered."

"No chance of escape, then?"

"Some will attempt it."

"And you?"

"For me, no. I must look after those that remain and see that they are treated humanely by the enemy."

"Of course," said Cogny. "General, I need not remind you that you must not surrender the garrison at all costs."

"Yes, sir. I understand."

"You have served with honor, General De Castries."

"Thank you, sir."

De Castries and the operator heard Viet Minh voices from outside the bunker. "I must go now, General. The enemy is here. We are destroying everything. Adieu," said De Castries.

The radio operator didn't wait for a response. He spun the dials, changing the frequency on all the radio sets. Together, De Castries and the operator rose and fired their weapons into the radios, destroying them.

The radio operator set his rifle down on the floor. De Castries instinctively holstered his pistol. He thought for a moment, then removed his pistol and set it on the ground with the radio operator's rifle. He would not surrender his weapon to a Viet Minh officer, which was a sign of capitulation. They waited in silence. It didn't take long.

A Viet Minh soldier entered the command bunker with his rifle at the ready to deal with any resistance. There was none. He looked over and saw the French general. None of the Viet Minh had ever captured a general before, and the soldier was nervous. "C'est fini?" asked the soldier.

"Yes. C'est fini," said De Castries.

The Viet Minh soldier smiled, grateful.

Outside the command bunker, several Viet Minh soldiers climbed on top of the curved, corrugated roof and took down the French flag, letting it fall to the mud. Their own flag was on the end of a pole, and they waved it proudly back and forth for all to see. Sporadic fighting around the garrison would continue for several more hours, and the Legionnaires on strongpoint Isabel would hold out for a few more days, but with the garrison's central command post and commanding general captured, the battle for the valley of Dien Bien Phu was over. The Viet Minh had won.

On the opposite end of the airfield, Coyle and Brigitte belly-crawled their way past a Viet Minh squad sitting in a trench, watching the destruction of the garrison. They crawled into the forest until they were sure they were out of the enemy's sight. Brigitte used the compass that Bruno had given her and studied her hastily-drawn map. She pointed the way to Coyle.
They kept low and moved deeper into the forest. They stayed off the footpaths as Bruno had instructed, wading through the undergrowth below the trees.

A Viet Minh soldier appeared from a grove of trees twenty feet in front of them, blocking their path. He had just finished taking a leak, and his hands were busy buttoning his pants when he saw Coyle and Brigitte. He fumbled for his rifle. Coyle drew his pistol and fired twice. The second bullet hit the soldier in the chest, and he dropped to the ground, badly wounded. A second soldier appeared and shot at Coyle with his rifle. Coyle shot back and killed him. Coyle knew there was only one bullet left in his revolver. He could hear more Viet Minh voices deeper in the woods. They were coming. "Run," he said.

Brigitte took off running through the trees, and Coyle followed close behind. The undergrowth made it slow going. The survivors of the Viet Minh patrol chased them and fired several times. Brigitte and Coyle heard the bullets zipping past their heads. The shots were close misses.

Brigitte saw a footpath up ahead and decided to follow it. She remembered Bruno's warning, but now was no time to be too cautious. She and Coyle jumped on the path and picked up speed, putting distance between them and the enemy patrol chasing them.

It was Brigitte's foot that caught the booby-trap's tripwire stretched across the forest trail. She stumbled to the ground. The tree branch that had been pulled back by the Viet Minh sappers was released and swung over her head, missing her by a couple of inches. It hit Coyle coming up behind her. The long branch had been rigged with several wooden stakes, each carved to a sharp point. One of the stakes plunged into Coyle's shoulder, impaling him and picking him up off the ground to pin him to another tree. He dropped his revolver. Brigitte screamed. The pain Coyle felt was intense, and he struggled to stay conscious. He pushed at the branch, hoping to free himself. Brigitte grabbed the branch and tried to help him. The tension on the branch was still too strong. It was hopeless. Coyle looked into Brigitte's eyes and said, "Go."

"I can't," said Brigitte.

"Can't or won't?" said Coyle with a weak smile.

Brigitte picked up the revolver and prepared to defend Coyle. Five Viet Minh appeared through the tree and raised their rifles. One of them shouted something at her in Vietnamese. Outnumbered, she dropped the revolver.

One of the soldiers ran up and tied her hands behind her back. He turned to Coyle and used his machete to cut through the branch. Each stroke sent waves of pain through Coyle. He groaned. Mercifully, he fainted after the third stroke. The branch broke, and two soldiers pulled the branch from Coyle's shoulder and placed a Russian field dressing on his wound. They cut off the staked end of the broken branch and tied Coyle's hands and legs to the middle of the pole. They carried him hanging from the pole through the forest with Brigitte by his side.

Two hundred Viet Minh engineers worked swiftly to repair the airfield. The French had agreed to fly in food and medical supplies, which were to be shared equally by both sides. A squad of French engineers would also arrive to repair the water purification unit and generator damaged in the final artillery barrage. The Vietnamese did not yet possess the technical expertise or the resources to save their own people. It was difficult for their commanders to admit they still needed the French.

Over six thousand French prisoners sat under the hot noonday sun. There was no shade or water. Many of the prisoners were suffering from concussions from the final artillery and rocket barrage. Others were badly wounded, and blue flies infested their blood-soaked bandages. The smell of putrid flesh and gangrene permeated the air to the point of choking, even the veterans. The stress of battle had been lifted, and most of the prisoners, no longer worried about snipers or falling artillery shells, dozed off wherever they sat.

Bruno sat with fellow paratroopers and watched the Viet Minh officers interrogating the prisoners and noting their names, ranks, and serial numbers. "Major, if they find you, you will hang," said one of the corporals.

The corporal waited until the sentries were looking elsewhere and motioned with a nod in a different direction. Bruno looked over at a medic closing the eyes of a dead Legionnaire sergeant missing both legs. Bruno observed that while the bottom of the sergeant's uniform was in tatters and covered in blood, the top of his uniform was relatively untouched. The corporal nodded to Bruno. Bruno hated the idea of giving up his paratrooper uniform, even if his chances of survival would vastly improve. Bruno waited until the medic had left and moved up beside the body of the sergeant. The corporal picked a fight with one of his paratrooper comrades. Bruno waited until the Viet Minh sentries looked in the direction of the fight, and he switched uniforms. He also swapped his dog tags for the sergeant's. Bruno had just joined the Foreign Legion. He was annoyed.

Outside the collapsed field hospital, Guinevere tended to Coyle's wound. The adrenaline his body had generated when wounded wore off after the first hour, and now Coyle was feeling the burning sensation of torn flesh and the sting of the dried blood that pulled at his bruised skin whenever he moved. There was no morphine or even simple aspirin to kill the pain. The Viet Minh had ransacked the hospital supplies and medicines.

Guinevere used tweezers to remove the pieces of bark and splinters that would otherwise cause an infection. "We have no more alcohol to irrigate the wound," said Guinevere as she finished up and covered the wound with a dressing. "You need to keep it as clean as possible. Use boiled water if you can. I'm sorry, but it is the best that I can do."

"You've done enough," said Coyle. "Any idea what will happen to you?"

"I will go with the prisoners if I am allowed. The Viet Minh don't even have enough medical personnel for their own wounded, let alone ours."

A Viet Minh major with two guards approached. "Are you American?" he asked Coyle.

Coyle nodded.

"You will come with me," said the major.

Coyle rose with Guinevere's help. "Good luck, Monsieur Coyle," said Guinevere.

"You, too," said Coyle. He followed the major down the hillside, escorted by two guards.

Coyle was brought to the Viet Minh command center in the same jeep Giap had used to arrive in the valley. He walked toward the waterfall and under the camouflage nets. Standing at the table, General Giap gave orders to several of his field commanders. The commanders saluted and left. Giap saw Coyle and said, "You are the American flyer?"

"Technically, I am a Foreign Legionnaire," said Coyle.

"I see. But you were an American flyer?"

"I am not at liberty to say."

"Are you at least willing to admit you are an American?"

"Yes. I am an American."

"My name is General Giap."

"I know who you are."

"And your name?"

"Tom Coyle."

"Are you wounded badly? I could have one of our doctors look at it."

"No, thank you. It's a bit tender, but nothing that won't heal."

"Please, have a seat."

Coyle sat down at a table, and Giap sat down across from him.

"There was a woman I was with when I was captured," said Coyle.

"The journalist, Brigitte Friang?"

"Yes. Is she all right?"

"Why wouldn't she be, Mr. Coyle? We are not barbarians."

"Thank you."

"You are an American. This is not your war. Why did you fight for the French?"

"It paid good."

"Not good enough, I think. But we must all make a living," said Giap. "I was a history teacher before the revolution. I'd like to return to my job one day when the French leave. Soon, I think. I brought you here to let you know that you will soon be released," said Giap as he handed Coyle a signed document that released him from prison. "A Red Cross plane is on its way here to inspect our prisoners and pick up the most seriously wounded. You will be on it when it returns to Hanoi."

"Why?"

"I wish you to deliver a message to your government and tell them what you saw here," said Giap. "Tell them that we mean America no harm. We just want to live in peace."

"I'll tell 'em, but I think they will find that hard to believe. You are Communists, and you follow Mao. He means to harm all that stand in his way, especially America."

"We are Vietnamese, and we follow Ho. Our struggle is for independence from the French. That will be achieved shortly. We have no quarrel with America or any other nation unless we are attacked. Tell your president to learn from the French mistakes and not to let history repeat itself. This generation has shed enough blood and deserves peace."

"I'll deliver your message."

"Then, you are free to go."

"I will not leave without Miss Friang."

"I am afraid that is not possible. She is a war correspondent for the French. There are many that believe her lies have cost the lives of thousands of Vietnamese."

"What will you do with her?"

"She will be tried."

"Then try me with her."

"You have committed no crime, Mr. Coyle."

"It was my plane that dropped napalm on your troops."

"I see," said Giap, remembering the screams of the men and women burning. "It is of no consequence. You will leave."

"I will not. Not without Brigitte."

"Then, I will have you shot."

"That would be a mistake for a nation that wants peace with America."

"You Americans think too much of yourselves as individuals. You have no concept of the collective good."

"Spoken like a true Communist."

Giap said something in Vietnamese to one of the guards. The guard walked over to Coyle and yanked off his dog tags.

"No one will know what happened to you, Mr. Coyle," said Giap. "As you said, technically, you are a Foreign Legionnaire. You will be buried in a mass grave along with hundreds of others, your name and deeds erased from history."

"Then so be it,"

"You Americans underestimate our resolve."

"And you ours," said Coyle.

Giap turned toward the two guards and barked out an order in Vietnamese. The guards grabbed Coyle by the arms and escorted him out. He was still feeling pain from his shoulder wound, and the guards' man-handling didn't help. Giap followed.

"Where are you taking me?" said Coyle.

"You made your choice, Mr. Coyle."

The guards took Coyle out of the command area and pushed him up against a tree. One of the guards leveled his rifle at Coyle's head and chambered a round. The end of the guard's rifle barrel was only an inch from the bridge of Coyle's nose.

"You can't just shoot me. It ain't right," said Coyle.

"I've just sacrificed eight thousand of my best men. You'd be surprised what I can do," said Giap. "Last chance, Mr. Coyle. Will you deliver my message?"

Coyle hesitated and prepared himself. "Not without Brigitte," said Coyle.

"Very well, Mr. Coyle," said Giap, nodding to the guard. "Have it your way."

The crack of a rifle rang out over the valley. A few birds that had returned to the mountain forests once again took flight. It was strange to hear just one shot after all the bombs, artillery, and mortar explosions. It seemed almost peaceful in a way.

The sun was hanging low over the mountains and shone in the eyes of the prisoners. Brigitte sat on the hillside with several other civilians from different nations, including the prostitutes from Algeria and Indonesia. Recent tears had washed away some of the dust and left clean tracts down her face. She watched the Red Cross plane land on the repaired airfield.

In the distance, Brigitte saw the silhouette of a man approaching, flanked by two Viet Minh guards. As he came closer, his face became clear. It was Coyle, holding two signed documents. The two guards talked to the soldiers guarding the civilians, and Coyle showed them the documents signed by General Giap. One of the soldiers walked up the hillside and over to Brigitte. "You, come," said the soldier.

Brigitte rose and walked down the hill with the soldier. When she reached Coyle, they embraced. "Now will you go?" said Coyle.

Brigitte nodded with tears in her eyes. Together, they walked toward the airfield and the waiting Red Cross plane. Their war was over.